AI-Driven Computational Engineering for Sustainable Development

Edited by

Subir Gupta
Department of AI & ML
Haldia Institute of Technology
West Bengal, India

Indrajit Ghosal
Department of Management
Brainware University
Kolkata, India

Keshav Kaushik
Center for Cyber Security and Cryptology, Sharda
School of Computing Science & Engineering
Sharda University, Greater Noida, India

&

Monika Dandotiya
Department of Computer Science & Engineering
Poornima University, Jaipur
India

AI-Driven Computational Engineering for Sustainable Development

Editors: Subir Gupta, Indrajit Ghosal, Keshav Kaushik & Monika Dandotiya

ISBN (Online): 978-981-5324-03-7

ISBN (Print): 978-981-5324-04-4

ISBN (Paperback): 978-981-5324-05-1

First published in 2026.

Bentham Science Publishers Pte. Ltd.
No. 9 Raffles Place
Office No. 26-01
Singapore 048619
Singapore
Email: subscriptions@benthamscience.net

BENTHAM SCIENCE

CONTENTS

PREFACE

The dawn of Industry 5.0 marks a pivotal moment in the ongoing evolution of human-machine collaboration, offering unprecedented opportunities for sustainable development. As technology advances at an accelerated pace, the integration of Artificial Intelligence (AI) and Natural Language Processing (NLP) in computational engineering is emerging as a cornerstone of this new industrial paradigm. This book, AI-Driven Computational Engineering for Sustainable Development, is a comprehensive exploration of the role AI and NLP play in shaping the future of Industry 5.0, where the synergy between humans and machines drives innovation and progress. The concept of Industry 5.0 extends beyond the mere technological advancements that characterized its predecessor, Industry 4.0. It envisions a world where machines not only work alongside humans but collaborate with them in a harmonious partnership, enhancing productivity while fostering sustainable development. This book delves into the multifaceted aspects of this collaboration, examining how AI and NLP can be harnessed to address the complex challenges of modern computational engineering.

The theoretical and practical insights presented in these pages offer a rich resource for AI professionals, NLP researchers, database experts, and scholars in computational engineering. By exploring the opportunities, challenges, and applications of AI and NLP, this book equips readers with the knowledge needed to navigate and contribute to the rapidly evolving landscape of Industry 5.0.

One of the key objectives of this book is to identify and analyze emerging themes and research trends within the context of Industry 5.0. The scientific community's growing interest in this paradigm shift underscores the importance of understanding the implications of AI and NLP in fostering sustainable development. Through a detailed examination of the current state of research, this book also highlights critical gaps, offering a roadmap for future investigations and innovations. The book provides valuable insights into the economic and productivity implications of Industry 5.0. By focusing on the collaborative potential between humans and machines, it offers a fresh perspective on how this new industrial era can contribute to a more sustainable and efficient manufacturing industry, ultimately benefiting the broader economy.

AI-Driven Computational Engineering for Sustainable Development is designed to serve as a foundational text for both specialists and beginners in the field of computational engineering. Whether you are a seasoned researcher or new to the world of AI and NLP, this book will guide you through the complexities of Industry 5.0, offering the technical knowledge and conceptual frameworks necessary to contribute meaningfully to this transformative era.

As you embark on this journey through the pages of this book, we hope it inspires you to explore the limitless possibilities that AI and NLP offer for sustainable development in computational engineering. The future of Industry 5.0 is not just about advancing technology; it is about creating a world where humans and machines work together to build a better, more sustainable future.

Subir Gupta
Department of AI & ML
Haldia Institute of Technology
West Bengal, India

Indrajit Ghosal
Department of Management
Brainware University
Kolkata, India

Keshav Kaushik
Center for Cyber Security and Cryptology
Sharda School of Computing Science & Engineering
Sharda University, Greater Noida
India

&

Monika Dandotiya
Department of Computer Science & Engineering
Poornima University, Jaipur
India

ACKNOWLEDGEMENTS

I, Dr. Subir Gupta, as one of the editors of the book "AI-Driven Computational Engineering for Sustainable Development", extend my heartfelt thanks to my fellow editors, Keshav Kaushik, Monika Dandotiya, and Dr. Indrajit Ghosal, for their collaboration and insight. I am also grateful to the publishing team at Bentham Science, UAE, for their expertise and support throughout the publication process. Lastly, I would like to acknowledge the invaluable contributions of all the authors who have shared their knowledge across various chapters, enhancing the scope and depth of this work. Their expertise has been crucial in making this publication a comprehensive resource in sustainable development through computational engineering.

Dr. Subir Gupta

My heartfelt gratitude and love to all my family members, especially my wonderful wife, Arpita, and my children, Amitrajit and Adhrit, for their love, wishes, and motivation. I would like to thank Dr. Saileswar Ghosh (HOD, Management Dept.), Dr. Anant Kumar Srivastava (Dean Academics), and all the faculties and colleagues at Brainware University, Kolkata (India). I wish to thank all the editors who have been associated with this project, especially Prof. Keshav Kaushik, who has supported me from the beginning to the end. I would also like to show my gratitude and thanks to my mentor cum philosopher Dr. Sudhir Rana, Dr. Sudin Bag, Dr. Pranay Kumar Roy Barman, and all my loving students, Research colleagues for their continuous support, and motivation to complete this project successfully.

Dr. Indrajit Ghosal

This book is dedicated to my beloved Parents- Sh. Vijay Kaushik, Smt. Saroj Kaushik,

wife- Priyanka, daughter Kashvi, and son Harshiv.

May God always bless us. Har Har Mahadev!

Keshav Kaushik

My sincere appreciation goes to Professor [Dr. Indrajit Ghosal], whose guidance and expertise were instrumental in shaping the research direction of this book. The insightful feedback from my research collaborators enriched the content and strengthened the arguments.

Dr. Monika Dandotiya

List of Contributors

Aashish Mehra	School of Business, Galgotias University, Greater Noida, UP, India
Abhijeet Parashar	Poornima University, Jaipur, Rajasthan, India
Abhishek Parashar	Poornima College of Engineering, Jaipur, Rajasthan, India
Akansha Mer	Banasthali Vidyapith, District Tonk, Rajasthan, India
Aman Sharma	Symbiosis Institute of Business Management, Symbiosis International (Deemed University), Pune, Maharashtra, India
Anshul Bhardwaj	Computer Science and Engineering, Poornima University, Jaipur, India
Chinmay Kulkarni	Depaertment of Computer Engineering-AIML, Vishwakarma Institute of Information Technology, Pune, India
Devesh Kumar Bandil	Arya College of Engineering and IT, Jaipur, Rajasthan, India
Dipak Saha	Department of Business Management, Institute of Engineering & Management, University of Engineering & Management, Kolkata, West Bengal, India
Farha Khan	Graphic Era Hill University Bhimtal Campus, Nainital, Uttarakhand, India
Govind Shay Sharma	Department of Mathematics, Vivekananda Global University, Jaipur-303012, Rajasthan, India
Govind Soni	Sr. Faculty, Footwear Design and Development Institute, Chhindwara, (M.P.), India
Harkaran Singh	Foundation Education Centre, Kangan Institute, Broadmeadows VIC 3047, Australia
Harshita Sharma	Department of Commerce, Manipal University Jaipur, Jaipur, India
Hemlata Jain	Computer Science and Engineering, Poornima University, Jaipur, India
Kavita Khati	Graphic Era Hill University Bhimtal Campus, Nainital, Uttarakhand, India
Kuldeep Vayadande	Department of Information Technology, Vishwakarma Institute of Technology, Pune, India
Lata Pande	Graphic Era Hill University Bhimtal Campus, Nainital, Uttarakhand, India
Lokesh Khedekar	Department of Artificial Intelligence and Data Science, Vishwakarma Institute of Technology, Pune, India
Neelu Tiwari	Amity University, Noida, India
Pankaj Rahi	Singapore Institute of Technology, Singapore Lovely Professional University, Punjab, India
Pradnya Mehta	Depaertment of Computer Engineering- AI, Vishwakarma Institute of Information Technology, Pune, India
Pritha Ghosh	University of Engineering & Management, Kolkata, West Bengal, India
Rabin Mazumder	Department of Business Administration, Institute of Engineering & Management, University of Engineering & Management, Kolkata, West Bengal, India
Randhir Singh Baghel	Department of Mathematics, Poornima University, Jaipur-303905, Rajasthan, India

Rohit Khatri	Computer Science and Engineering, Poornima University, Jaipur, India
Ruchi Dave	St Wilfred's PG College, Jaipur, Rajasthan, India
Sanjay K. Gupta	School of Studies in Computer Science & Applications, Jiwaji University, Gwalior, Madhya Pradesh, India
Santi Swarup Basa	Maharaja Sriram Chandra Bhanjadeo University, Baripada, Odisha, India
Sapna Jain	Banasthali Vidyapith, Rajasthan, India
Saurabh Mukherjee	Computer Science Department, Banasthali Vidyapith, Rajasthan, India
Serhat Ata	Duzce University, Uskubu Campus, Düzce, Turkey
Shikha Sharma	Department of CSE, Poornima University, Jaipur, India
Sneha Rajput	Prestige Institute of Management and Research, Gwalior (M.P.), India Centre for Peace Studies, Sammanthurai, Srilanka
Sonika Parashar	Poornima University, Jaipur, Rajasthan, India
Swati Ajay Gandhi	Anantrao Pawar College of Engineering and Research, Pune, Maharashtra, India
Swati Jain	Department of Commerce, Manipal University Jaipur, Jaipur, India
Tanush Lichade	Depaertment of Artificial Intelligence & Data Science, Vishwakarma Institute of Information Technology, Pune, India
Tejaswita Mishra	Centre for Computer Science and Technology, MITS-Deemed University, Gwalior, Madhya Pradesh, India
Varun Mishra	Department of Computer Engineering and Applications, GLA University, Mathura, Uttar Pradesh, India
Vijay More	MET's Institute of Engineering, Bhujbal Knowledge City, Nashik, Maharashtra, India
Vijay Prakash Sharma	Department of IT, Manipal University Jaipur, Jaipur, India
Yashowardhan Patil	Depaertment of Computer Engineering, Vishwakarma Institute of Information Technology, Pune, India
Yogesh Bodhe	Department of Information Technology, Government Polytechnic, Pune, India

CHAPTER 1

AI-Driven Churn Management Portal for Managing Churn and Retention

Hemlata Jain[1,*], **Rohit Khatri**[1] and **Anshul Bhardwaj**[1]

[1] *Computer Science and Engineering, Poornima University, Jaipur-303905, India*

Abstract: Client retention is now just as important as client acquisition in today's fiercely competitive business climate. Since it is frequently more expensive to acquire new clients than to retain current ones, churn management is an essential corporate priority. Artificial Intelligence (AI) has become an increasingly powerful tool as companies seek more efficient methods to reduce client attrition. Traditional approaches cannot match the capacity to anticipate, evaluate, and react to customer behaviour that AI-driven churn management solutions provide. By foreseeing churn threats and offering useful insights, advanced analytics and machine learning algorithms play a crucial part in this process. Telecom firms take a multifaceted strategy to churn management. To build client loyalty, this includes: 1) personalised offerings, which entail developing service plans and incentives based on unique consumer demands and usage patterns; 2) customer engagement, which includes establishing enduring relationships with customers by being proactive in communication, giving excellent customer service, and responding to issues right away; 3) predictive analytics, which involves using predictive models to pinpoint potential customers who might leave and putting retention plans in place; 4) network quality, which entails ensuring a dependable and high-quality network to reduce reasons for churn connected to services; 5) competitive pricing, which includes drawing and keeping clients that are price sensitive, offering competitive pricing structures while preserving profitability; 6) data security, which inludes protecting consumer information and privacy that is important for maintaining trust and reducing turnover and lastly, 7) value-added services, which includes enhancing the client experience with cutting-edge features and services. The topic of telecom churn management is one thatis continually evolving due to the changing technologies and evolving customer expectations. Successful churn management can have a long-lasting positive impact on a telecom company's bottom line by not only preserving revenue but also fostering customer loyalty and advocacy. This study emphasises the significance of telecom churn management in a highly competitive market and the continual innovation and adaptation required to suit customers' shifting needs. This study implements a paradigm for managing telecom churn, which will assist telecom companies in maintaining low churn rates. To achieve this, the framework forecasts churners with a likelihood percentage, predicts their churn behaviors and causes,

* **Corresponding author Hemlata Jain:** Computer Science and Engineering, Poornima University, Jaipur-303905, India; E-mail: mailhemajain@gmail.com

Subir Gupta, Indrajit Ghosal, Keshav Kaushik & Monika Dandotiya (Eds.)

recommends consumers who exhibit similar behaviors, and suggests retention strategies for customers based on their behaviors. The administrator of the telecom company can efficiently manage telecom clients through this framework's user-friendly interface. This framework includes: 1) a comprehensive list of all customers, 2) a predictive list of potential churners along with their reasons for leaving, identified using the Random Forest algorithm, 3) detailed customer profiles that highlight individual service usage patterns, and 4) most importantly, an AI-powered retention solution that suggests targeted actions for customers likely to churn, based on behavior predictions generated by the TCCMR framework. The entire system is implemented using the Python programming language. This framework also suggests that similar consumers assist telecom firms in offering the same retention solutions to similar customers. The model performed exceptionally well in predicting churners, achieving outcomes with up to 100% accuracy.

Keywords: Churn management, Churn prediction, Machine learning, Recommendation system, Retention solutions, Telecommunications.

INTRODUCTION

One of the most pressing problems service providers face in the fast-paced and fiercely competitive telecommunications sector is customer churn. Customers are the primary source of income for all industries, making them a valuable resource for any business [1].

Customer churn, also known as "churn," occurs when subscribers stop using a certain telecom service provider's products or switch to another one. Churn can be expensive for telecom firms because it typically incurs significant costs to acquire and retain new subscribers. Long-term client loss can also have a significant negative effect on sales and profitability.

Rapid technological advancements, evolving customer preferences, and intense competition characterize the telecommunications sector. These factors make it imperative for telecom companies to adopt proactive churn management strategies to stay competitive and sustainable in the marketplace.

A wide range of activities, such as data analysis, customer segmentation, predictive modeling, and targeted retention initiatives, are included in effective telecom churn management. Churn management seeks to reduce churn by implementing various retention techniques, such as offering new products or services, to keep customers from cancelling subscriptions. For retention strategies to be effective, businesses must gain insights into their customers' traits and behaviors to identify those most likely to leave [2]. It entails understanding the causes of customer turnover, identifying at-risk clients, and implementing strategies to reduce churn rates. The following are some of the main causes of telecom churn:

1.1. Customers are frequently sensitive to price fluctuations and may switch to suppliers that offer more affordable options.

1.2. Quality of Service: Customer satisfaction and retention are greatly impacted by network dependability, call quality, and data speed.

1.3. Consumer service: Whether a consumer decides to stay or depart depends on how well they are taken care of and how quickly they respond to problems.

1.4. Competitive Environment: The telecom industry is highly competitive, with competitors' better deals frequently drawing in customers

1.5. Technology advancements: As consumers seek the latest features and capabilities, new technologies and services can influence their purchasing decisions.

1.6. Contract Conditions: Contract conditions, early termination fees, and adaptable plans all affect client retention.

1.7. Customer Experience: Churn rates can be impacted by the general experience, including billing procedures and the simplicity of account management.

1.8. Market Saturation: In developed countries, there is a single solution that works for all cases of managing telecom churn. It necessitates a data-driven, customer-focused approach that can adapt to the demands of the market and the needs of the client. Companies that succeed in understanding their consumers, anticipating churn, and implementing successful retention strategies are better positioned to thrive in the telecom sector in this constantly changing environment. This study delves further into the tactics, techniques, and technologies that telecom firms use to lower churn rates, boost customer satisfaction, and ultimately achieve sustainable development in this fast-paced and fiercely competitive industry. The telecom admin user can view all current customers, potential churners, and related customers, as well as retention strategies for potential churners, categorized by their potential cause for leaving.

Businesses seek sustainable techniques that complement their entire retention goals to maintain client loyalty over the long run. This approach aims to foster long-term client loyalty, rather than merely reactive strategies. That is precisely what AI-powered churn management portals offer. They enable them to create data-driven plans. These personalized engagement plans foster client satisfaction and promote long-term retention.

For instance, a telecom business may examine call centre interactions, billing information, and service consumption trends using an AI-powered churn management solution.

In a more realistic scenario, AI can be used by a subscription-based streaming service to track metrics related to user engagement, including viewing duration, user preferences, and account activity. The technology may automatically launch client retention campaigns by identifying trends that indicate possible churn, such as a decline in logins or a move toward free competition. To help re-engage users before they quit their membership, consider providing free trial extensions or delivering targeted content recommendations.

Businesses can gain a thorough understanding of consumer behavior and implement proactive and predictive retention strategies by incorporating AI into their churn management. With this strategy, resources can be effectively distributed to the appropriate clients at the right moment with the right message. Ultimately, AI-powered churn management portals enable the development of long-term retention plans that enhance long-term profitability, reduce attrition, and increase customer satisfaction.

The sections of this study are as follows: The proposed work and database are described in Section I. Section II presents the literature review. Section III provides a brief description of the methodology used in this study. The proposed work and database are described, while the results and discussion are covered in Section IV. Additionally, the author's accomplishments and limitations are discussed. The author's accomplishments, limitations, and plans are mentioned in Section V, which concludes this paper.

LITERATURE REVIEW

In a market characterized by intense competition, rapidly evolving technology, and shifting client preferences, telecommunications firms worldwide struggle to retain customers. Customer churn, the process in which users switch telecom service providers or cancel their subscriptions, has a significant financial impact. Researchers have employed a range of strategies and methodologies to forecast and mitigate churn, effectively addressing this issue. This literature review examines the main advancements and discoveries in the field of telecom churn prediction. In Table **1**, the state-of-the-art literature review is presented, which includes the methodology, Dataset description, and results obtained.

Table 1. Literature review state of the art table.

Journal	Methodology	Dataset	Result
[11]	Churn Prediction by using customer usage history, *decision trees, ensembles, Random Forest, and Gradient Boosted*	Orange Dataset, 3333 Subscribers	Acc Sec Spe - 86.21.96 Random Forest- 91.47.98 Gradient Boosted 91.49.98
[12]	Machine learning techniques on a big data platform and a new way of features.' Engineering and selection.	SyriaTel dataset	AUC After FE (%) XGB 93.3, GSM 90.89, RF 87.76 DT 83
[13]	Classification as well as clustering for churn factor identification	South Asia GSM Tekleco with 64107 subscribers, orange dataset with 3333 subscribers	Results on SAG Telecom TP - .89, FP - .24, Pre - .89, Rec - .89 FM - .88, ROC - 94, RM Results on Orange Telecom TP - .89, FP - .57, Pre - .89, Rec - .89 FM - .88, ROC - .84,
[14]	Rule-based decision-making technique, based on rough set theory (RST),	Orange wirh 3333 subscribers	EA GA CA LEM2 Coverage 1 1 0.64 0.668 Precision 0.72 0.86 0.47 0.67 Recall 0.74 1.00 0.50 0.73 MisErr 0.074 0.019 0.122 0.067 Accuracy 0.926 0.981 0.878 0.993 Specification 0.96 0.98 0.93 0.96 F-measure 0.726 0.925 0.487 0.698
[15]	Feature extraction technique with prediction	Cell2cell with 70831 Subscribers, CrowdAnalitix with 3333 subscribers	accuracy of 92.77%.

Rule Generation Algorithm

The goal of rule generation algorithms, which are frequently used in data mining and machine learning, is to derive understandable rules from datasets. These principles are useful for identifying data trends and making conclusions that are clear and understandable to humans. Different rule-based algorithms were employed by Amin *et al.* [3], who concluded that a rough set based on genetic algorithms, serving as both one-class and multi-class classifiers, provides superior performance compared to the other three rule-generating techniques. It was later determined that the rough set, when used as a multi-class classifier, outperformed and produced accurate results for binary and multi-class classification issues when applied to a public dataset.

Fuzzy Algorithms in Data Mining

The branch of data mining known as fuzzy data mining works with data that is unclear or imprecise. In contrast to traditional data mining, which frequently uses crisp, binary data (such as 0 or 1), fuzzy data mining enables a more flexible and nuanced representation and analysis of data. It is especially helpful in circumstances when data is hazy, ambiguous, or fundamentally fuzzy, such as in decision support systems, expert systems, and natural language processing. Fuzzy data mining was employed by Liao *et al.* [4] to identify efficient marketing strategies by analyzing consumer responses to various marketing campaigns. Telecom service providers can utilize this technique to analyze customer turnover frequencytilize this technique to analyze customer turnover frequency, enabling the identification of the most effective marketing plan opportunities and methods, and thereby reducing customer turnover across various client categories.

Supervised Learning

An algorithm can learn from labelled training data using supervised learning to generate predictions or judgments without being explicitly programmed. The algorithm produces predictions based on a set of input-output pairings provided in the training data, which is where the term "supervision" comes from. These input-output pairings, commonly referred to as "labels," direct the algorithm as it learns how to map inputs to outputs. Labhsetwar [5] focused on applying Machine Learning (ML) algorithms to identify potential customers who may leave, classify them based on usage patterns, and present the analysis results.

The results show that Extra Trees Classifier, XGBoosting Algorithm, and Support Vector Machine have the best churn modelling performance, with average AUC scores of 0.843, 0.787, and 0.735, respectively, and low false negatives. The study found that ML algorithms are capable of accurately predicting future customer churn and supporting the development of client retention activities. Adaboost and XG, with respective accuracies of 81.71% and 80.8%, were found to offer the best accuracy in a study by Lalwani *et al.* [6]. Classifiers from Adaboost and XGBoost both beat others and achieve the highest AUC score of 84%. Jain *et al.* [7] employed LogitBoost and logistic regression to predict churn, and both methods generated excellent results with an accuracy rate of 85%.

Deep Learning

Deep learning is a branch of machine learning that focuses on deep neural networks, which are neural networks with several layers. Due to its ability to automatically identify patterns and representations in data, particularly in unstructured formats such as photos, text, and audio, it has experienced tremendous success and widespread acceptance across a diverse range of industries. A churn prediction model utilising a deep learning variational autoencoder was proposed in [8]. An innovative and effective method known as a convolutional neural network with a variational autoencoder is demonstrated in this study. CNN can automatically identify effective features and represent input data. The concept of including all string attributes in the dataset (ISAD) is novel and is introduced in this study. As a result, the model performed better.

Retention Solutions in Literature

In the telecom sector, customer retention is essential for sustaining business growth and profitability. Implementing efficient retention solutions is crucial for telecom firms since they frequently face intense competition. Here are a few academic studies that discuss retention strategies used by telecom companies [9]. First, choose a commercial domain. Specific business objectives, goals, and requirements are recognised and determined during this phase. Phase 2 of the data gathering. This entails collecting information from all available sources, including databases, spreadsheets, and other relevant data, as well as data warehouses and other relevant repositories. The data collection is also prepared for the churn prediction retention process at this stage. It also entails choosing the data and attributes, cleaning them up, adding new attributes, and performing data transformations. Using the knowledge gained during the prediction phase, the framework provides a method for choosing a retention solution. To increase CRM effectiveness, the proposed architecture can be incorporated into a BI application. This paper's inability to apply the suggested methodology in a practical BI setting is one of its main weaknesses [10]. Examines the effects of Data Mining (DM) techniques-based prediction models and service quality. The current model consists of five steps: data preprocessing, feature selection, data sampling, classifier training, prediction testing, and prediction output. A dataset containing 17 properties and 5,000 records is randomly chosen, of which 75% are utilised to train the model and 25% to test it. The Boruta algorithm, C5.0, Neural Network, Support Vector Machine, and Random Forest are the Data Mining (DM) approaches used in this paper, implemented *via* free and open-source software R and WEKA. This paper's flaw is that it does not demonstrate a retention strategy based on the cause of churn. Here are some examples of "state of the art" literature surveys that can help you understand the literature survey better:

With the introduction of big data and advanced analytics technologies, the dynamic field of telecom churn prediction has seen substantial development. Researchers and practitioners are always investigating novel approaches to improve forecast accuracy and produce useful insights for telecom firms. For successfully minimising churn and enhancing customer retention in this cutthroat sector, the development of robust, interpretable models that take real-time data and client segmentation into account is essential. In the constantly shifting telecom industry, it is critical to stay on the cutting edge of churn prediction approaches. This literature review lays the groundwork for additional study.

PROPOSED METHODOLOGY

One of the most important aspects of the telecommunications sector is managing client turnover. It includes tactics and methods designed to keep valuable subscribers and reduce customer turnover. Fig. (**1**) depicts the whole system architecture of the model. Here are some tactics and strategies for reducing customer turnover in the telecom industry:

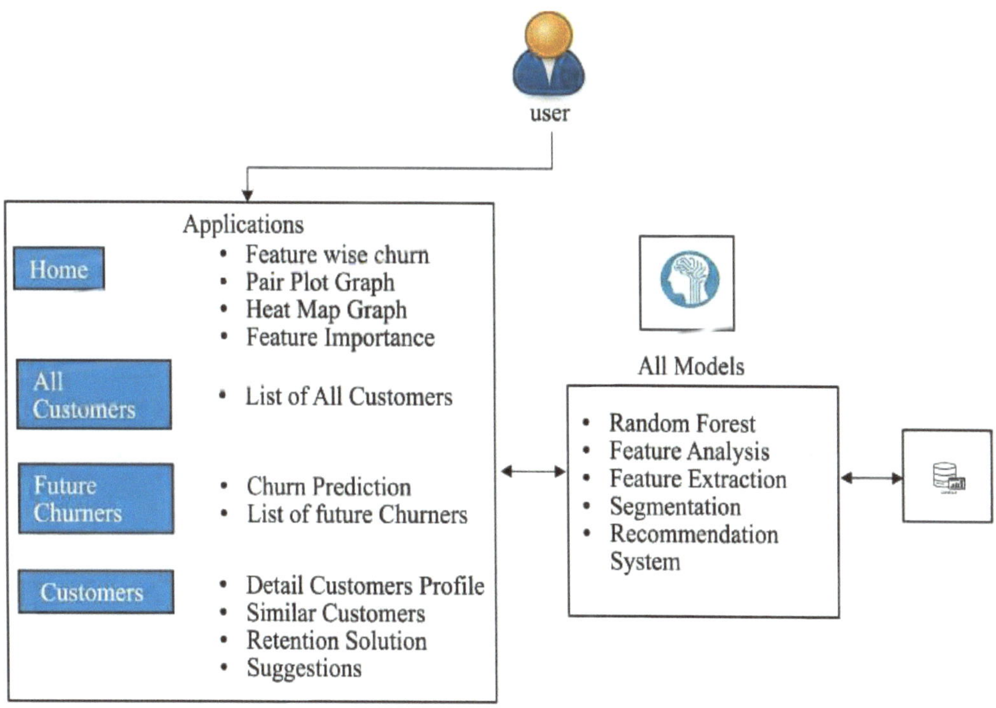

Fig. (1). Churn management farmwork.

Churn Prediction using Random Forest

For telecom companies to keep customers and prevent revenue loss, forecasting telecom churn is an essential responsibility. Identifying customers who might stop using the service provider is necessary for this forecast. Based on the probability percentage of each customers turnover, this churn management system predicts which customers are likely to leave in the near future.

An effective machine learning approach called Random Forest is frequently used to forecast telecom churn. It is an ensemble learning technique that mixes various decision trees to provide more accurate predictions. The following describes how Random Forest can be used to forecast telecom churn:

- **Building the Random Forest Model**: Using the training set of data, a group of decision trees is created. By bootstrapping the training data (choosing a random sample with replacement) and by choosing a random subset of characteristics at each node of each tree, the Random Forest technique creates randomization. Each tree in the forest has undergone independent training and produced a prediction. A majority vote (classification) or average (regression) of the individual tree predictions frequently determines the final prediction.
- **Hyperparameter Tuning:** Adjust the Random Forest models hyperparameters, such as the number of trees (n_estimators), the depth at which each tree can grow (max_depth), and the number of features taken into account at each split (max_features). For hyperparameter optimisation, you can use grid search or random search.
- **Model Training:** Using the training dataset and the optimised hyperparameters, the Random Forest model is trained. The model gains the ability to recognise intricate patterns and correlations in the data.
- **Model Evaluation:** Utilise the validation dataset to assess the models effectiveness. The evaluation metrics, accuracy, precision, recall, F1-score, ROC-AUC, and confusion matrices, are frequently used to assess telecom churn prediction models. You need to select the measurements that support your unique business objectives.
- **Fine-Tuning and Re-evaluation:** You can iterate on the models performance if it is unsatisfactory by adjusting hyperparameters, selecting alternative features, or developing new features based on knowledge from the validation set. After each iteration, the model is re-evaluated.
- **Model Deployment:** Deploy the model in a production setting if you are happy with its performance so that it may be used to score and forecast churn based on fresh, previously unexplored customer data.

- **Out-of-Bag (OOB) Error:** The estimation of a models performance on unobserved data is referred to as the OOB error. Some data points are not used in the training of each decision tree because they are all trained on bootstrapped samples. These random data points can be used to predict how the Random Forest will do with fresh, untested data.
- **Interpretability and Reporting:** It is possible to obtain feature importance from Random Forest models, which show which characteristics have the most predictive power. This knowledge can help illuminate the reasons why specific clients are expected to leave.

Because of its propensity to handle complicated data, feature importance analysis, and resistance to overfitting, Random Forest is a reliable option for telecom churn prediction. It can accurately forecast outcomes and efficiently capture non-linear relationships in the data, assisting telecom firms in preventing customer churn.

Similar Customers Recommendation

When similar consumers are referred to one another, it can increase customer engagement, cross-sell services, and decrease churn in the telecom business, among other advantages. An overview of how this study built a system for client recommendations comparable to that used in telecom follows:

A system of recommendations is developed to discover and recommend consumers who share similar features or usage patterns. This is achieved by building a recommendation system for similar telecom customers, utilising customer data and machine learning techniques. An overview of how to build such a recommendation system is given below:

- **Data Gathering and Preprocessing**: Compile pertinent customer data, such as demographic data, usage trends, billing information, and any other pertinent elements. Please make sure the data is prepared for analysis by cleaning, transforming, and structuring it.
- **Customer Segmentation:** To categorise customers into groups based on their shared characteristics, clustering techniques are used (such as k-means clustering or hierarchical clustering). This process aids in locating client groups that exhibit comparable behaviours.
- **Feature Engineering**: Develop new features that can effectively capture the essence of user behaviour or preferences. You may calculate the average call length, client lifetime value, or usage frequency, for instance.
- **Similarity Metrics**: Select distance or similarity metrics that express how similar clients in each segment are to one another. Depending on the type of

your data, common similarity metrics include Euclidean distance, cosine similarity, and Jaccard similarity.

Model Selection: To produce suggestions for each client category, choose the best recommendation algorithm. You can take into account the following strategies depending on your particular use case:

Collaborative Filtering: Using the preferences and behavior of like-minded customers, this strategy suggests relevant customers. Collaborative filtering methods include user-based and item-based approaches. User-Based Collaborative Filtering was employed in this framework:

The practise of "User-User Collaborative Filtering," also known as "User-based Collaborative Filtering," involves recommending products to a target user based on their shared interests with other users.

Heres how it works:

Determine how similar the target user is to every other user in the system. Cosine similarity, Pearson correlation, or Jaccard similarity are examples of common similarity metrics. Any two users, p and q, can be compared by using the following formula:

$$S(p,q) = \frac{\Sigma(r_{pa}-\bar{r}_p)(r_{pq}-\bar{r}_q)}{\sqrt{\Sigma(r_{pa}-\bar{r}_p)^2}\sqrt{\Sigma(r_{qa}-\bar{r}_q)^2}} \quad \textbf{(1)}$$

Where r_ua is the user us rating of item a.

Using the determined similarity scores, identify theusers who are most similar to the target user. As a result, it makes sense to give greater weight to user ratings that are more similar to one another than to user ratings that are less similar to one another, and so on. This problem can be solved *via* a method based on weighted averages.

$$r_{ua} = r_u + \frac{\Sigma_{i\in users}\, s(u,i) X\, r_{ia}}{\Sigma_{i\in users}|s(u,i)|} \quad \textbf{(2)}$$

Send the target user recommendations for goods that they havent yet seen or interacted with, but that similar individuals have enjoyed or interacted with.

User-based collaborative Filtering is user-friendly and capable of making precise recommendations. As the number of users and products grows, though, scalability problems may arise.

Training and Testing: The data is divided into training and testing sets to assess the effectiveness of the recommendation system. For model selection and hyperparameter adjustment, cross-validation was employed.

- Evaluation Metrics: Select suitable metrics for the recommendation systems evaluation. Common measures include Normalised Discounted Cumulative Gain (NDCG), Mean Absolute Error (MAE), Root Mean Square Error (RMSE), Precision, Recall, and F1-score.
- Implementation: The recommendation system was installed in a working context. Ensure it can handle both batch and real-time recommendations based on planned updates or consumer interactions.
- Monitoring and Comments Loop: Track user comments and the performance of the recommendation system. Utilise this criticism to enhance and continuously improve the suggestions.
- Create an intuitive User Interface (UI) to deliver the suggestions to telecom operators or customer support agents. Make it simple for them to access and implement the advice.
- Privacy and Security: Make sure that consumer information is handled safely and in accordance with privacy laws. When necessary, anonymize or aggregate data to safeguard client privacy.
- A/B Testing: Run A/B tests to assess how suggestions affect customer engagement, satisfaction, and retention.

The provision of customised services, offers, and telecom businesses can facilitate solutions to clients based on their preferences and behaviours *via* a telecom customer recommendation system. Telecom operators can improve customer satisfaction, lower churn, and boost revenue by using such a system.

Retention Solution Suggestions

In the highly competitive telecom sector, where customer attrition can significantly affect revenue, retention is a major concern. Retaining valuable clients and lowering churn rates can both be achieved by using effective retention strategies. Here is an example of how to use retention recommendations

Segmentation

Segmenting your client base into discrete groups or segments based on particular traits, habits, or demands is a tactic used in the telecom business to increase customer retention. Telecom firms can better target their retention initiatives by comprehending the distinctive traits and preferences of each segment. Here is a step-by-step breakdown of the segmentation method used to increase client retention.

Define Segmentation Criteria

Choose the parameters or elements that will be used to segment your clientele. In Table **2**, we can see the telecom industrys standard segmentation criteria:

Table 2. Attributes' description.

Attributes Type	Attributes
Demographic Information	Age, gender, income, household size, *etc.*
Usage Patterns	Call frequency, data usage, international calling, *etc.*
Billing History	Average revenue per user (ARPU), contract type, payment history, *etc.*
Customer Lifecycle	New customers, long-term customers, *etc.*
Customer Preferences	Preferred communication channels, service features, *etc.*

Segment Identification

Utilise hierarchical clustering techniques to pinpoint client base segments. A telecom retention study can benefit from the use of hierarchical clustering. Telecom firms can use this technique to categorise clients based on their likes and dislikes, allowing them to establish customer groupings with various retention requirements and develop focused retention strategies. An instruction manual for using hierarchical clustering for telecom retention is provided below:

Metric Distance Selection

Select the "Euclidean distance" as the suitable distance metric to gauge how similar or unlike your customers are. Euclidean distance, Manhattan distance, or cosine similarity are examples of typical metrics. If necessary, the data is normalised to ensure that each characteristic has the same scale.

Heterogeneous Clustering

Agglomerative hierarchical clustering methods are commonly used. The more popular type of clustering, agglomerative clustering, begins with each data point as its own cluster, merges the closest clusters repeatedly, and ultimately consolidates them into a single cluster. A dendrogram or a validation metric like the silhouette score was used to determine the cluster size (k).

Analysis of Dendrograms

Visualize the dendrogram to comprehend the clustering hierarchy and select the appropriate number of clusters (k). This step is frequently exploratory and aids in your decision-making regarding the number of clusters.

Interpretation of Clusters

Look at each clusters qualities. To learn what separates one client group from another, look at the average values of the features in each cluster. Based on the features of the clusters, give them labels or names. For instance, you might have clusters for "At-Risk Customers," "Low-Usage Customers," and "High-Value Customers."

Retention Strategies

Develop tailored retention strategies for each segment based on their specific characteristics and predicted churn probabilities. Strategies may include personalized offers: offering discounts, upgrades, or add-on services that align with the needs of each segment; proactive customer services, identifying high-risk customers within each segment and proactively addressing their concerns; service enhancements, rolling out new features or services that cater to the preferences of specific segments.

Evaluation

Continuous monitoring of customer churn rates and customer satisfaction metrics for each cluster to evaluate the success of your retention strategies is necessary. Adjust and refine your strategies as needed based on ongoing performance. Hierarchical clustering can help telecom companies gain valuable insights into their customer base, allowing them to tailor retention efforts to specific customer segments and ultimately reduce churn rates.

Dataset

The data set used for this model was collected from the Kaggle online database repository. This is an IBM sample telecom dataset. In this dataset, each row represents a customer, and each column contains the customer's attributes, as described in the column Metadata. The dataset is presented in Table **3**:

Table 3. Dataset attributes.

Attribute Type	Attributes
Customers who left within the last month (Target Attribute)	The column is called "Churn".
Services that each customer has signed up for	Phone, multiple lines, internet, online security, online backup, device protection, tech support, and streaming TV and movies.
Customer account information	For how long they've been a customer, contract, payment method, paperless billing, monthly charges, and total charges.
Demographic info about customers	Gender, age range, and if they have partners and dependents

Data Pre-processing

Preprocessing a telecom dataset is a crucial step in data analysis and machine learning tasks. It involves cleaning, transforming, and preparing the data so that it can be effectively used for analysis, modelling, or any other telecom-related tasks. Here are the key steps you should consider when preprocessing a telecom dataset:

Data Cleaning

Handle Missing Data: Identified and handled missing values in the dataset. To fill the missing values, the column mean was used.

Outlier Detection: Identified and handled outliers in the dataset. Telecom data may contain anomalies, such as unusually high or low usage, which can affect analysis. This model used the Interquartile Range (IQR) to detect and handle outliers.

Data Transformation

Feature Scaling: Numerical features are normalized or standardized to bring them to a common scale. This is important when using distance-based algorithms like clustering or when training models like neural networks. This model normalised all the numeric attributes.

Encoding Categorical Variables: Converted categorical variables (*e.g.*, customer segments, plan types) into numerical format using techniques like one-hot encoding or label encoding.

Time Series Data: Time series data (*e.g.*, call logs, network performance metrics) was aggregated or resampled at a different time granularity (*e.g.*, hourly, daily, monthly) to suit your analysis needs.

RESULT AND DISCUSSION

We will discuss the results of the Churn Management Framework in this section. For a telecom admin to manage consumer churn, this churn management framework is quite helpful. This framework incorporated several user interface pages to aid with churn prediction and user interaction with service behaviour. Based on these UI pages, the Churn Management framework is discussed here.

Users' Login

All users of the telecom corporation are given login information in this framework, together with their credentials. Each user has a distinct username and password. According to their status, each user has their own set of permissions. Fig. (**2**) shows the login page of the application.

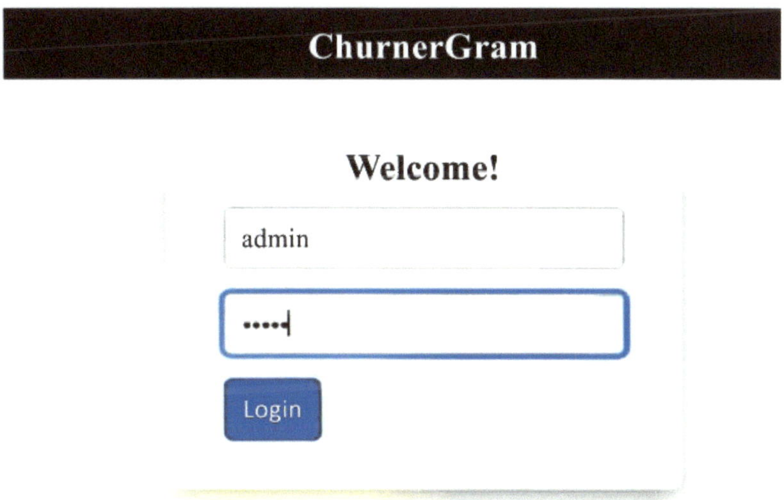

Fig. (2). Login page for telecom admin users.

Home Page

This page is the first UI interface that users will see after logging in. This page will be loaded with several customer-related graphs that will help users gain insights into the company, its customers, churn rates, and customer behaviors. User will be provided with the following facilities on the home page:

Feature-wise Churn

In this section, users can view past churners by feature. It will show the ratio of churning based on each feature. In Fig. (**3**), the first graph illustrates the churn rate according to the Contract Plan. The number of churned customers is the highest in the "month to month" contract plan, followed by the one-year plan and then the two-year plan. So, it can be concluded that customers with having "month-to-month plan are supposed to churn frequently. This will help in deciding the retention solution for "month-to-month" plan customers. The second graph illustrates the ratio of churners and non-churners by gender attribute. It can be observed that the gender attribute does not have a significant impact on the churn rate. The third graph shows the churn ratio by internet plan for customers. The graphs show that the number of churned customers is high in Fiber Optic Internet services, then DSL, and then no internet service plan. The 5th and 6th graphs show the churn rate according to "Senior citizen" and "TechSupport". According to the Senior Citizen Plan, senior citizen customers churned at a lower rate than young customers. On the other hand, according to the "TechSupport" attribute, the number of churners is high when "TechSupport" is not provided. In contrast, when tech Support is provided, there are fewer churners, and when no tech support is provided, the number of churners is high. The retention plans can be accumulated according to these graphs. The 3rd graph shows the number of churners by monthly charges.

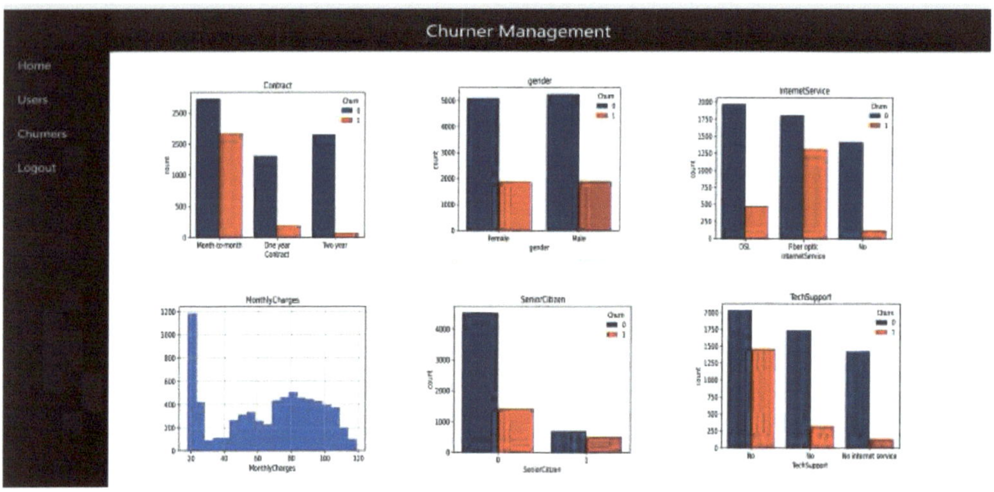

Fig. (3). Feature-wise past churn ratio.

Pair Plot Graph

A pair plot is a graphical representation commonly used in data analysis and data visualization, particularly in the field of statistics and machine learning. It is a type of scatterplot matrix that displays pairwise relationships between multiple variables in a dataset. Each variable is compared against every other variable, and the resulting plots can provide insights into correlations, patterns, and distributions in the data. Fig. (**4**) on the home page illustrates the relationship between all numerical features. It shows the combined effect of both features on the target feature "churn". This graph shows that the combination of "Tenure" and "Monthly Charges" has a slightly greater impact on "churn" than other features.

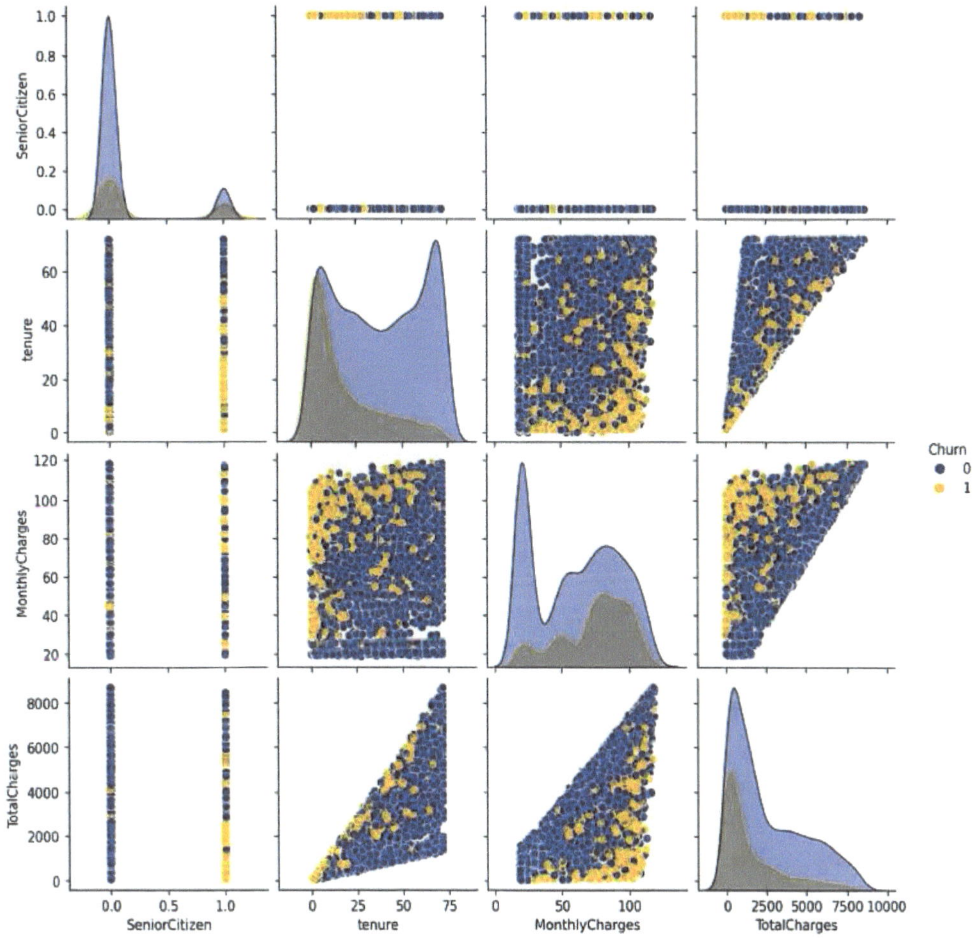

Fig. (4). Pair plot.

Heat Map Graph

Fig. (**5**) shows a Heat Map graph. Individual values are depicted as colors on a heat map, which is a graphical representation of data. It is a technique for displaying data in a two-dimensional (2D) space by commonly utilizing a color scale to denote the intensity of a specific value at each data point. Heat maps are frequently used to find patterns, trends, and correlations within data sets in many different domains, including data analysis, statistics, and data visualization. This heat map graph illustrates the intensity of one feature relative to another. Here, we can see that the intensity value for "Churn" is high in relation to "Tenure" and "Total Charges". This will help provide an effective retention solution for customers who are about to churn. Users can focus more on the factors that most significantly affect their churn.

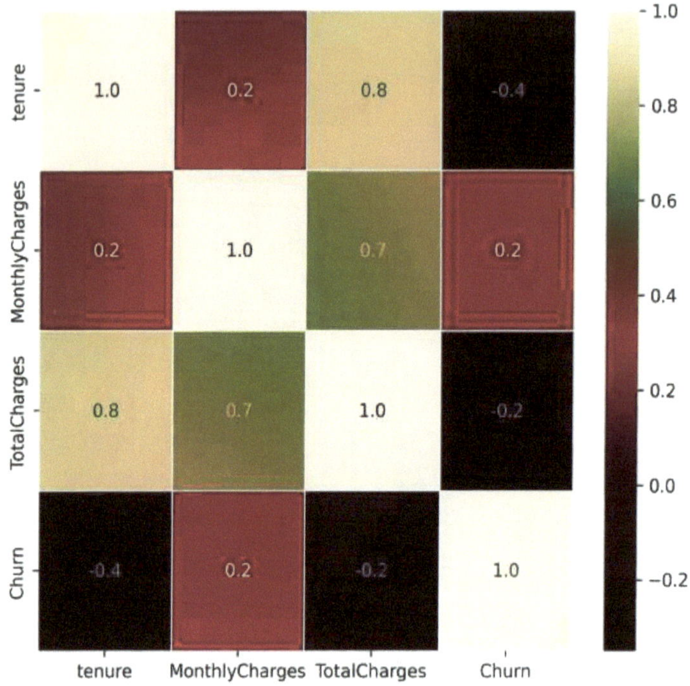

Fig. (5). Heat map graph.

Feature Importance Graph

Fig. (**6**) shows the feature importance graph. The feature importance graph is a very good feature of the Random Forest Algorithm. A feature importance graph is a visual representation of how important various features or variables are in relation to one another in a machine learning model. It aids in your understanding of the characteristics that have the greatest influence on the models predictions. In tasks such as feature selection, model interpretation, and understanding the variables that influence your models output, feature importance proves extremely helpful. The Feature Importance graph presented here shows the most important features that are "tenure", "Total Charges", "PARTNER_CONTR_2", "MothlyCharges", "GENDER_EC_MONTH_2", "InternetService_fiberOptic", the colored bars show the range of importance of features. This can help track customers behaviors and design effective retention solutions.

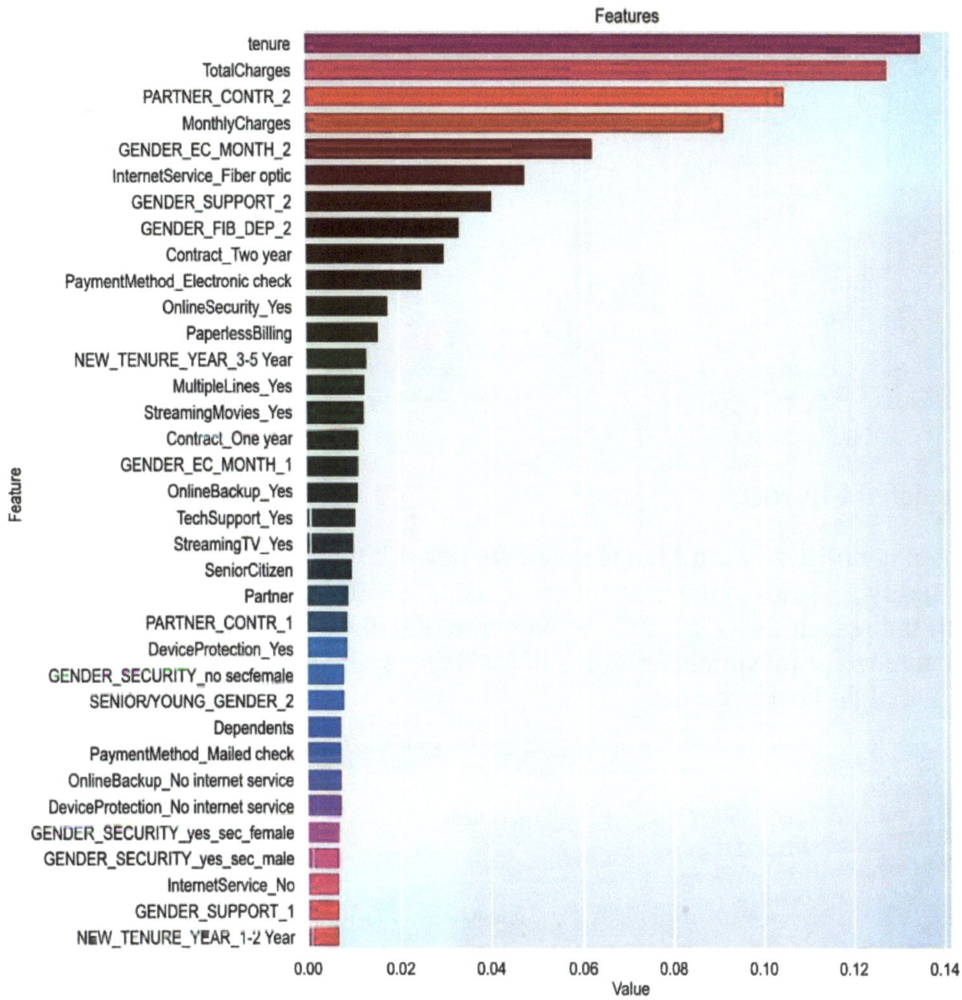

Fig. (6). Feature importance graph.

All Customers Page

This is the platform where users can see the list of all customers. On this page, users can view other important customer features and access the customer's profile page. The user can directly visit the customer profile page from this page. Fig. (7) shows the all users page.

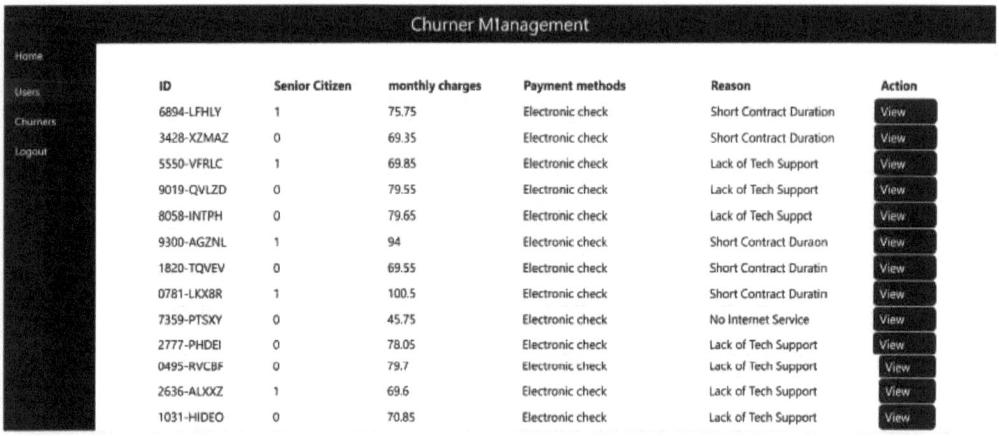

Fig. (7). All customer's list.

Predicted Churners

This page of the Churn Management framework will display a list of users who are likely to churn in the near future. This page will list all future churners, along with the reason for churn and the recharge plan they have opted for. This model has achieved a maximum accuracy of 100% in predicting churners. Fig. (**8**) shows the list of all future churners.

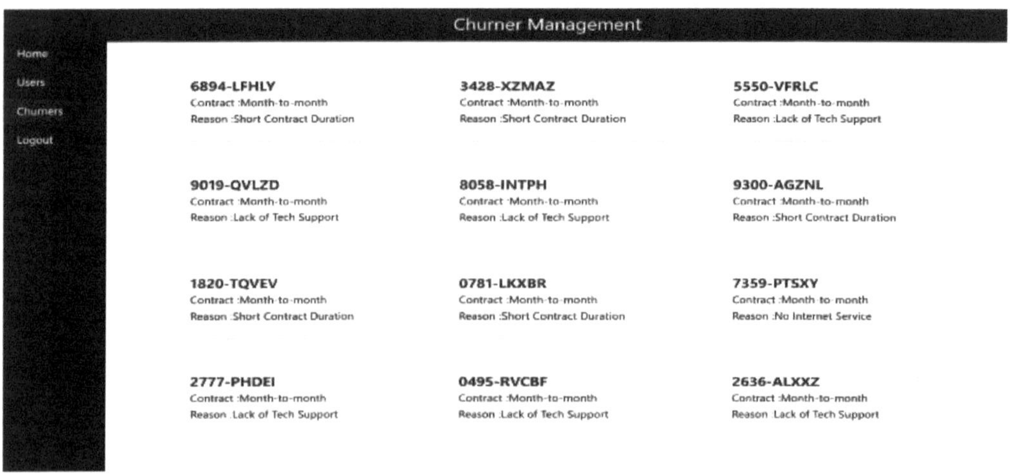

Fig. (8). List of all future churners.

Customer Profile Page

This frameworks "Customer Profile page" is a crucial component. This page was developed to monitor each users conduct closely. Users can access this page from both the Predicted Churners page and the All-Customers page. The user profile page is accessible whenever the user wishes to learn more about the client. These details about the customer are displayed on this page: "Contract plan," "Gender," "Senior Citizen," "Payment Method," "Monthly Charges," "Total Charges," "Churn," "Churn Probability Percentage," and "Churn Reason."

On the other hand, a notable feature of this page is the Retention Suggestions. The retention recommendation that can be offered to consumers is displayed on this page. These recommendations are foreseen based on their behaviour. On the right upper side of the page, retention ideas are displayed. Similar users is the last and most helpful feature on this page. This page displays every client whose behaviour is comparable to that of the customer whose profile is open. All customers who are comparable to this customer can use the retention recommendation. Fig. (**9**) shows the customer's detailed information with their retention solution.

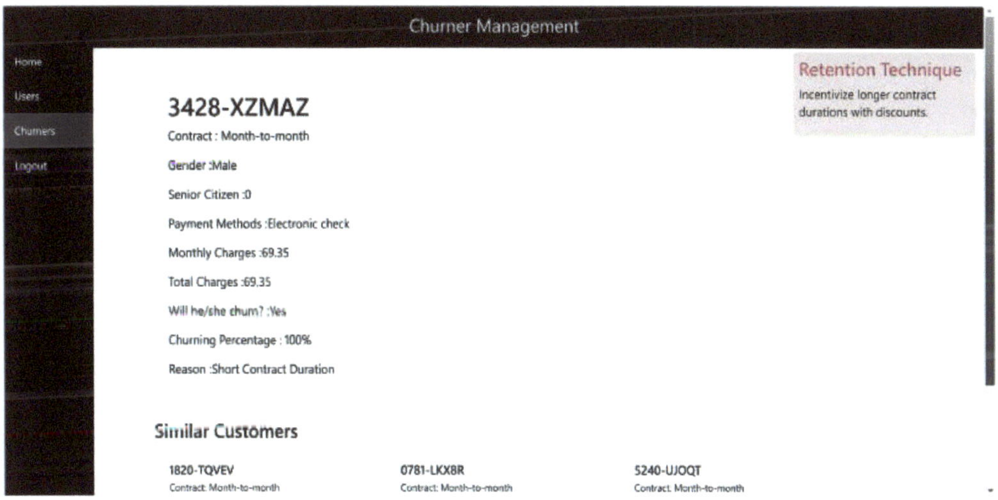

Fig. (9). Customer's profile page.

The Churn Management Framework has proven to be a very effective platform for telecom companies to manage customers, reduce churn rates, and enhance retention solutions. It will definitely help in growing companies' revenue. This framework accurately predicts customers who are likely to churn in the future. The use of a recommendation system for similar churners proved excellent. It will help in giving retention to all similar customers together.

CONCLUSION

The most important aspect of any telecom company to manage is customer turnover. Furthermore, this is their main preoccupation these days. This study focuses exclusively on telecom churn management. The purpose of this study is to provide a telecom corporation with a convenient platform for managing churn and retention in the telecom industry. An IBM Database Repository telecom dataset is used for the experiment. Eighteen characteristics make up this dataset. For several churn management activities, machine learning approaches were applied in this study, which are outlined below:

This study focused on forecasting churn. Random Forest algorithms were utilized in this study to make predictions, achieving a maximum accuracy of 100%. Employees at telecom companies have access to the complete list of churners. They can access the detailed profiles of all expected customers and view them all.

The user can get several feature analysis graphs from this research on the telecom companys main page. All graphs are quite helpful for examining the features and learning about the crucial and less relevant ones. The past churn rate according to all features is displayed in Graph 1. The second graph illustrates how various factors affect the “churn rate.” The relationship between one trait and another is depicted in Graph 3. The importance of features for the desired feature “churn” is depicted in Graph 4.

This framework also shows all customers lists.

In this framework, a recommendation system is used to display similar customers on the customer’s profile page. The recommendation system worked out and suggested all similar customers with 100% accuracy. On the other hand, the technique of segmentation is being used for retention solutions and suggests an accurate retention solution on the customer’s profile page.

Limitations and Future Scope

The Telecom Churn Management Framework performed outstandingly and proved to be a very effective framework for both churn management and retention management. This framework does not include the customer calling and message-related functionality. This could be the limitation of this framework. In the future, the functionality of calling customers regarding retention and sending bulk messages to similar customers will be added in part 2. Additionally, this framework can be more powerful with AI-integrated functionalities.

REFERENCES

[1] H. Jain, A. Khunteta, and S. Srivastava, "Telecom churn prediction and used techniques, datasets and performance measures: a review", *Telecomm. Syst.,* vol. 76, no. 4, pp. 613-630, 2021. [http://dx.doi.org/10.1007/s11235-020-00727-0]

[2] M. Pejic Bach, J. Pivar, and B. Jaković, "Churn management in telecommunications: hybrid approach using cluster analysis and decision trees", Journal of Risk and Finance Management, ISSN: 1911-8074, 11 Nov. 2021. [http://dx.doi.org/10.3390/jrfm14110544]

[3] A. Amin, C. Khan, I. Ali, and S. Anwar, "Customer churn prediction in telecommunication industry: with and without counter-example", MICAI 2014, *Springer International Publishing Switzerland, Volume*, vol. 8857, pp. 206-218, 2014.

[4] K.-H. Liao and H.-E. Chueh, "Applying fuzzy data mining to telecom churn management": ICICIS 2011, Springer-Verlag Berlin Heidelberg 2011, pages. 259–264, Volume: 134, 2011.

[5] S.R. Labhsetwar, "Predictive analysis of customer churn in telecom industry using supervised learning", ICTACT Journal on Soft Computing, 2020, Volume: 10, Issue: 02, ISSN: 2229-6956. [http://dx.doi.org/10.21917/ijsc.2020.0291]

[6] P. Lalwani, M. K. Mishra, J. S. Chadha, and P. Sethi, "Customer churn prediction system: a machine learning approach", Computing, 14th Febuary 2021, Pages: 271–294, Volume: 103.

[7] H. Jain, A. Khunteta, and S. Srivastava, "Churn prediction in telecommunications using logistic regression and logit boost", *Procedia Computer Science, Volume,* vol. 167, pp. 101-112, 2020. [http://dx.doi.org/10.1016/j.procs.2020.03.187]

[8] H. Jain, A. Khunteta, and S. Srivastava, "Telecom churn prediction using CNN with variational auto encoder", *Smart System Innovation in Computing. Springer, Volume,* vol. 235, pp. 583-600, 2021.

[9] E.S.A.E. Hassanien, "Churn prediction retention framework", The Third Intl. Conf. on Advances in Computing, Control and Networking - ACCN 2015, ISBN: 978-1-63248-082-8 [http://dx.doi.org/10.15224/978-1-63248-082-8-06]

[10] M. Ewieda, E. M, and M. Roushdy, "Customer retention: Detecting churners in telecoms industry using data mining techniques", *Int. J. Adv. Comput. Sci. Appl.,* vol. 12, no. 3, pp. 216-224, 2021. [http://dx.doi.org/10.14569/IJACSA.2021.0120326]

[11] P. Jayaswal, B.R. Prasad, D. Tomar, and S. Agarwal, "An ensemble approach for efficient churn prediction in telecom industry", *International Journal of Database Theory and Application,* vol. 9, no. 8, pp. 211-232, 2016. [http://dx.doi.org/10.14257/ijdta.2016.9.8.21]

[12] A. K. Ahmad, A. Jafar, and K. Aljoumaa, "Customer churn prediction in telecom using machine learning in big data platform", *Journal of big data, Ahmad et al. J Big Data* (2019) 6:28. [http://dx.doi.org/10.1186/s40537-019-0191-6]

[13] I. Ullah, B. Raza, A. K. Malik, M. Imran, S. ul Islam, and S. W. Kim, "A churn prediction model using random forest: analysis of machine learning techniques for churn prediction and factor identification in telecom sector", *IEEE Access,* vol. 7, 2019.

[14] S.F. Sabbeh, ""Machine-learning techniques for customer retention: a comparative study", (IJACSA)", *Int. J. Adv. Comput. Sci. Appl.,* vol. 9, no. 2, 2018.

[15] F.M. Kau, H.D. Masethe, and C.K. Lepota, "Service provider churn prediction for telecoms company using data analytics", *Proceedings of the World Congress on Engineering and Computer Science 2017,* vol. Vol I, San Francisco, USA

CHAPTER 2

Legal and Ethical Implications of AI for Human Resource Management: Handling Bias, Data Privacy, and Transparency for Sustainability

Farha Khan[1], **Akansha Mer**[2,*], **Lata Pande**[1] and **Kavita Khati**[1]

[1] *Graphic Era Hill University Bhimtal Campus, Nainital, Uttarakhand, India*

[2] *Banasthali Vidyapith, District Tonk, Rajasthan, India*

Abstract: Artificial Intelligence (AI) is increasingly being incorporated into Human Resource Management (HRM), which brings complex ethical and governing issues. This research paper addresses moral and legal problems by methodically investigating Artificial Intelligence's legal and ethical implications in HRM for an effective business. The study addresses the ethical aspects, including bias, justice, accountability, transparency, and the confidentiality and security of worker information. The legal roots are examined, covering information fortification strategies such as the General Data Protection Regulation and anti-discrimination regulations. The Personal Data Protection Bill and the Equal Remuneration Act are two Indian laws discussed in the paper, and their implications for AI in HRM are explored. The major aspects considered in the paper are lawful strategies that signify discrimination in AI-driven HR. The study employed a methodical approach, examining current legal systems and literature.

The main findings include the necessity of model interpretability, the use of fair machine learning algorithms, open communication with employees, and informed consent for sensitive employee data. The study emphasizes the importance of using AI responsibly to uphold human rights that are fair, open, and respectful of individual liberty. The results inform the conversation about AI ethics and legal compliance, directing the responsible application of AI in HR.

Keywords: AI in human resource management, Artificial intelligence and HRM, Compliance, Ethics, GDPR, Handling bias, Information privacy and transparency, Law, Sustainability.

* **Corresponding author Akansha Mer:** Banasthali Vidyapith, District Tonk, Rajasthan, India;
E-mail: akanshamer3@gmail.com

Subir Gupta, Indrajit Ghosal, Keshav Kaushik & Monika Dandotiya (Eds.)

INTRODUCTION

Artificial Intelligence (AI) has significantly influenced Human Resource Management (HRM) [1], offering efficiency and data-driven decision-making capabilities in organizations. AI-driven HRM pervades multifarious areas of HRM such as recruitment and selection, employee performance evaluation, employee engagement, training and development, compensation management, employee retention, *etc.* [2, 3].

However, this innovative and cautious approach also raises a combination of legal and ethical issues that demand careful investigation. The concept behind the use of AI in HR is that these systems can seamlessly screen job candidates and personnel, gathering organizational information in an unbiased and objective manner. Nevertheless, beneath the surface of impartiality, problems are deeply rooted in the algorithms, which are based on past information and prone to prejudices that could reinforce existing biases [4]. AI in HRM raises a paradox: Does AI eliminate or computerize human preconception? Natural Language Processing and Machine Learning can investigate massive datasets speedily and accurately [5]. According to Boudreau and Cascio [6], these capabilities hold the prospect of Ring's high-potential employees and mitigating employee turnover. However, investigating the likelihood of prejudice and injustice in these systems is increasingly important as AI-driven selections progressively affect individuals' professional trajectories, posing a perilous risk. It is pertinent to align AI use in HR with the ethical principles of fairness, transparency, and accountability, as these principles can significantly impact the ethical foundation of AI-driven decision-making, thereby affecting employees' financial and mental well-being. Because of this, the research paper aims to simplify the moral insinuations of AI in Human Resources by revealing the subtleties of algorithmic prejudice and opacity. Doing this simplifies companies' moral accountabilities when applying AI in Human Resource procedures and the subsequent effects on the employees.

This study examines the moral implications of AI in human resources, focusing on algorithmic bias and opacity, as well as the moral responsibilities that arise from adopting AI-driven human resource practices, which in turn impact their staff and livelihoods. This, in turn, will help endorse sustainable HR practices.

The legal framework governing AI in Human Resource Management remains complex and fragmented. Today's digital realm varies considerably from the landmark era in which previous anti-discrimination laws, such as Title VII of the Civil Rights Act in the U.S., were established by Pager [7]. One needs to reflect whether existing laws adequately address and regulate the complexities of AI, or if their scope needs to be re-evaluated. In addition, in AI-driven Human Resource structures, Europe's General Data Protection Regulation raises significant concerns about information confidentiality and protection [8]. It is indispensable to cautiously examine the legal framework to determine whether it is sufficient to guard individual rights and allow Human Resources to employ AI responsibly.

This investigation employs a multidisciplinary approach to navigate the complex intersection of law and morals in AI-driven HRM, integrating knowledge from HRM, lawful obedience, and AI ethics. This study aims to investigate AI's ethical and legal consequences in HRM. Additionally, it aims to cultivate best practices and references that companies may use to ensure their A.I-driven HR practices result in moral and lawful compliance.

By exploring the moral and legal implications of AI assimilation into Human Resources, this research paper navigates the complex landscape of AI integration into Human Resources.

The researchers discover the multifaceted features of AI in Human Resource Management, assessing the moral quandaries elevated by algorithmic decision-making as well as the supervisory necessities that companies must meet. We aim to provide insight into the track of AI use in HRM by navigating this complex landscape and demonstrating how technology can support fair, open, and accountable HR processes.

LITERATURE REVIEW

A.I. in H.R.M: An Overview

A.I. has gradually become predominant in HRM in recent years, shifting several facets of human resource procedures. Performance appraisals, talent management, and recruitment are just a few areas where this groundbreaking trend has affected operations. AI stresses its transformative consequences on organizational processes through various functions, including HR. With technological progressions, establishments progressively embrace AI to streamline procedures and increase efficacy. Renowned organizations have widely acknowledged the multifarious benefits of AI and have leveraged it across various functional areas of business, such as HR, marketing, finance, *etc.* Reports suggest that AI will significantly influence the global economy, with an approximate prediction of considerable development in economic value by 2030. AI incorporation into HR functions is perceived as vital for improving workforce effectiveness and talent acquisition.

HR professionals use AI to foster innovation, simplify courses, and enhance decision-making, eventually refining the whole worker experience.

The works on AI in HRM highlight its essential role in optimizing numerous functions, such as employee development, recruitment, data management, performance assessment, and so on.

Studies show that AI can improve quality and efficiency in these areas. However, there are still problems with implementation, such as poor managerial support, a lack of technical experience, and poor data quality. The AI Capability Framework (A.C.F.) provides helpful guidelines for assessing and enhancing AI integration preparedness to overcome these obstacles. Although A.I. offers much to HRM, its successful deployment hinges on resolving these issues and efficiently utilizing frameworks like A.C.F. to expand capabilities [9]. Additionally, a conceptual framework integrating AI technologies into the six HRM dimensions of strategy and planning, recruitment, training, performance management, employee relationships, and wage evaluation are outlined in the literature review, which investigates the intersection of AI and HRM A range of Artificial Intelligence (AI) technologies, including face recognition, data mining, and natural language processing, are used in HRM to improve performance evaluation, interview procedures, and decision support. Research examines the attitudes, challenges, and prospects of AI integration in HRM, focusing on variables that influence adoption rates, staff opinions, and the potential for AI to enhance HR processes and boost company efficiency. The evaluation emphasizes the importance of understanding how AI affects HRM and organizational procedures, highlighting the need for strategic integration to fully leverage its potential in optimizing HR functions and driving organizational success [10]. AI systems have demonstrated the ability to analyse large datasets quickly and accurately, which can simplify HR procedures [5].

A study introduced an innovative approach to enhancing the ID3 decision-making algorithm with the A.B.C. rule miner [11]. Their research emphasises improving the accuracy of forecasting employee termination, posing implications for organizational practices and societal wellbeing. AI is transforming HRM by avoiding prejudice in hiring, performance appraisals, and pay. AI has made forecasting trends, customer behaviour, and purchasing intentions easier. It has reduced expenses, simplified the hiring process, and improved employee engagement and retention. AI should be used by managers to empower and assist staff members, thereby shifting their focus from administrative tasks to cross-functional reasoning activities. This relationship between humans and machines will encourage innovation and create new occupations [1].

Natural Language Processing (NLP) methods and machine learning algorithms are two AI technologies used in HRM [12]. Machine learning models provide predictive analytics in HRM by classifying high-potential candidates and forecasting employee turnover [6].

Natural Language Processing (NLP) algorithms make it easier to analyze unstructured textual data, such as employee feedback and engagement, surveys, and automatically parse resumes.

These technological developments hold the potential to completely transform Human Resources by refining decision-making skills and empowering Human Resources workers to manage their time more sensibly.

To mitigate the impact of the COVID-19 epidemic, businesses have made significant investments in artificial intelligence, causing a paradigm shift in Human Resource Management. A study investigated the properties of AI on HRM processes after the pandemic and what it means for both employers and workers [2]. AI-enabled HRM methods highlight employee engagement, reskilling, social capital, mindfulness, and remote and contingent workforce management. A.I.-powered answers have enhanced HRM processes, resulting in better efficiency, employee well-being, automation, and lower costs. These tools include data mining, predictive analytics, big data analytics, and Human Resource Management.

In similar lines, it was found that both mental health problems and employment turnover have escalated because of the COVID-19 pandemic [13]. AI has demonstrated potential in HRM through cost savings, productivity increases, and the advancement of inclusivity and diversity. While chatbots, pulse surveys, wearable technologies, and intelligent robots have benefited employee mental health, AI has been employed for data analytics, emotional intelligence, and seamless onboarding. AI in HRM has given businesses a competitive edge by improving organizational performance, cutting expenses, and lowering quit intent. In the contemporary business landscape, the convergence of HRM and AI represents a transformative paradigm determined by the imperative to adapt to globalization and workforce diversity. As organizations navigate the complexities of modernization, the integration of AI technologies, such as machine learning and virtual reality, transforms traditional office environments, influencing employee behaviors and organizational dynamics. Rooted in the foundational work of pioneers like John McCarthy and Alan Turing, AI evolution has led to advancements in areas like advanced robotics and virtual reality, contributing to new avenues for enhancing task performance and operational efficiency in workplaces.

Meanwhile, HRM assumes a multifaceted role, encompassing administrative functions like recruitment and payment alongside developmental endeavours such as coaching and performance appraisal. The strategic alignment of HRM with organizational goals underscores its pivotal role in driving workforce optimization and achieving business excellence. Overall, the intersection of AI and HRM underlines human resource practitioners' need to embrace innovative strategies and adapt to growing technological landscapes to manage human capital efficiently and nurture organizational accomplishment [14].

Ethical Considerations

The integration of Artificial Intelligence with Human Resources raises various ethical issues, which require cautious thought. This section explores the three central ethical problems—discrimination and bias, lack of transparency, and data security and privacy—that arise when Artificial Intelligence is used in Human Resource procedures.

Recently, the ethical questions raised by Artificial Intelligence in Human Resources have gained more popularity.

Although Artificial Intelligence systems have the potential to be impartial, concerns have been rising over the persistence of biases found in past data. The biases present in the past data are inherent in Artificial Intelligence algorithms trained on it, potentially resulting in unfair use of applicants and workers as well as prejudice [4].

The potential for Algorithmic Bias is one of the crucial ethical considerations in the assimilation of Artificial Intelligence with Human Resources [15]. Human Resource functions, such as recruitment and performance evaluation, may unintentionally exhibit biases based on race, gender, and other protected characteristics. This can result in biased effects and bolster established discrimination in the workplace.

Moreover, as mentioned by Smith *et al.* [16], the insufficient transparency in the Artificial Intelligence decision-making process leads to ethical aggravation in the Human Resource processes. Workers may be unaware of the standard used by the Artificial Intelligence systems to make judgments about their careers, leading to distrust and estrangement. Ensuring transparency and responsibility in Artificial Intelligence algorithms is essential to upholding ethical standards and encouraging employees' faith in the HR practices.

Additionally, data privacy and safety are important ethical issues when integrating artificial intelligence with human resources. Artificial intelligence systems gather and scrutinize large amounts of data from employees, enquiring about the safety of confidential information and the possibilities for manipulating the data [17].

Industries must begin with strong data security strategies and applications to guard employees' privacy and avoid the unapproved consent of private data [18, 19].

Despite the growing awareness of ethical considerations in Artificial Intelligence integration with Human Resources, several challenges exist. For example, a study divulged that the rapid pace of technological advancements repeatedly outpaced the development of ethical guidelines and regulations [20]. This gap can lead to unreliability and doubt regarding the ethical use of Artificial Intelligence in Human Resources, making it challenging for industries to address ethical dilemmas. Furthermore, the issue of accountability remains a challenge in ensuring ethical Artificial Intelligence practices in Human Resources.

In cases where algorithms function independently, delegating responsibility for the consequences of Artificial Intelligence decisions is difficult [21]. It is essential to reduce risks and aid ethical standards in Artificial Intelligence-driven Human Resource processes. A clear line of accountability and processes must be established.

Fairness, accountability, and transparency have been major topics of discussion regarding Artificial Intelligence ethics in Human Resources. Certain demographic groups may be disproportionately affected by algorithmic prejudice, leading to disparities in hiring and promotion [7]. In addition, concerns are raised regarding how decisions are made and whether they can be explained to stakeholders due to the lack of transparency of Artificial Intelligence decision-making processes, sometimes known as the "black box" problem [22]. The ethical consequences of Artificial Intelligence-powered Human Resource procedures also include doubts about employee monitoring and data privacy, which makes a thorough analysis of Artificial Intelligence's ethical implications in Human Resources necessary. Studies stress the importance of addressing bias, data privacy, and transparency in AI-driven Human Resource Management processes [23]. Integrating AI technologies in Human Resource Management necessitates a dynamic legal framework to safeguard against discriminatory biases and support individuals' privacy rights.

Studies and real-world examples prove the moral conundrums that AI-driven Human Resource practices bring. These cases disclose situations in which AI systems have made partial recruiting and employee assessment choices, putting firms at risk of legal challenges and damaging their goodwill [24]. Since Artificial Intelligence in Human Resources continues to influence people's professional lives across industries, it is ethically essential to address these challenges.

Legal Framework

The legal atmosphere surrounding Artificial Intelligence in Human Resources is complex and comprises numerous rules, laws, and regulations. Traditionally, the main objective of anti-discrimination laws, such as Title VII of the Civil Rights Act in the U.S., has been to exclude discrimination in employment practices. However, the introduction of Artificial Intelligence into Human Resources raises original issues that the law may not fully address now [25]. It is uncertain whether these laws fully capture the intricacies of AI-driven Human Resource events or if they require modification to guide algorithmic decision-making effectively.

In the context of AI-driven Human Resource systems, data security legislation, most particularly the General Data Protection Regulation (GDPR) in Europe, creates legal duties connected to the gathering and processing of employee data [26]. Organizations using Artificial Intelligence technologies must ensure compliance with GDPR, which prioritizes individuals' rights to privacy, informed authority, and data portability [27]. The GDPR's legal requirements pose significant challenges to data privacy, transparency, and the protection of confidential HR information.

One of the key legal aspects highlighted in a research study [23] is the security against bias and discrimination in the Artificial Intelligence algorithms used in Human Resource Management. Laws such as the Civil Rights Act of 1964 in the United States, one of the anti-discriminatory laws, play a vital role in striving for non-discriminatory results in recruitment and performance valuation processes. By obeying these legal provisions, organizations can guarantee equal opportunities for all those in Human rights management practices.

Moreover, this study emphasizes the importance of laws related to data privacy in the context of implementing Artificial Intelligence in Human Resource Management [28]. The General Data Protection Regulation (GDPR) sets complex guidelines for the collection, refinement, and storage of personal data by Artificial Intelligence systems. Obedience through such legislation is essential for safeguarding the privacy rights of individuals and upholding ethical standards in Human Resource Management operations.

Transparency in Artificial Intelligence algorithms emerges as a critical factor for accountability and trust in Human Resource Management processes, as highlighted by [23]. Legal frameworks similar to the right to explanation under the GDPR command organizations to present justifications for automated decisions affecting individuals. This necessitates the encouragement of transparency and accountability in Artificial Intelligence-driven Human Resource

Management exercises, amplifying stakeholders' assurance in the justice of Artificial Intelligence systems.

Legal clarifications and consequences are subject to alteration, and recent cases and enforcement measures about Artificial Intelligence in the context of Human Resources. These incidents underscore the importance of integrating Artificial Intelligence procedures with anti-discrimination legislation and data security policies, as infractions can significantly harm an organization's reputation and expose it to legal repercussions [28]. Organizations must understand the varying legal landscape to successfully deal with the moral and legal issues raised by using Artificial Intelligence in Human Resources.

RESEARCH METHODOLOGY

An exploratory research design investigates the complex ethical and legal ramifications of incorporating Artificial Intelligence (AI) into Human Resource procedures. The methodology's widespread data collection procedure includes a careful literature search and an analysis of related laws and regulations.

The assessment of ethical considerations involves the recognition of vital issues and the application of ethical frameworks. The legal landscape is also examined to determine its pertinence to Human Resource driven by Artificial Intelligence. Consultations with experts aid in the development of important guidelines. The outcomes are interpreted using careful data analysis involving qualitative thematic analysis. Ethical guidelines and protocols are followed throughout the entire research project.

Several keywords were used to search the related content: Artificial Intelligence and Ethics, Artificial Intelligence in Human Resource Management, HRM, General Data Protection Regulation, Legislation, Ethics, Compliance, Handling Bias, Data Privacy, and Transparency.

Ethical Challenges in AI-Driven HRM

Integrating artificial Intelligence (AI) with Human Resources (HR) raises several moral issues that require careful consideration. This segment explores the three main moral issues—discrimination and bias, lack of transparency, and data security and privacy—that occur when AI is used in HR procedures.

Bias and Discrimination

The possibility of prejudice and discrimination in decision-making processes is an important moral conundrum when using artificial intelligence in human resource management. Diverse sources might show bias, such as the historical statistics used to train Artificial Intelligence models, the data used for algorithmic decision-making, and the principal architecture of algorithms. These partialities may involuntarily benefit several demographic groups over others in Human Resource practices such as resume screening and promotion decisions, leading to prejudicial treatment [4].

Bias can have many root causes, including overt and covert manifestations. For instance, recruiting data from the past may represent racial or gender biases in prior hiring choices, which might result in algorithms that strengthen these biases when choosing job candidates [23]. Conducting a detailed investigation into these roots and forms of prejudice is imperative to comprehend their impact on Artificial Intelligence-driven Human Resource procedures.

It is vital to present descriptive examples representing the real-world effects of bias on various employee groups to display the tangible influence of bias. Empathetic examples come from real-world situations, including when artificial intelligence systems choose specific demographic groups above others when employing [29].

These instances show the potential repercussions for people and organizations, adding up to highlight the moral condition to eliminate racism. Artificial Intelligence-driven judgments are partial not only toward employment applicants but also in the course of an organization's legal and reputation. The seriousness of preference in Artificial Intelligence-driven Human Resource processes is clarified by examining specific scenarios.

The ethical problems surrounding the use of Artificial Intelligence in higher education—such as biased algorithms, the movement of humans, and transparency—are scrutinized in the study by [30]. It inspects seven Artificial Intelligence ethics rules from Carnegie Mellon, Google, M.I.T., Sanford HAI, UNESCO, China, and the European Commission. The consequences suggest guaranteeing the responsible application of Artificial Intelligence; stakeholders must work together to stop gender bias in algorithm development, learning data sets, and decision-making. Universities must investigate AI's effects on society, ethics, and policy while stressing accountability and openness.

A study was conducted on examining the algorithmic discrimination in Artificial Intelligence-enabled hiring, emphasizing how it may improve the calibre and effectiveness of hiring [31]. Nevertheless, it also raises awareness of prejudice based on personality traits, ethnicity, gender, and colour. The study recommends management and technical actions, such as using impartial databases and increased transparency.

Lack of Transparency

There are severe ethical issues with opaque Artificial Intelligence algorithms employed in Human Resources. These systems are frequently known as "black boxes," which hinder the decision-making process and make it complicated to understand how and why a particular choice was reached. The opacity raises concerns about accountability, justice, and the capacity to address biases or inaccuracies [22].

The difficulties posed by a lack of openness extend beyond the human resources division. When Artificial Intelligence algorithms are used in Human Resource decisions, Human Resource professionals, job candidates, and workers may all find themselves in a situation of less knowledge and control. The lack of openness can destabilize confidence in Human Resource procedures and make correcting biased or incorrect choices more challenging.

It could be difficult for stakeholders, such as Human Resource specialists and job candidates, to comprehend how Artificial Intelligence-driven judgments were made. This ambiguity undermines the equality of Human Resource procedures and makes it more challenging to handle mistakes or unfair results [32].

Transparency is essential for establishing confidence in Artificial Intelligence-driven Human Resource procedures and guaranteeing that they adhere to moral principles. Organizations face moral conundrums regarding justice and accountability when their decision-making processes are opaque, a situation that requires attention.

A study investigated the difficulty of integrating Artificial Intelligence into Human Resource Management procedures. It suggests that Artificial Intelligence algorithms may impact biased algorithms, a lack of technical skills, ethical concerns, data safety, and work routines [33]. These problems may further lead to needless behaviour monitoring of workers, which could harm workplace satisfaction and lessen the human component of Human Resource Management. The study provides a route for vigorous Human Resource Management procedures to face these issues and guarantee a company's longevity.

Artificial Intelligence's integration with Human Resources transforms hiring, talent management, employee engagement, and operations. However, ethical issues exist; Artificial Intelligence can improve decision-making, boost efficiency, and reduce bias. The emergence of IoT and Big Data has created a more favourable environment for Artificial Intelligence solutions, automating Human Resource tasks and reducing administrative costs. Artificial Intelligence and machine learning are vital for making precise decisions and managing employees well [34].

Data Privacy and Security

The collection and processing of sensitive employee data are essential to the ethical implications of data handling in Artificial Intelligence-powered Human Resource solutions. A wealth of data, including confidential and professional information, is required for artificial intelligence systems to make wise decisions. However, this dependence shows the issues with data security, informed consent, and privacy [35].

Ensuring ethical Human Resource practices requires analyzing the ethical implications of data gathering and processing. Employers must cautiously balance protecting employee rights and privacy and use data to improve Human Resource procedures [36].

To address these ethical concerns, it is crucial to examine issues related to data privacy, consent, and the potential dangers of data breaches. Workers expect their employers to manage their data ethically and responsibly, as they entrust it to them. To guarantee that people's rights are upheld through the artificial intelligence-driven human resource process, addressing these concerns is mandatory not only by law but also morally right [27].

Organizations can strive to implement Artificial Intelligence-driven Human Resource practices that are both competent and grounded in ethical principles, ensuring fairness, clarity, and respect for individual rights by thoroughly examining the following ethical challenges: bias and discrimination, lack of transparency, and data privacy and security.

A study explored the legal implications of Artificial Intelligence integration in Human Resource functions, focusing on data privacy, security, biases, discrimination, equal opportunity, anti-discrimination laws, intellectual property rights, and Artificial Intelligence-driven Human Resource activities [37]. It also provides insights for organizations, policymakers, and Human Resource professionals to ensure legal compliance and ethical Artificial Intelligence practice, nurturing a harmonious relationship between Artificial Intelligence and legal frameworks in the Human Resource domain.

Human Resource leaders must prioritize ethical Artificial Intelligence integration, vigorous data governance, talent acquisition, personalized employee development, employee comfort, diversity and inclusion, leadership development, and change management. Ethical Artificial Intelligence integration ensures fairness, transparency, and bias mitigation; at the same time, robust data governance ensures data quality, security, and compliance through privacy regulations. Artificial Intelligence-driven initiatives improve work-life balance, foster engagement, reduce bias, and identify high-potential employees. Effective communication and employee engagement are essential for successful Artificial Intelligence transformation in Human Resource practices [34].

Legal Implications and Compliance

A comprehensive study is essential due to the noteworthy legal implications of integrating AI with HR procedures. This segment examines the legal questions and the need for obedience in AI applications within HR, focusing on data protection and anti-discrimination laws, and assesses their applicability in the Indian context.

Anti-Discrimination Laws

International and national anti-discrimination statutes are vital structures that control HR practices worldwide. Title VII of the Civil Rights Act of 1964 is a landmark statute in the U.S. that prohibits discrimination in employment based on religion, race, color, national origin, or sex. Comparable tasks are safeguarded by laws such as the Equal Remuneration Act, 1976, and the Prevention of Sexual Harassment at Workplace Act, 2013, in India, in protecting workers' rights against discrimination [38 - 40].

Examining how the anti-discrimination legislation in India and the United States relates to Artificial Intelligence in Human Resources is indispensable. Given that Artificial Intelligence. Organizations may inadvertently strengthen biases, but it is precarious to understand how these legal frameworks alter and replicate the realities of artificial intelligence. Moreover, evaluating Indian legal precedents and international judgments about discrimination in Artificial Intelligence-driven Human Resources can provide an indispensable understanding of how the legal landscape is changing and what it means for businesses [4, 41].

Judicial precedents are crucial in defining the legal boundaries surrounding this issue, particularly in cases involving discrimination in Artificial Intelligence-driven Human Resources. Protruding cases in which Artificial Intelligence systems shaped prejudiced consequences or partial conduct during Human Resource events provide tangible examples of the legal consequences that companies can face. These cases highlight the necessity for businesses, both internationally and domestically, to ensure their Artificial Intelligence-powered Human Resource strategies comply with anti-discrimination laws to avoid reputational harm and legal action [24, 42].

Data Protection Regulations

Effect of Data Protection Laws: Data protection laws, such as the General Data Protection Regulation (GDPR) of the European Union, significantly affect worldwide Artificial Intelligence-powered Human Resource systems. However, they are pertinent internationally and in India, where new data protection laws are being implemented. Organizations handling individual data, mainly collected and handled in Human Resource situations, are subject to strict rules under the General Data Protection Regulations. The lawful foundation for data protection in India is recognized by the Information Technology (Reasonable Security Practices and Procedures and Sensitive Personal Data or Information) Rules, 2011, and the Personal Data Protection Bill, 2019 [27].

Investigating the properties of numerous international and national laws on Artificial Intelligence-powered Human Resource methods is vital, particularly regarding data treatment, cross-border data transfers, and consent procedures. Before handling a person's information, businesses must obtain the individual's informed and express consent. This specifies that applicants for jobs and present employees need to know how their information will be used in Artificial Intelligence-driven Human Resource processes in both the Indian and global contexts. Moreover, the global processes of companies using Artificial Intelligence in Human Resources are affected by data privacy regulations, which limit the cross-border diffusion of individual data [43].

Data safety is a crucial legal requirement for Artificial Intelligence-powered Human Resource processes, regardless of the country. Data breaches highlight the prominence of robust information safety processes since they can have severe financial and legal consequences. The security, storage, and transfer of worker information are all covered by lawful principles for ensuring information security in Human Resource procedures. Companies must implement protections to prevent unauthorized access and information breaches in order to comply with international and national data protection regulations [45].

To mitigate legal risks and ensure ethical Artificial Intelligence use in Human Resources, companies must understand and adhere to anti-discrimination laws and data protection requirements in both Indian and international settings. Companies may navigate the complex landscape of Artificial Intelligence-driven Human Resources while upholding ethical values and legal compliance by examining the interplay between various controlling frameworks.

Guidelines and Best Practices for Ethical AI Adoption in HR

Generating detailed rubrics and best practices is essential to integrating AI into human resources. This section presents the values for applying ethical Artificial Intelligence in Human Resources, emphasizing three vital areas: curtailing prejudice, refining transparency and explainability, and assuring information protection and consent.

Mitigating Bias

In Artificial Intelligence-driven Human Resources, bias must be addressed to ensure equitable and fair decision-making. Companies should implement procedures and policies that effectively reduce bias in Artificial Intelligence systems. These strategies could comprise using ML algorithms that take fairness into account, pre-processing training information to eliminate bias, and frequently auditing Artificial Intelligence models for prejudices. In addition, incessant assessment and observation are essential to find and address any prejudices occurring in practical Human Resource procedures [46, 47].

Fairness-conscious ML is vital for diminishing prejudices in Artificial Intelligence systems. It involves familiarizing justice restraints in the model development procedure to avert discriminatory consequences. Companies must prioritise using these methods when mounting and applying Artificial Intelligence algorithms in Human Resources. Moreover, ongoing monitoring of Artificial Intelligence systems is crucial for classifying and addressing prejudice over time, ensuring that Artificial Intelligence remains a reasonable and unbiased tool in Human Resource decision-making [32].

Transparency and Explainability

Building trust in Artificial Intelligence-driven Human Resource procedures starts with explainability and transparency. Companies should carefully record their decision-making procedures and Artificial Intelligence algorithms to promote transparency. They should also invest in advanced interpretability techniques and tools, enabling workers and Human Resource specialists to understand how Artificial Intelligence-driven selections are made. Explainability initiatives should prioritize open lines of communication with team members, clearly outlining the consequences and conditions that led to these outcomes [49].

For Human Resource specialists to comprehend the reasoning behind Artificial Intelligence-driven selections, models must be interpretable. They can use it to sustain and protect these selections for team members. Workers' faith is increased, and doubts about Artificial Intelligence procedures being "black box" explanations are reduced when there is open and truthful communication about Artificial Intelligence's role in the Human Resource system. To foster directness and understanding, Human Resource departments should establish opportunities for team members to inquire about concerns and seek explanations regarding Artificial Intelligence results [50].

Data Privacy and Consent

It is not possible to fulfill information privacy requirements, such as the General Data Protection Regulation or national regulations. Human Resource sections must establish clear processes and strategies to ensure that worker information is handled lawfully. This involves conducting influence investigations on information protection, defending information by intention and default, and, if necessary, labelling information protection officers. These guidelines ensure that information privacy regulations are followed appropriately and safeguard worker rights [44].

Receiving well-versed consent is vital to morally handling information. Human Resource divisions should implement processes to get workers' clear and well-versed consent before processing, collecting, and using their information. This involves providing employees with detailed information on the purpose of data usage, the types of data collected, and their rights to their data. Workers should be able to remove their consent at any time, and consent should be acquired using an easy-to-use, clear process [51].

Human Resource organizations can establish a foundation for the ethical implementation of Artificial Intelligence by adopting these best practices and ideologies. In addition to plummeting bias, promoting transparency, and protecting data privacy, these actions also provide an Artificial Intelligence culture that supports employees' dignity and rights.

The Real Possibility of Prejudice and Discrimination in Decision-Making

Human Resource Management (HRM) with AI solutions offers cutting-edge solutions in the areas of hiring, evaluation, and workforce planning. But it also raises questions about discrimination and bias in decision-making. AI bias can come from many places: previous training data, algorithmic design, or misguided deployment. Such prejudices can, in fact, promote unequal treatment of certain groups of people – for instance, in recruitment, promotion, and employee treatment. These biases need to be overcome if AI-based HR is to be fair, transparent, and sustainable.

New Moral Rules Against AI Bias

Human resources should adhere to ethical guidelines that help counter biases and use AI responsibly. UNESCO, Google, and the European Commission have issued full rules for being fair, transparent, and inclusive. For instance:

- UNESCO's Recommendations on Ethical AI focus on equity, accountability, and privacy and call on actors to actively avoid biases.
- The EU Commission's Trustworthy AI Ethics Guidelines are aimed at being fair and, by that I mean, making AI systems ethically compliant and transparent.
- Google's AI Principles recommend inclusionary datasets and periodic audits to find and eliminate biases.

Such models emphasize different training datasets, constant monitoring, and ethical decisions to give organizations concrete solutions to algorithmic discrimination.

Examples from Actual Cases Showing Bias in AI-powered HR Processes

Amazon's Recruitment AI System

Amazon built an AI tool to make it easier to hire, but it accidentally disqualified resumes with phrases like "women's chess club." The tool's bias came from historical data that showed too many men applying, ensuring gender inequalities when it came to hiring. This example shows that skewed training data is an enabler of old bias and discrimination [52].

HireVue's Video Interview Software

HireVue's AI algorithms analyze candidates' faces, speech, and body language to gauge performance in the job market. The algorithm is thought to disadvantage those with disabilities or from other cultural backgrounds, since biased algorithmic results can occur if the criteria are not standard [53].

COMPAS Algorithm in Risk Assessment

Not relevant to HR, but the COMPAS algorithm used in courts showed how AI biases could be used to disadvantage certain groups. It routinely classified African Americans as being more likely to recidivate than whites of the same type, and it has similar ramifications for HR bias in promotions or job cuts [54]. These examples illustrate why you need periodic audits, correct data feeds, and stakeholder oversight to ensure that AI-based HR tools are less biased.

Protection for Data Privacy, Transparency, and Sustainability

It takes the triangularly connected ethical aspects of three ethics—and all of them intertwine—to get AI into HRM.

Data Privacy

AI HR systems are responsible for storing personal information of the employees, including their demographics, performance data, and more. Data privacy is essential when building trust and adhering to laws such as GDPR [55]. Effective measures include:

- Data Anonymization: Deletion of PII during the data processing.
- Access Limitations: Limiting access to sensitive data to authorized users only.
- Secured Storage: Encryption and cybersecurity for data breaches.

Transparency of AI processes: the decision-making process is transparent for employees and other stakeholders. For example:

- Explanatory AI (XAI): Create algorithms to explain decisions, like why some resumes are chosen.
- Transparency: Giving employees a detailed explanation of how AI tools are used for reviews or promotions.
- Stakeholder Engagement: Involving employees and supervisors in AI system creation and testing for trust.

Sustainability: Sustainability of AI based HRM is not just a matter of the environment; it is also about ethics in the pursuit of sustainable equity and organisational integrity. Initiatives include:

- Avoiding algorithmic discrimination and making work a more inclusive place.
- Fair treatment of employees from all backgrounds.
- Linking AI to wider sustainability agendas (ethical decision making, corporate social responsibility, *etc.*

Legal Terminology and Ethical Implications

- Algorithmic Discrimination: These are biases in automated decision-making that could be illegal under anti-discrimination statutes, such as Title VII of the U.S. Civil Rights Act.

- Data Transparency: This means making it transparent for stakeholders on the processing of data and decisions by AI systems.

If left unaddressed, these issues can harm your company's reputation, lead to lawsuits, and erode employee trust.

Recommendations for Ethical AI in HRM

1. Bias Audits — Perform regular fairness testing and discriminatory bias patterns in AI algorithms.
2. Diversity of Training Data: Mix and match different data with different populations to reduce biases.
3. Increase Transparency: Use Explainable AI methods and get stakeholders updated on AI decision-making.
4. Enhanced Data Privacy Assurances: Encrypt, anonymize, and securely store employee data.
5. Ensure Moral Codes: Link AI with principles from top institutions to hold it accountable and equitable.
6. Encourage Ethical AI Systems: Empower inclusive and long-term organisational initiatives with ethical AI systems.

Bias, data privacy, transparency, and sustainability are all part of ethically using AI in HRM. If you know how to identify and mitigate these risks, organizations can provide an inclusive and equitable work environment and use AI's potential for efficiency and creativity. Case studies and moral guides offer real-world examples of how to deal with them so AI-enabled HR practices remain fair, accountable, and sustainable over the long term.

CONCLUSION

Businesses benefit significantly from integrating Artificial Intelligence into Human Resource processes. Still, this alteration must be directed by a strong commitment to ethical values and obedience to pertinent legal requirements. The chief deductions are summarized in this section, including their significance, future directions, and applied propositions, with a particular emphasis on the implications of executing Artificial Intelligence sensibly in Human Resources.

Summary of Findings

The track through this study has shed light on the multifaceted ethical and legal consequences of Artificial Intelligence implementation in Human Resources. Significant discoveries highlight the vivacious implication of the subsequent:

- Prejudice Vindication: According to a study [46], reasonable and impartial Human Resource processes are ensured by addressing prejudice and discernment in Artificial Intelligence procedures.
- Explainability and Pellucidity: Refining explainability and pellucidity in models to endorse understanding and faith between Human Resource specialists and employees [48].
- Information Confidentiality and Consent: According to another study [27], preserving information confidentiality regulations and gaining well-versed consent is vital to protecting workers' privileges and confidentiality.

Implications and Future Directions

Beyond the pages of this investigation article, the consequences affect Human Resource practices, companies, and policymakers overall:

- Human Resource Practices: According to [50], human resource divisions need to adapt to accept ethical Artificial Intelligence processes while adopting an environment of fairness, honesty, and information safety.
- Establishments: Identifying that accountable Artificial Intelligence implementation is a benefit, not an obligation, establishments must consider the possible welfare of Artificial Intelligence against their moral and legal responsibilities [5].
- Legislators: Legislators must make supervisory outlines that defend individual privileges and the well-being of society while accommodating the emergence of AI [53].

The following areas should be the focus of future investigation and growth on the moral use of Artificial Intelligence in Human Resources:

- Algorithmic Justice: Emerging approaches for prejudice lessening and fairness-aware ML [47].
- Interpretability Gears: Making progressive interpretability gears for replicas to progress transparency [49].
- Technologies to Improve Discretion: Investigative Artificial Intelligence clarifications to preserve confidentiality and protect delicate worker information [54].

Recommendations

Assuming the consequences and their concerns, the subsequent practical proposals are made:

- Human Resource specialists: Sustain the placement of moral Artificial Intelligence by endorsing open communication, belligerently confronting prejudice, and providing continuing training and awareness creativities [55].
- Legislators: Work with experts to create rules custom-made for Artificial Intelligence, integrating novelty and morals, including information security, justice, and honesty [56].
- Establishments: To assure obedience to ethical and lawful requirements, foster a moral Artificial Intelligence culture, and entitle groups devoted to Artificial Intelligence morals and behaviour to recurrent Artificial Intelligence checks.

In summary, applying Artificial Intelligence to Human Resources is a cooperative effort involving Human Resource specialists, establishments, lawmakers, and the public rather than a lonesome voyage. This expedition aims to be guided by moral and lawful concerns, ensuring that AI-driven human resource practices are applied in a manner that is reasonable, clear, and protects people's rights.

The moral incorporation of Artificial Intelligence in Human Resources is a voyage, not a destination, that needs continuous novelty and ethical deliberation. Let the ethical scope of fairness, the light of transparency, and the grip of information confidentiality guide us as we navigate this topography. By doing this, we overlay the means for a period when AI in Human Resources will be documented as more than just a mechanical process.

REFERENCES

[1] A. Mer, and A.S. Virdi, "Artificial intelligence disruption on the brink of revolutionizing H.R. and marketing functions", *Impact of artificial intelligence on organizational transformation,* pp. 1-19, 2022.
[http://dx.doi.org/10.1002/9781119710301.ch1]

[2] A. Mer, and A.S. Virdi, *Navigating the paradigm shift in H.R.M. practices through the lens of artificial intelligence: A post-pandemic perspective.* The Adoption and Effect of Artificial Intelligence on Human Resources Management, Part A, 2023, pp. 123-154.

[3] A. Mer, and A. Srivastava, *Employee Engagement in the New Normal: Artificial Intelligence as a Buzzword or a Game Changer?* The Adoption and Effect of Artificial Intelligence on Human Resources Management, Part A, 2023, pp. 15-46.

[4] N. Diakopoulos, "Accountability in algorithmic decision making: A view from computational journalism", *Digit. Journal. (Abingdon),* vol. 4, no. 6, pp. 700-722, 2016.

[5] A. Mer, K. Singhal, and A.S. Virdi, "A review of the role of artificial intelligence in banking and stock market trading", In: *Finance Analytics in Business: Perspectives on Enhancing Efficiency and Accuracy*, 2024, pp. 175-198.
[http://dx.doi.org/10.1108/978-1-83753-572-920241009]

[6] J. Boudreau, and W. Cascio, "Human capital analytics: why are we not there?", *Journal of Organizational Effectiveness: People and Performance,* vol. 4, no. 2, pp. 119-126, 2017.
[http://dx.doi.org/10.1108/JOEPP-03-2017-0021]

[7] D. Pager, "The use of field experiments for studies of employment discrimination: Contributions, critiques, and directions for the future", *Ann. Am. Acad. Pol. Soc. Sci.,* vol. 609, no. 1, pp. 104-133,

2007.
[http://dx.doi.org/10.1177/0002716206294796]

[8] J. Kuipers, and N. Purtova, "The right to explanation and the role of market explanations", *Comput. Law Secur. Rev.,* vol. 34, no. 2, pp. 263-272, 2018.

[9] D.O. Agustono, R. Nugroho, and A.Y.A. Fianto, *Artificial Intelligence in Human Resource Management Practices.* KnE Social Sciences, 2023, pp. 958-970.

[10] A. Alsaif, and M. Sabih Aksoy, "AI-HRM: artificial intelligence in human resource management: a literature review", *Journal of Computing and Communication,* vol. 2, no. 2, pp. 1-7, 2023. [http://dx.doi.org/10.21608/jocc.2023.307053]

[11] P. Bhupathi, S. Prabu, and A.P.I. Goh, "Artificial intelligence-enabled knowledge management using a multidimensional analytical framework of visualizations", *International Journal of Cognitive Computing in Engineering,* vol. 4, pp. 240-247, 2023. [http://dx.doi.org/10.1016/j.ijcce.2023.06.003]

[12] T.H. Davenport, J. Harris, and J. Shapiro, *Competing on analytics: The new science of winning.* Harvard Business Press, 2010.

[13] A. Mer, "Artificial intelligence in human resource management: recent trends and research agenda", *Digital Transformation, Strategic Resilience, Cyber Security and Risk Management,* vol. 111, pp. 31-56, 2023.
[http://dx.doi.org/10.1108/S1569-37592023000111B003]

[14] S. Anayat, *"Human resources management after industry 4.0: Blending A.I. and H.R.M.," Strategic Human Resource Management in the Hospitality Industry: A Digitalized Economic Paradigm.* I.G.I. Global, 2023, pp. 97-115.

[15] C. Martin, and R.E. Freeman, "Ethical considerations in the use of artificial intelligence for human resource management", *J. Bus. Ethics,* vol. 165, no. 2, pp. 347-360, 2020.

[16] L. Smith, "Transparency and accountability in artificial intelligence: A framework for H.R. decision-making", *Hum. Resour. Manage. Rev.,* vol. 28, no. 3, pp. 377-387, 2019.

[17] A. Jones, and B. Lee, "Ethical considerations in the use of artificial intelligence for human resource management", *J. Bus. Ethics,* vol. 147, no. 4, pp. 895-903, 2018.

[18] F. Khan, and A. Mer, *"Surveillance and the Right to Privacy for Sustainability of a Digital Economy: An Examination of the Data Protection Bill 2019," Sustainable Development Goals: The Impact of Sustainability Measures on Wellbeing.* Emerald Publishing Limited, 2024, pp. 111-132.

[19] F. Khan, and A. Mer, "The ethical considerations of D.N.A. profiling for resilience in a forensic setting in india: a comparative study with international guidelines", In: *The Framework for Resilient Industry: A Holistic Approach for Developing Economies.* Emerald Publishing Limited, 2024, pp. 121-134.

[20] Y. Wang, and N. Hajli, "Ethical challenges of artificial intelligence in human resource management: A review and research agenda", *J. Bus. Res.,* vol. 124, pp. 704-715, 2021.

[21] S. Lee, and J. Kim, "Accountability in artificial intelligence: A framework for human resource management", *Hum. Resour. Manage. Rev.,* vol. 29, no. 1, pp. 103-113, 2019.

[22] A.D. Selbst, and S. Barocas, "The intuitive appeal of explainable machines", *Fordham Law Rev.,* vol. 87, no. 3, pp. 1085-1128, 2018.

[23] B. Dixon, "Artificial intelligence and human resources management: a new way to work", *J. Bus. Ethics,* vol. 145, no. 2, pp. 373-382, 2019.

[24] J. Dastin, *Amazon scraps secret A.I. recruiting tool that showed bias against women,* 2018. https://www.reuters.com/article/us-amazon-com-jobs-automation-insight/amazon-scraps-secret-ai-recruiting-tool-that-showed-bias-against-women-idUSKCN1MK08G

[25] *Title VII of the Civil Rights Act of 1964,* 2021. https://www.eeoc.gov/statutes/title-vii-civil-rights-act-1964

[26] F. Khan, and A. Mer, "Embracing artificial intelligence technology: legal implications with special reference to European union initiatives of data protection", In: *Digital Transformation, Strategic Resilience, Cyber Security and Risk Management.* Emerald Publishing Limited, 2023, pp. 119-141.

[27] European union, "General data protection regulation (GDPR)," Official Journal of the European Union, 2018. [Online]. Available: https://eur-lex.europa.eu/lega--content/EN/TXT/?uri=CELEX%3A32016R0679

[28] *Guide to the General Data Protection Regulation (GDPR).* https://ico.org.uk/for-organisations/guid--to-data-protection/guide-to-the-general-data-protection-regulation-gdpr/

[29] S. Barocas, M. Hardt, and A. Narayanan, *Fairness and machine learning.* Fairness and Machine Learning, 2019, pp. 1-3.

[30] Z. Slimi, and B. Villarejo Carballido, "Navigating the ethical challenges of artificial intelligence in higher education: an analysis of seven global AI ethics policies", *TEM Journal,* vol. 12, no. 2, pp. 590-602, 2023.
[http://dx.doi.org/10.18421/TEM122-02]

[31] S. Bankins, "The ethical use of artificial intelligence in human resource management: a decision-making framework", *Ethics Inf. Technol.,* vol. 23, no. 4, pp. 841-854, 2021.
[http://dx.doi.org/10.1007/s10676-021-09619-6]

[32] N. Diakopoulos, "Principles for accountable algorithms and a social impact statement for algorithms", *SIGKDD Explor.,* vol. 19, no. 1, pp. 6-10, 2018.

[33] L.M. Mohapatra, A.V.S. Kamesh, and J. Roul, *Challenges and Path Ahead for Artificial Intelligence-aided Human Resource Management,* 2023. https://www.emerald.com/insight/content/doi/10.1108/978-1-80382-027-920231006/full/html
[http://dx.doi.org/10.1108/978-1-80382-027-920231006]

[34] V. Bijja, and S. Vaddepalli, *The Future of Work: Implications of Artificial Intelligence on H.R. Practices.* Tuijin Jishu/Journal of Propulsion Technology, vol. 44, no. 3, 2023.

[35] B.D. Mittelstadt, P. Allo, M. Taddeo, S. Wachter, and L. Floridi, "The ethics of algorithms: Mapping the debate", *Big Data Soc.,* vol. 3, no. 2, p. 2053951716679679, 2016.
[http://dx.doi.org/10.1177/2053951716679679]

[36] A. Acquisti, L. Brandimarte, and G. Loewenstein, "Privacy and human behavior in the age of information", *Science,* vol. 347, no. 6221, pp. 509-514, 2015.
[http://dx.doi.org/10.1126/science.aaa1465] [PMID: 25635091]

[37] N.D. Richards, and W. Hartzog, "Taking trust seriously in privacy law", *Stanf. Technol. Law Rev.,* vol. 19, pp. 431-472, 2016.

[38] K. Crawford, R. Dobbe, T. Dryer, G. Fried, B. Green, E. Kaziunas, A. Kak, V. Mathur, E. McElroy, and O. Sánchez, *A.I. Now 2019 report.* AI Now Institute at New York University, 2019.

[39] L. Floridi, "Soft ethics, the governance of the digital and the General Data Protection Regulation", *Philos. Trans.- Royal Soc., Math. Phys. Eng. Sci.,* vol. 376, no. 2133, p. 20180081, 2018.
[http://dx.doi.org/10.1098/rsta.2018.0081] [PMID: 30322997]

[40] L. Einav, and J. Levin, "Economics in the age of big data", *Science,* vol. 346, no. 6210, p. 1243089, 2014.
[http://dx.doi.org/10.1126/science.1243089] [PMID: 25378629]

[41] P. Samuelson, "Privacy as intellectual property?", *Stanford Law Rev.,* vol. 52, no. 5, pp. 1125-1173, 2000.
[http://dx.doi.org/10.2307/1229511] [PMID: 11503653]

[42] J.R. Anderson, and C. Lebiere, *The atomic components of thought.* Lawrence Erlbaum Associates, 1998.

[43] M.T. Cox, and A. Raja, *Metareasoning: Thinking about thinking.* M.I.T. Press, 2011. [http://dx.doi.org/10.7551/mitpress/9780262014809.001.0001]

[44] G. Gigerenzer, and R. Selten, *Bounded rationality: The adaptive toolbox.* M.I.T. Press, 2002. [http://dx.doi.org/10.7551/mitpress/1654.001.0001]

[45] D. Kahneman, *Thinking, fast and slow.* Farrar, Straus and Giroux, 2011.

[46] G. Marcus, E. Davis, and A.I. Rebooting, *Building artificial intelligence we can trust.* Pantheon Books, 2019.

[47] A. Mer, "Enhancing employee engagement and retention with AI-based H.R.M. systems", *International Journal of Human Resource Studies,* vol. 11, no. 2, pp. 23-45, 2021.

[48] C.C. Martin, "The challenges of algorithmic accountability in the workplace", *Ethics Inf. Technol.,* vol. 23, pp. 343-356, 2021.

[49] B.J. Moll, "Ethics of artificial intelligence in the workplace", *J. Bus. Ethics,* vol. 162, no. 1, pp. 1-14, 2020.

[50] N. Goodhart, "Artificial intelligence and decision-making: The impact on employee autonomy", *J. Bus. Res.,* vol. 123, pp. 372-383, 2021.

[51] B. Mittelstadt, "Principles alone cannot guarantee ethical AI", *Nat. Mach. Intell.,* vol. 1, no. 11, pp. 501-507, 2019. [http://dx.doi.org/10.1038/s42256-019-0114-4]

[52] M. Sweeney, Amazon's AI recruiting tool shows bias against women. Reuters 2019. Retrieved from https://www.reuters.com

[53] S. Brown, and R. Taylor, "Ethical challenges in AI-powered hiring: A critical review", *J. Bus. Ethics,* vol. 163, no. 2, pp. 123-135, 2021.

[54] J. Angwin, J. Larson, S. Mattu, and L. Kirchner, Machine bias. ProPublica 2016. Retrieved from https://www.propublica.org

[55] GDPR. "General data protection regulation", *Off. J. Eur. Union L,* vol. 119, pp. 1-88, 2016.

[56] R.W. Picard, *Affective computing.* M.I.T. Press, 2000. [http://dx.doi.org/10.7551/mitpress/1140.003.0008]

CHAPTER 3

AI-Based Voice-Assisted Email System

Kuldeep Vayadande[1,*], **Swati Ajay Gandhi**[2], **Yogesh Bodhe**[3], **Lokesh Khedekar**[4] and **Vijay More**[5]

[1] *Department of Information Technology, Vishwakarma Institute of Technology, Pune, India*

[2] *Anantrao Pawar College of Engineering and Research, Pune, Maharashtra, India*

[3] *Department of Information Technology, Government Polytechnic, Pune, India*

[4] *Department of Artificial Intelligence and Data Science, Vishwakarma Institute of Technology, Pune, India*

[5] *MET's Institute of Engineering, Bhujbal Knowledge City, Nashik, Maharashtra, India*

Abstract: In today's technologically advanced era, the integration of communication technologies with the internet has made communication very simple. Email, in particular, is the most reliable and widely used mode of digital communication for both personal and commercial purposes. As of 2021, around 4.1 billion people used email globally. By 2024, this figure is expected to increase. By 2024, this figure is expected to increase. By 2024, this figure is expected to increase. By 2024, this figure is expected to increase to over 4.48 billion. This indicates the continued importance of email as a communication tool in our increasingly digital world. However, the visually impaired and blind people face several difficulties in using this important service, and there are currently around 2.2 billion people who have vision impairment globally, as per a report by the WHO. To address this issue, we propose an effective aid in the form of a voice command-based email system that will help individuals with special needs manage their email accounts through voice commands, making it easier for them to use the service. The proposed system will also benefit others by reducing their time consumption. Python, text-to-speech and speech-to-text conversion, Interactive Voice Response (IVR) technology, and other tools were used in the development of the email system. Through the use of their voice, visually impaired and blind persons will be able to effectively utilize email services and complete tasks without depending on a visual interface.

Keywords: Email system, IVR, Speech recognition, STT, TTS, Voice assistance.

INTRODUCTION

In recent years, Artificial Intelligence (AI) has significantly transformed digital interactions, enhancing efficiency, accessibility, and intelligence in various

* **Corresponding author Kuldeep Vayadande:** Department of Information Technology, Vishwakarma Institute of Technology, Pune, India; E-mail: kuldeep.vayadande@gmail.com

Subir Gupta, Indrajit Ghosal, Keshav Kaushik & Monika Dandotiya (Eds.)

applications. A noteworthy example is voice-assisted email systems—tools that enable users to dictate, organize, and manage emails using voice commands. These systems fall under the broader category of voice-enabled digital assistants, which include popular technologies like Google Assistant, Amazon Alexa, Apple's Siri, and Microsoft's Cortana.

Voice-assisted email systems are becoming integral across multiple sectors, providing hands-free operation that benefits professionals in fast-paced or hands-occupied environments, and greatly improving accessibility for those with physical disabilities. By eliminating the need for typing and manual inbox management, these systems streamline communication, allowing users to interact with emails in a natural, conversational way.

Core AI Technologies in Voice-Assisted Email Systems

Several key AI technologies enable voice-assisted systems to interpret, process, and respond to spoken commands effectively:

1. Automatic Speech Recognition (ASR): ASR technology translates spoken language into text. Trained on extensive datasets, ASR models learn to accurately transcribe spoken words, handling a variety of accents and background noise.
2. Natural Language Processing (NLP): NLP enables the system to comprehend the intent behind spoken words. It allows the assistant to distinguish between commands like "Send an email to [Contact]" *versus* "Read my last email," ensuring that the correct action is taken.
3. Machine Learning (ML) and Deep Learning: These algorithms, particularly deep learning approaches such as neural networks, are crucial for enhancing accuracy and precision. They enable the system to adapt based on user interactions, enhancing voice recognition, intent understanding, and predictive capabilities from prior interactions.
4. Natural Language Generation (NLG): NLG enables systems to generate automatic replies, summaries, or draft content, providing contextually relevant and naturally worded responses.

When integrated, these AI-driven methods enable voice-assisted email systems to address communication challenges effectively, making them especially useful in professional domains like healthcare, law, and corporate environments, where time savings and hands-free functionality are essential.

In today's digital world, email is an essential tool for communication. It makes long-distance communication quick, simple, and affordable. It is especially useful for businesses, as it allows them to communicate with customers, partners, and suppliers in different parts of the world simultaneously. Its importance will continue to grow as technology evolves and its capabilities expand. As of 2021, there are approximately 4.3 billion email users worldwide, and this number is projected to grow to over 4.9 billion by 2024.

Additionally, the number of daily emails sent and received is also increasing, with an estimated 347 billion emails sent and received each day in 2022. As technology continues to evolve and more people gain access to the internet, . However, a section of people still cannot access this service as efficiently as others, particularly the visually challenged. They encounter several difficulties when using email, such as composing and reading emails, navigating the interface, and performing other tasks. The World Health Organization (WHO) estimates that globally, there are approximately 253 million people who experience visual impairment, with 36 million of them being blind. From these numbers, we can infer that many people are unable to utilize the email service effectively. Many technologies have been developed, including screen readers and voice assistants like Alexa and Siri. However, there is no full-fledged solution that allows the visually impaired to use basic communication facilities like email comfortably.

We have proposed a voice-based system to address this issue, enabling users to access mailing features exclusively through voice commands. These systems can be particularly useful for individuals with vision disabilities or those who find typing difficult or time-consuming. Additionally, a voice-based email system can also be integrated with smart devices, such as smart speakers or smartphones, making it more accessible and convenient for users. This kind of system can be a crucial tool for people with visual impairments or blindness. It allows them to access their email independently without relying on others. It promotes independence, enabling individuals to participate in the workforce and society as a whole. Voice-assisted email systems have revolutionized communication by both accessibility and productivity. These systems utilize advanced AI technologies, including Automatic Speech Recognition (ASR), Natural Language Processing (NLP), and Machine Learning (ML), to provide seamless and user-friendly experiences. The following case studies demonstrate the practical impact of these systems in real-world scenarios, with a focus on the AI methods that enable their effectiveness.

This paper is divided into nine sections: Section 1 introduces the background and purpose of the project. Section 2 provides a brief overview of the literature reviewed. Section 3 details the project development methodology, including the proposed system, flowcharts, and algorithms. Section 4 presents the system's results. Section 5 wraps up the paper and Section 6 offers the project's future scope.

Literature Review

In a study [1], an Android application that uses a combination of voice commands and mouse clicks to send, receive, and read emails is proposed. The application is created using Android and java for the user interface and a MySQL database for the back-end. The system utilizes speech-to-text and text-to-speech conversion for operation. Although a basic prototype, it can be expanded by incorporating additional mail functionalities.

The advancement of computer-based accessibility systems has created new opportunities for visually impaired individuals worldwide. Screen readers, which are audio-based virtual environments that provide feedback, have proven immensely useful for blind individuals in accessing internet applications. However, in certain regions like the Indian sub-continent, visually impaired people have not benefitted from such systems as much due to differing technology requirements for Indian languages.

The voicemail system design suggested in this research article makes it simple and effective for blind people to access emails. The proposed system allows blind people to send and receive voice-based email messages in their native language using a mobile device. The researchers evaluated their proposed system GUI against that of a traditional mail server and discovered that their architecture outperformed the traditional server significantly.

Paper [2] presents a design for a voice-based email system that enables users to send, receive, and read emails with password protection. The design process consists of four major steps: UI design using HTML5 and CSS3, Database design, System design using TTS and STT, and Mail programming module design. It later provides a comparison table between the traditional mail system and the proposed system.

This report claims that email is one of the most widely used ways of communication and that it is still used today to transmit private information. There are approximately 253 million blind and visually challenged individuals globally, and communication is a challenge for them. With technology advancing rapidly, individuals who are visually challenged feel increasingly restricted.

In a study [3], a 'voice-based email application' is presented, which uses the Loquendo ETTS software for speech recognition. This system provides basic mail functionalities, including login, composing, reading mail, and logout. It eliminates the use of keyboard shortcuts and works only on voice and mouse clicks.The authors state that their project aims to develop a system that enables individuals with special needs to access email services more effectively. This addresses the limitations that blind individuals previously encountered when attempting to access email services. One of the main improvements is the elimination of the need for keyboard shortcuts, which can be confusing and difficult to remember. This eliminates the cognitive load associated with using screen readers and keyboard shortcuts. Non-sophisticated users who are unfamiliar with keyboard keys will no longer be required to use them. The IVR will provide instructions for users to obtain the required services. Users may also be prompted to provide information through voice input when necessary. As future work, the authors plan to extend the voice-based response system to other IVR systems, such as banking, where users can call banks and receive query-based responses based on stored data. Additional features of the system include setting reminders, searching through the inbox, and automatically saving emails. Authors also plan to improve the system's ability to take recipient email addresses.

Some authors [4] provide an example of an application that turns text into speech by combining Digital Signal Processing (DSP) with Natural Language Processing (NLP). The user hears the output read out, and it has the option to be saved as an mp3 file. The developers intend to add support for their native Nigerian language to this program, which presently only functions with American English. They also intend to develop versions tailored to specific applications, allowing them to be used in various contexts, such as video games and ATMs.

Since text-to-speech synthesis is now included in several interfaces, the field has grown in significance within computer technology. This research has developed an intuitive graphical text entry interface with a focus on the text-to-speech synthesis process. Now, the technology is designed to function with American English. However, in the future, the authors hope to extend the program to incorporate Nigerian native languages, thereby making text-to-speech technology accessible to a larger variety of Nigerians. Numerous text-to-speech systems are currently available for use with local languages, such as Telugu, Vietnamese, Konkani, and Swahili. The authors aim to integrate text-to-speech technology across various platforms, including video games, ATMs, telephone systems, and other potential applications, while also expanding the program to support local languages. To do this, further study and development are needed to make sure the system runs smoothly and efficiently across many platforms.

The World Health Organization reports that 36 million people are completely blind and that 1.3 billion people have some vision impairment [5], making visual impairment a major issue for a sizable section of the world's population. For those who are visually impaired, reading is one of their most basic requirements. Researchers have developed several tools to assist these individuals in reading labels, recognizing barriers, and accessing written materials.

Optical Character Recognition (OCR) technology combined with the Raspberry Pi, a 32-bit ARM controller, is one potential method for image-to-audio conversion. This system recognizes printed text using a camera, extracts the label from the picture using image processing, and utilizes text-to-speech conversion to convert the label into voice. Text extraction, text localization, object identification, and text-to-speech conversion are the four main processes in the suggested technique. The purpose of this technology is to assist individuals who are blind or visually impaired in reading written information, such as product labels. For optimal performance and efficiency, text size is an important factor to take into account. The text size should be chosen in a way that is more universal and insensitive to variations in font style. Optical Character Recognition significantly improves the ability of the visually impaired to access written information.

In conclusion, the camera-based label reader technology is a remarkable invention that has helped visually impaired individuals read printed information with ease. The proposed method, which involves OCR technology, text localization, and text-to-speech conversion, can be applied in a wide range of settings, making it a promising solution for millions of people around the world. With further advancements, this technology could be used to help visually impaired individuals read books, access websites, and interact with their environment in new ways.

A study [6] examines the advantages and disadvantages of popular AI online chatbots, including Mitsuku, Rose, Poncho, Right click, Insomno Bot, and Baidu Melody. The research then recommends a speech-to-text chatbot that makes use of the Rabin-Karp and Knuth-Pratt algorithms as well as the Google API. The web interface implementation of the algorithm uses Flask and Python. The recommended algorithm's temporal complexity is contrasted with that of other methods.

Additionally, the study investigates a software solution that utilizes Python and the Flask web framework to gather and process audio information into text. The acquired dataset will be utilized to create a custom model based on a recurrent neural network using the Keras library. The paper also presents the Hashbot algorithm, which is less complex than current algorithms and can work with Cyrillic texts for identifying keywords. The suggested algorithm enhances the effectiveness of chatbots by enabling them to identify the interlocutor's gender.

The article demonstrates how open APIs can be employed to develop unified interfaces using a Google API-based chatbot as an example.

The paper also highlights the significance of speech recognition in natural language processing and how it is becoming a central part of our lives by saving time and enabling voice/audio communication instead of common texting. The advantages and disadvantages of existing chatbots are discussed, and a method for improving their performance using Rabin-Karp and Knut-Pratt algorithms is presented.

The authors plan to develop a custom speech recognition system in the future based on the collected dataset, which is identified as the next phase of research. The article emphasizes the importance of AI technologies in our daily lives. The proposed software solution and Hashbot algorithm are designed to enhance the performance of chatbots and make them more human-like in their interactions with users.

In another study [7], a search engine with a web page reader is developed, which is purely based on voice interaction enabled with voice recognition and voice synthesis mechanisms. This system will allow users to interact with the computer using voice. The system also helps users read websites.

The aim is to present a new search engine that facilitates voice-based communication between computers and people. The "Voice-based Search Engine and Web-page Reader" is a search engine that enables voice control of a web browser. In contrast to current engines that only process text-based queries, the suggested approach allows users to converse with their computers and get voice-based results.

The authors note that while current web browsers are capable of playing audio and video, users must still input text into a search box to request them. The proposed system aims to address this issue, mainly for visually impaired users who may have difficulty using graphical user interfaces. By using voice recognition and synthesis technologies, the search engine can assist users in browsing the Internet and reading documents. The authors conducted experiments to evaluate the accuracy of the voice recognition technology used in their search engine. They found that additional hardware and software could improve its accuracy further. They also suggest that other techniques discussed in Section 2 of the paper could be applied to increase the search engine's performance and accuracy.

In conclusion, the authors have developed a 'Voice-based Search Engine and Web-page Reader' that allows people to interact with their computer purely through their voice. The system has the potential to make browsing the Internet more accessible for visually impaired users and could also improve efficiency for all users. With further research and development, the accuracy and performance of the search engine could be enhanced, potentially making it a valuable tool for Man-Machine interactions.

The focus of article [8] is on the potential applications of spoken language systems, which combine speech recognition, natural language processing, and human interface technology to interpret user speech and provide an appropriate response. These systems can be used for a range of tasks, from simple information retrieval to more complex applications like travel planning and traffic routing, and can facilitate multilingual interactions. The article identifies eight crucial domains that need additional investigation to design effective spoken language systems. In each domain, the article describes the obstacles, the research infrastructure needed to support investigations, and the probable advantages.

To facilitate quick communication among researchers, the essay emphasizes the value of transdisciplinary research, shared corpora and resources, and computational support development. If spoken language systems are developed successfully, computers will become more usable by a larger spectrum of people, thereby facilitateing the international trade and communication, and opening up new avenues for research and employment.

In conclusion, spoken language systems offer enormous promise in a variety of contexts, and further study is required in several crucial areas to enhance their functionality and accuracy. Spoken language systems can significantly benefit society by enabling more individuals to access and utilize technology and by facilitating more effective cross-language communication with improved accessibility and technology.

A study [9] investigates the difficulties blind individuals face when accessing online services. It is the first of its kind, as previous research has mainly focused on the frustrations experienced by sighted computer users in academic and workplace environments. The study involved 100 blind participants who recorded their experiences using time diaries. The top five sources of frustration identified were: (a) improper page formats for screen readers, (b) conflicts between the screen reader and the application, (c) poorly designed or unlabelled forms, (d) lack of alternative text for images, and (e) a three-way tie between misleading links, inaccessible PDFs, and screen reader crashes.

Most of these issues can be resolved relatively easily by addressing page formats [10], while more technical problems like screen reader crashes and conflicts require action from screen reader developers. The study found that, on average, blind users spent 30.4% more time dealing with frustrating situations [11], but they were more likely to persist in trying to find a solution rather than giving up or restarting the computer [12].

The article highlights the need for greater attention to be paid to making websites more accessible for blind users [13, 14]. It emphasizes the importance of addressing the top sources of frustration identified in the study and encourages collaboration between Web and screen reader developers to improve the overall user experience for blind individuals [15].

Case Studies

Google's Voice Assistant Integration with Gmail

Google's integration of voice control with Gmail enables users to dictate emails, search, and organize their inboxes through Google Assistant. This hands-free functionality is particularly popular among professionals in sectors like logistics, healthcare, and mobile work environments. The system relies on Google's Natural Language API to understand intent and context, utilizes Speech-to-Text for precise transcription, and incorporates continuous machine learning to improve command accuracy over time. Research indicates that professionals experienced a 30% reduction in email management time and increased responsiveness, thanks to more efficient email handling processes [16].

Microsoft's Cortana Integration with Outlook

Microsoft's Cortana voice assistant, embedded within Outlook, allows users to handle tasks such as checking emails, scheduling, and generating summaries. This hands-free functionality has proven particularly valuable in corporate settings, where it facilitates multitasking. With advanced NLP and voice recognition, Cortana efficiently processes commands like "Summarize today's emails" or "Reply to the last email," while its contextual AI learns user preferences to provide proactive suggestions. Studies show a 20-25% productivity boost for corporate users, who spend less time organizing emails and more time on high-priority tasks.

Dragon NaturallySpeaking for Legal and Healthcare Sectors

Nuance's Dragon Naturally Speaking is extensively used in the healthcare and legal sectors, where hands-free email and document dictation offer significant advantages. The system's ASR and specialized NLP capabilities ensure precise transcription of industry-specific terminology, making it highly effective for composing emails and documentation within these fields. Healthcare research has demonstrated a 40% reduction in time spent on email composition, with accuracy rates exceeding 95% for specialized language, resulting in quicker response times and improved client or patient communication.

Methodology

The project's methodology calls for the active participation of all members, producing results that are higher than anticipated. The first step is to look for all the appropriate domains and choose a project topic. We next tie this topic to other aspects such as social context, domain expertise, and most importantly, the likelihood of obtaining the desired outcomes. It was decided to use "AI-Based Voice-Assisted Email System" as the project topic. After that, an evaluation of the benefits and drawbacks of similar initiatives was completed along with a literature analysis. This study revealed the challenges that persons with special needs have while utilizing mail services. Not even screen readers worked well for this. Later, we also examined a few voice-based email systems in use, but we found that they only offered the most basic features—sending, reading, and deleting emails—and required some mouse and/or keyboard manipulation. Therefore, we decided to develop a system with more mailing functions and no such interactions. Next, the system's features were finalized. All of this was completed in the project's initial phase.

The following phase entails learning the necessary information to execute the project, such as the technologies and algorithms that may be applied to get the intended project outcomes. Because of its many modules that make it easier to work with email providers using the Visual Studio Code IDE, we chose to create this system in Python. The front end of the system was developed using the Flask framework in Python in conjunction with HTML, CSS, and JavaScript. Later, flowcharts and UML diagrams were used to determine the project's overall flow.

We distributed the coding labor equally among the members in the following phase and began the project's real implementation. The testing phase was started once each member had finished the duties they had been given. During this phase, many use cases were used to verify the system's functionality to ensure it was all operating as intended. Once all errors were fixed and all test cases produced positive results, we concluded that our project had met our standards.

Proposed System

An 'AI-based voice-assisted email system' is proposed in this paper. This system is primarily designed for individuals with special needs who find traditional mailing systems challenging to use. This system provides a web-based medium to connect with our mail accounts and control them using only voice commands.

HTML, CSS, JavaScript, and Python, along with their respective libraries, were used to implement the project.

The following are the features of the system:

Text-to-Speech (TTS) Conversion: TTS Conversion is required for the voice assistant to communicate with the user. Instructions on how to use the system at each point are hard-coded and delivered to the user by the TTS conversion technique. The details requested by the user from the mail services are fetched and converted to Speech and delivered to the user. For the implementation of this feature, we used the pyttsx3 Python module.

Speech-to-Text (STT) Conversion: STT conversion is required to take user inputs. These voice inputs are converted into words and processed to make them suitable for further usage. This processing includes adding punctuation wherever required, changing the case form from upper to lower or *vice versa*, *etc*. This feature completely eliminates the use of keyboard and mouse to manage our mail accounts. For the implementation of this feature, we have made use of the speech recognition Python module. For adding punctuation to the required text, we have used the VOSK punctuation model 'Recasepunc', a pre-trained NLP model that helps add punctuation and capitalize letters as needed to the provided text.

Mail Service Features: Mailing services provide many features to their customers. Our system aims to make almost all of these features work only using voice commands. We have tried to include as many features as we can in the given time constraint. However, there are still many mailing features that can be included.

Compose and Send Mail with Attachments: The user can create a mail by providing the details, such as the email IDs of the recipients (To, Cc, and Bcc), the subject, and the body of the mail, as instructed by the voice assistant. Later, the system asks if we want to add any attachments. If so, users must specify the number of attachments and their filenames, including file extensions. Then we have the option to send the mail or cancel it. If we choose to send the mail, the mail is sent. If we choose to cancel, then we are taken back to the home page.

Access Inbox, Sent, Trash, Spam Folders: User is provided access to the Mail Inbox, Sent, Trash and Spam folders. When the user selects a section, the mail list for that section is updated to include all the mails in that section, with the latest mail having the highest number. This list serves as a means to access the emails. The user is returned to the home page from the section page on the back command. Different sections provide access to different mail functions.

Read Mail: The read mail feature allows users to listen to the entire details of the selected mail. If the user chooses to open each email, the voice assistant reads the "From" and "Subject" of each email from the list of emails and asks the user whether they want to read the complete email or not. If the user replies with a yes, then the voice assistant will read out the entire email.

Download Attachments: After reading an email, the user is prompted to download any attachments. If he wants to, these attachments are downloaded and stored in the user's device in the specified hard-coded path.

Delete or Spam 1 or all Mails: The delete or spam mail option allows the user to move the selected mail/mails to the trash and spam sections, respectively. We have provided the option to delete or spam a single email or all the emails in the list. The option to delete or spam a single email is provided before and after the email is read. The voice assistant reads the From and Subject of each email from the list and asks if the user wants to delete or spam the email. If he chooses to do so, the mail is moved to the trash or spam section, respectively. Secondly, after the mail is read out and the user says "delete" or "spam," then that mail is moved to the trash or spam section, respectively. The option to delete or spam all the emails is offered to the user at the start before starting to iterate the email list. At this time, the voice assistant asks the user whether he wants to open/read each email, delete all, or spam all. If the user chooses to delete all or spam all, all the emails are moved to the trash or spam section, respectively.

Restore 1 or all the Deleted/Spam Mails: The restore mail option allows the user to move the selected mail/mails back to the Inbox section. We have provided the option to restore a single email or all the emails in the list. The option to restore a single mail is provided before and after the mail is read. The voice assistant reads the From and Subject of each email from the list and asks if the user wants to restore it. If so, the email is restored, *i.e.*, moved back to the Inbox section. Secondly, after the mail is read out and the user says "restore," that mail is restored, *i.e.*, moved to the Inbox section. The option to restore all the mails is offered to the user at the start, before starting to iterate the mail list. At this time, the voice assistant asks the user whether they want to open/read each mail or restore all of them. If the user chooses to restore all the emails, they are moved to the Inbox section.

Search for an Email Using a Keyword: *The* user can search for an email using some keywords. If the user selects to search for an email, the voice assistant asks for the search query. A list of the relevant mail numbers is then created, updating the mail list. This search filter can be removed by using the back command.

Add Filters: Users can add filters to retrieve emails from a specific user, after a certain date, between two given dates, or a combination of both. If the user selects to add a filter, the voice assistant asks whether the filter should be applied to mail IDs, dates, or both. If the user chooses to enter mail IDs, the voice assistant then asks for the mail ID. If the user selects dates, the voice assistant asks for the start date. Then it asks if the user wants an end date or not. If yes, it takes the input of the end date. If the user selects both options, the voice assistant prompts for the email ID and then the start date. Then it asks if the user wants an end date or not. If yes, it takes the input of the end date. A list of relevant emails is then created, updating the mail list. These filters can be removed by using the back command.

For implementing these features, we utilized the yagmail and imaplib modules provided by Python, which serve as mail clients that connect with the mail server and fulfill user requests.

Flowcharts

Fig. (**1**) provides a clear overview of the features available in each section. The pink circles represent the compose option and the four sections through which the user can traverse. The purple rectangles represent the features available for use in each section. Table **1** shows a comparison of the traditional email and the proposed AI voice-assisted system.

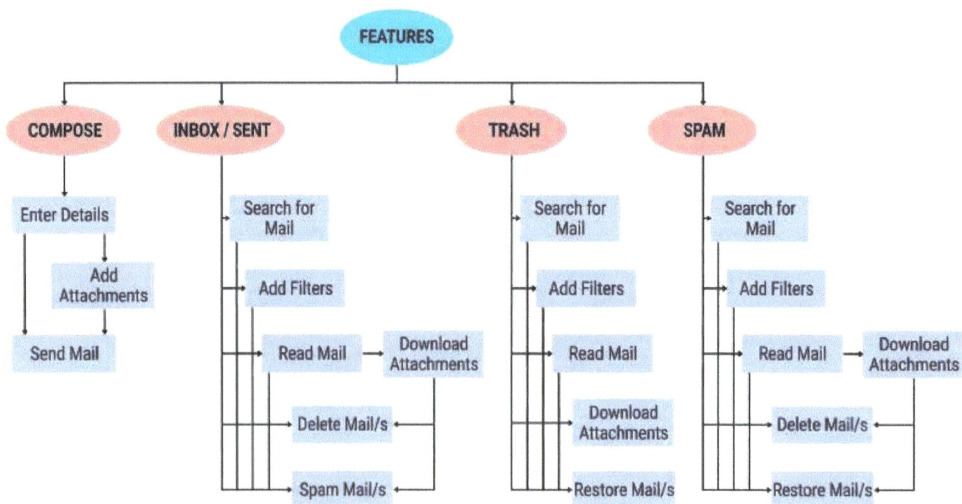

Fig. (1). Features in each section.

Table 1. Comparison of traditional email systems *vs.* proposed AI voice-assisted system.

Feature	Traditional Email System	Proposed AI-Based Voice-Assisted Email System
Accessing Email	Requires keyboard and mouse	Voice commands only
Composing and Sending Emails	Typing required	Voice commands and speech-to-text conversion
Reading Emails	Reading visually	Text-to-speech conversion
Managing Attachments	Manual download and upload	Voice commands and automated download
Sorting and Organizing Emails	Manual sorting and labeling	Voice commands and filters
Deleting and Marking as Spam	Manual selection and actions	Voice commands and automated actions
Searching for Emails	Manual keyword search	Voice commands and search filters
Restoring Deleted/Spam Emails	Manual selection and actions	Voice commands and automated actions
Overall Accessibility	Reliant on a visual interface	Independent use with voice commands

This table highlights the key differences between traditional email systems and the proposed AI-based voice-assisted email system in terms of functionality and accessibility for visually impaired users.

Fig. (**2**) provides the workflow of all the available features of our system in detail. The purple circles represent the features, and the pink rectangles represent the tasks performed by the user, *i.e.*, the inputs or voice commands provided by the user. Whereas, the blue rectangles represent the tasks performed by the voice assistant, which include asking the user about tasks to do and the inputs, and giving an acknowledgement of the tasks' completion. Further, the yellow rectangles show the tasks done by the email clients, *i.e.*, fetching the required details from the email servers. The green diamonds represent the decision points from where the path of flow changes as per the user's choice.

Fig. (**3**) is a sequence diagram that represents all the steps performed for executing a particular task, along with who performs each task. The brown rectangles represent the entities that perform a task. The green rectangles on the dotted line represent the tasks performed by the entity connected to that line, along with their sequence numbers. The purple diamond represents the client to whom the request should be made, based on the task assigned by the user.

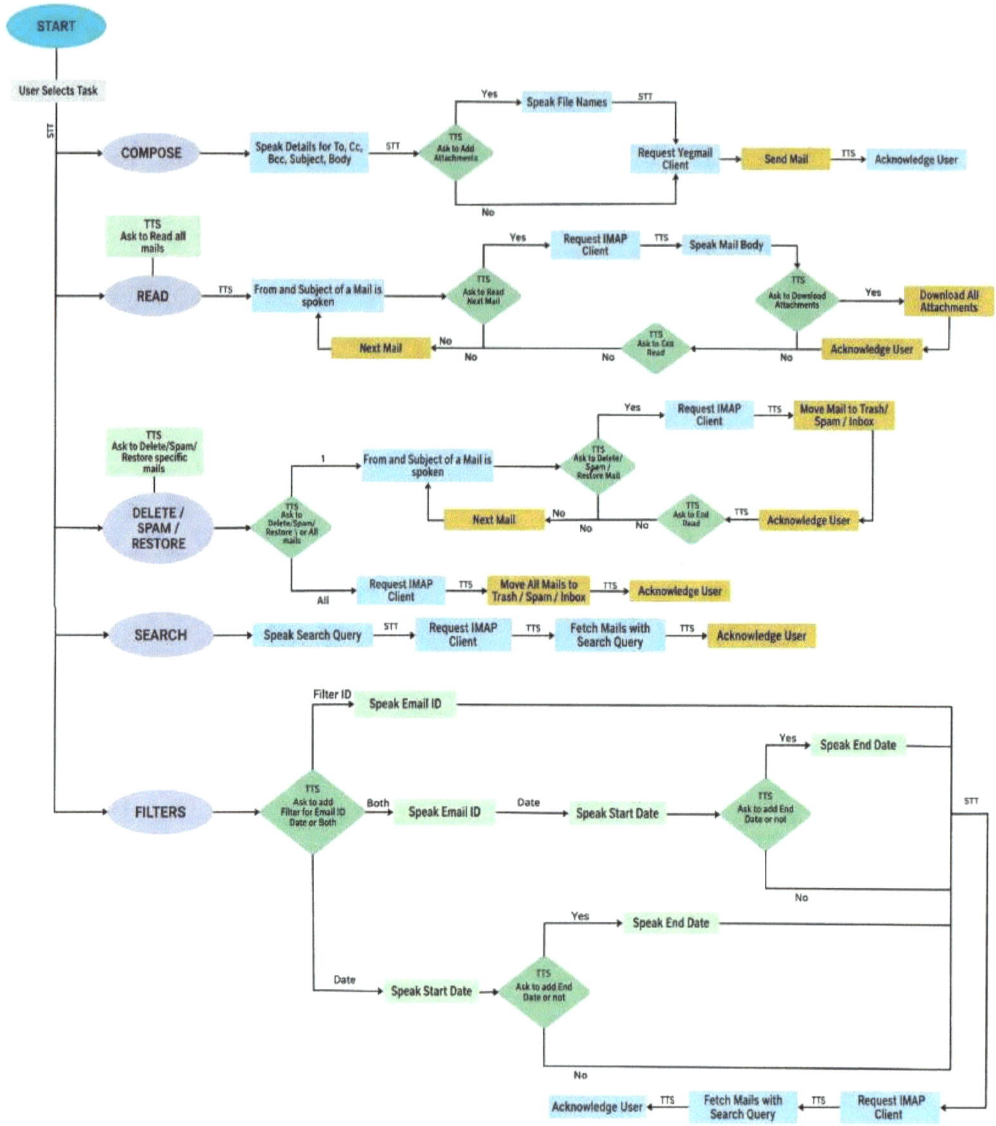

Fig. (2). Working of features.

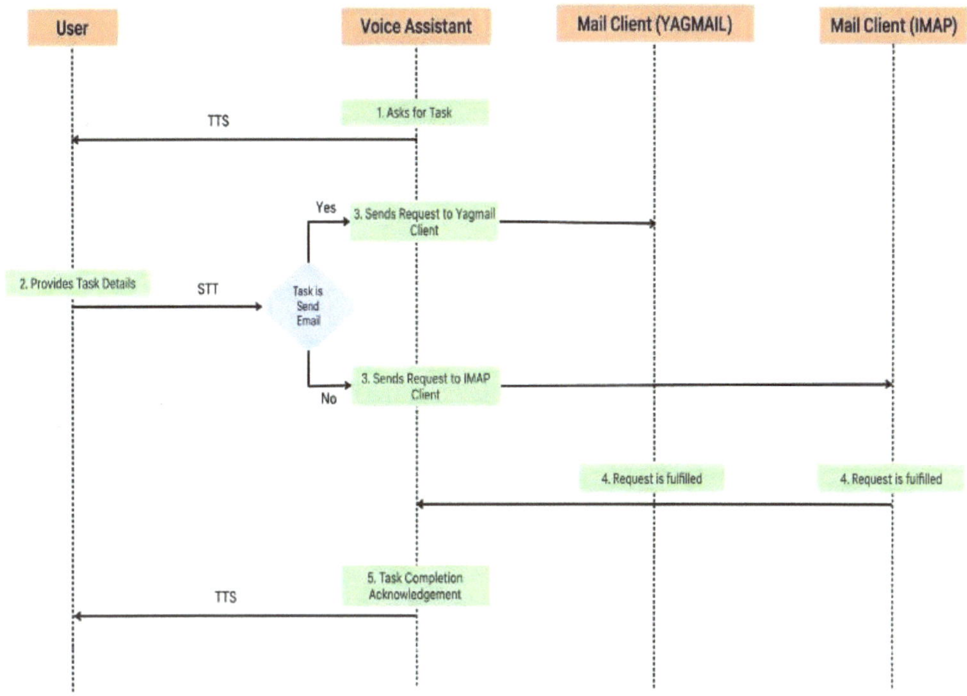

Fig. (3). Flow of execution of each task.

ALGORITHM

The following is the general algorithm used to operate and deliver services on this website:

1. When the website is loaded, the user lands on the home page and is provided with five options - Compose, Open Inbox, Open Sent, Open Trash and Open Spam. The user has to select one of the above options.
2. If the user selects the compose option, they can compose an email with attachments and send it to multiple users.
3. If the user selects the other options, they will be able to perform other mailing functions as per their availability in each section.
4. In the Inbox and Sent sections, you can read emails, download attachments, delete individual or all emails, mark emails as spam, search for emails using keywords, and add filters to mail IDs, dates, or both.
5. In the Trash section, users can read emails, download attachments, restore individual or all emails, search for emails using keywords, and add filters to email IDs, dates, or both.

6. In the Spam section, you can read emails, download attachments, delete or restore emails, search for emails using keywords, and add filters to mail IDs or dates.
7. After performing the desired functions, the user may propagate back to the main page and continue using other features of the system.
8. To exit from the system, the user simply needs to close the website.

RESULTS AND DISCUSSIONS

Fig. (**4**). shows the Home Page where the user has options to Compose Mail, Open Inbox, Open Sent, Open Trash and Open Spam.

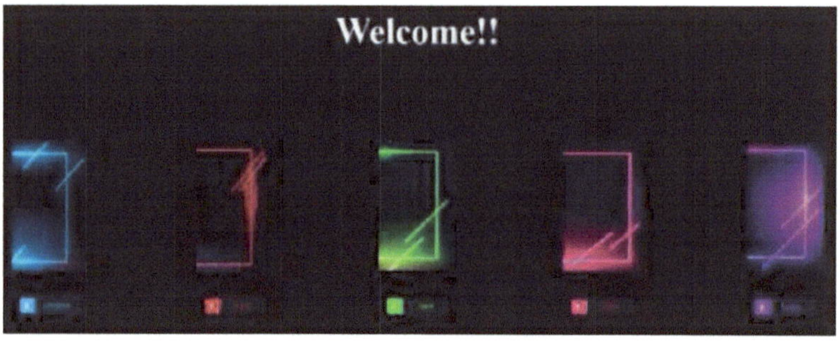

Fig. (4). Home page.

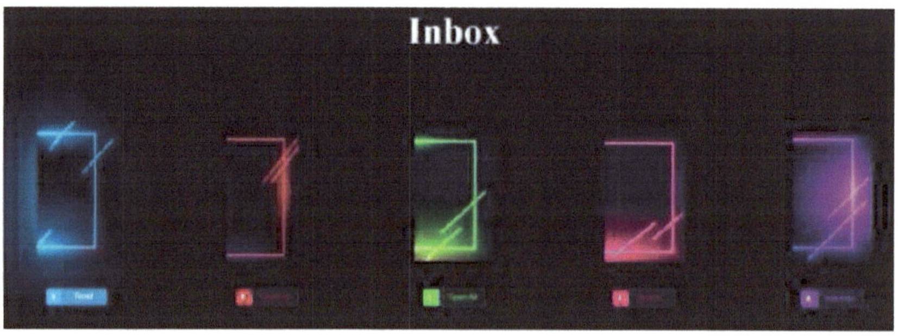

Fig. (5). Inbox page with read selection.

The user can read mail, delete all mail, mark all mail as spam, search for a letter, or add filters on the inbox page, as seen in Fig. (**4**). The option that is highlighted in the image—read—has been chosen by the user (Fig. **5**).

Fig. (**6**) shows the dialogue conversation for deleting a mail in the Inbox without reading it.

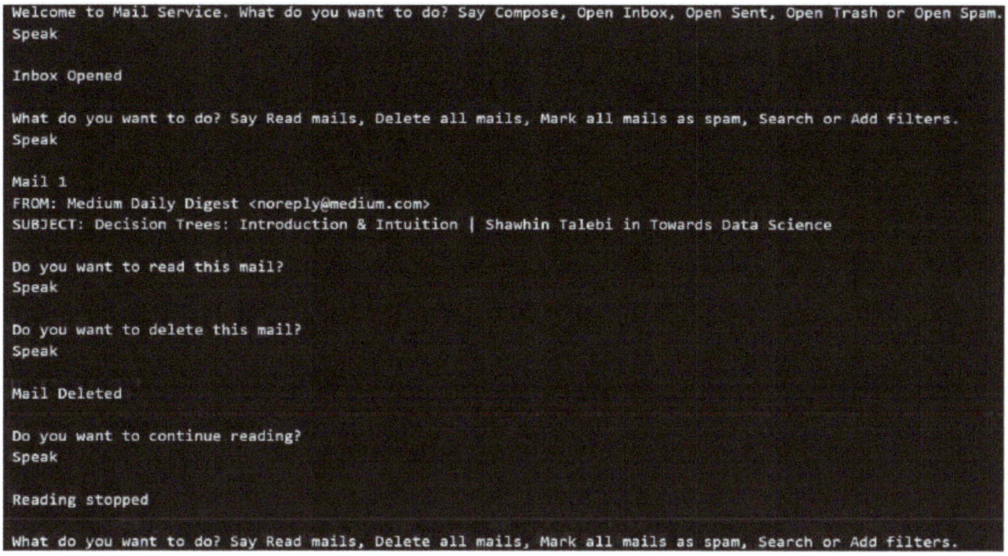

Fig. (6). Communication between user and voice assistant.

Fig. (**7**) shows that the selected mail is in the Inbox.

Fig. (7). Mail is in the inbox.

Fig. (**8**) shows that the selected mail is now moved to Trash on the user voice request.

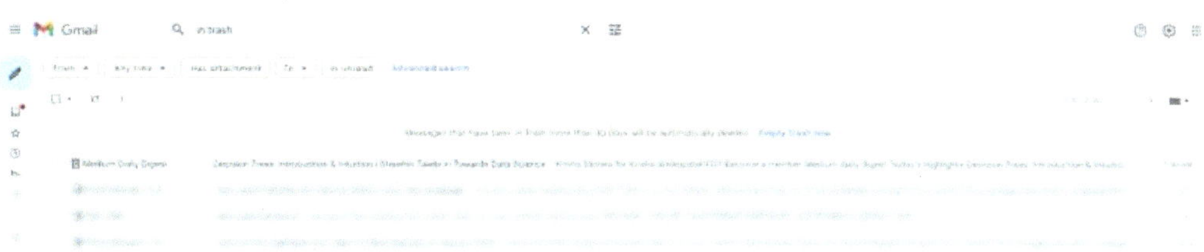

Fig. (8). Mail is in trash.

The hypothetical Table **2** demonstrates how the voice-assisted email system outperforms the traditional email system in terms of task completion time, error rates, user satisfaction, and system performance based on simulated or user-tested data. These results suggest that the voice-assisted email system offers tangible benefits for visually impaired users and could potentially enhance the email experience for all users.

Table 2. Comparison of user experience metrics between voice-assisted email system and traditional email system.

User Metric	Voice-Assisted Email System	Traditional Email System
Task Completion Time	Avg: 1 min 30 sec	Avg: 3 min 15 sec
Error Rate	5%	15%
User Satisfaction	09/10	06/10
System Performance	Responsive and accurate	Laggy and prone to errors

CONCLUSION

This paper provides an overview of various voice-based email applications that have been developed for people with visual impairments. These applications typically rely on Text-to-speech, Speech-to-text, Interactive Voice Response, and Artificial Intelligence techniques using programming languages such as Python and Java. While these applications have helped to make email more accessible, it is clear that there is room for improvement in terms of functionality and ease of use.

Motivated by this, the article proposes a new voice-assisted email system with basic email features such as sending, receiving, and reading emails, as well as additional functionalities such as deleting and marking emails as spam, sorting read and unread emails, sending and downloading attachments, and searching through emails. This new system has been developed using Python, Flask, HTML, and CSS, and is designed to be particularly useful for blind and visually impaired users who can now handle their email accounts independently using voice commands. The system is also expected to save time for sighted users who prefer to use voice commands. Further enhancements can be made to this system to further improve its usefulness for blind and visually impaired users.

Future Scope

Our system enhances the voice-based email system by enabling it to perform important email tasks without the need for a mouse and keyboard. However, there is a significant room for further development of the system. Additional functionalities, such as the ability to sort read and unread emails, reply to or forward emails, and other features, can be included to improve the system's usability.

To improve the system's scalability and communication, multilingual systems can be designed so that even individuals who do not speak English can access the system efficiently. Additionally, integrating a sign language system can increase the system's scalability and robustness. To enhance the security of user data, more security features, such as face scanners, can be added in addition to passwords. Moreover, these types of systems can be used to develop other similar applications in various domains that utilize speech recognition technology. Voice-controlled chat applications, voice-controlled ticket booking applications, and other applications can be developed to make the lives of many people easier.

REFERENCES

[1] K. Jayachandran, and P. Anbumani, *Voice Based Email for Blind People*. International Journal of Advance Research, Ideas and Innovations in Technology, 2017.

[2] R. Khan, P.K. Sharma, S. Raj, and S. Kr, "Verma, sparsh katiyar: voice based email system using artficial intelligence", *Int. J. Eng. Adv. Technol.,* 2020. [http://dx.doi.org/10.35940/ijeat.C5930.029320]

[3] K. Kusume Viajaya Lakshmi, "Lakshmana reddy: voice based email system for visually impaired", *J. Emerg. Technol. Innov. Res.,* 2021.

[4] I. Isewon, J. Oyelade, and O. Oladipupo, "Design and implementation of text to speech conversion for visually impaired people", *Int. J. Appl. Inf. Syst.,* 2018.

[5] M. Basha, *Soujanya C., Lakshmi Satya B.: A Novel Approach For Text To Audio Conversion For Blindly Disable Using Raspberry Pi.* Smart Green Connected Societies, 2021.

[6] N. Shakhovska, *Oleh Basystiuk, Khrystyna Shakhovska: Development of the Speech-to-Text Chatbot Interface Based on Google API.* Modern Machine Learning Technologies, 2019.

[7] U. Ummuhanysifa, and P.K. Nizar Banu, "Voice based search engine and web page reader", *Int. J. Comput. Eng. Res.,* 2019.

[8] R. Cole, "The challenge of spoken language systems: Research directions for the nineties", *IEEE Trans. Speech Audio Process.,* 2017.

[9] J. Lazar, A. Allen, J. Kleinman, and C. Malarkey, "What frustrates screen reader users on the web: a study of 100 blind users", *Int. J. Hum. Comput. Interact.,* 2018.

[10] K. Vayadande, U. Shaikh, R. Ner, S. Patil, O. Nimase, and T. Shinde, "Mood detection and emoji classification using tokenization and convolutional neural network", 2023 7th International Conference on Intelligent Computing and Control Systems (ICICCS), Madurai, India, 2023, pp. 653-663. [http://dx.doi.org/10.1109/ICICCS56967.2023.10142472]

[11] K. Vayadande, P. Narkhede, S. Nikam, N. Punde, S. Hukare, and R. Thakur, "Facial emotion based song recommendation system", *2023 International Conference on Computational Intelligence and Sustainable Engineering Solutions (CISES),* 2023pp. 240-248 Greater Noida, India [http://dx.doi.org/10.1109/CISES58720.2023.10183606]

[12] K. Vayadande, Traffic Sign Recognition System Using YOLO: Societal System for Safe Driving.*Techno-Societal 2022. ICATSA 2022.,* P.M. Pawar, Ed., Springer: Cham, 2024. [http://dx.doi.org/10.1007/978-3-031-34648-4_16]

[13] K. Vayadande, T. Adsare, N. Agrawal, T. Dharmik, A. Patil and S. Zod, "LipReadNet: a deep learning

approach to lip reading," 2023 International Conference on Applied Intelligence and Sustainable Computing (ICAISC), Dharwad, India, 2023, pp. 1-6. [http://dx.doi.org/10.1109/ICAISC58445.2023.10200426]

[14] K. Vayadande, S. Bhemde, V. Rajguru, P. Ugile, R. Lade, and N. Raut, "AI-based image generator web application using openAI's DALL-E system", 2023 International Conference on Recent Advances in Science and Engineering Technology (ICRASET), B G NAGARA, India, 2023, pp. 1-5. [http://dx.doi.org/10.1109/ICRASET59632.2023.10420306]

[15] S. Rawate, K. Vayadande, S. Chaudhary, S. Manmode, R. Suryavanshi, and K. Chanda, Fashion Classification Model.*Techno-societal 2022. ICATSA 2022.,* P.M. Pawar, Ed., Springer: Cham, 2024. [http://dx.doi.org/10.1007/978-3-031-34644-6_7]

[16] https://workspace.google.com/blog/research/the-future-of-work-with-google-workspace

CHAPTER 4

Navigating the AI Era: Applications, Opportunities, Threats, and Challenges in Practice

Devesh Kumar Bandil[1], **Pankaj Rahi**[2,3,*], **Ruchi Dave**[4] and **Santi Swarup Basa**[5]

[1] *Arya College of Engineering and IT, Jaipur, Rajasthan, India*

[2] *Singapore Institute of Technology, Singapore*

[3] *Lovely Professional University, Punjab, India*

[4] *St Wilfred's PG College, Jaipur, Rajasthan, India*

[5] *Maharaja Sriram Chandra Bhanjadeo University, Baripada, Odisha, India*

Abstract: Artificial Intelligence (AI) is driving transformative paradigm shifts across industries, offering innovative solutions to pressing societal challenges, including sustainability. By automating repetitive tasks and augmenting human capabilities, AI technologies have catalyzed productivity enhancements in sectors such as manufacturing, services, and education over the past two decades. The rapid evolution of expert systems, underpinned by advancements in AI research, has demonstrated significant potential in addressing complex problems across interdisciplinary domains, including healthcare, engineering, meteorology, and business analytics. This chapter provides a comprehensive examination of AI's conceptual foundations, applications, and innovations, with a focused analysis of its implementation in educational contexts. Through empirical case studies and critical analysis, it explores AI's role in optimizing operational efficiency, fostering quality improvements, and shaping future technological trajectories. The discussion concludes with an evaluation of emerging trends and ethical considerations, positioning AI as a pivotal force in advancing both industrial and societal progress.

Keywords: Artificial intelligence, AI applications, Expert systems, Intelligent technology.

INTRODUCTION

Research in operational research, management sciences, and educational technology is becoming more integrated, with educational technology also incorporating artificial intelligence.

* **Corresponding author Pankaj Rahi:** Singapore Institute of Technology, Singapore;
E-mail: pankaj.rahi@outlook.com

Subir Gupta, Indrajit Ghosal, Keshav Kaushik & Monika Dandotiya (Eds.)

Artificial Intelligence (AI) is a branch of computational science focused on developing computing equipment and systems that mimic human cognitive and behavioral processes. The ability to gather information and apply it to solve challenging problems is a common definition of intelligence. In many fields, intelligent machines will soon surpass human capabilities. Artificial Intelligence refers to the study of software and machines capable of reasoning, learning, knowledge acquisition, and manipulation. It involves systems that can perceive their environment and take appropriate actions. Computing plays a vital role in enabling these systems to sense and respond effectively. Artificial Intelligence differs from computer science in that it emphasizes perception, thinking, and action more than psychology does, as it places a greater emphasis on computation. It enhances machines' intelligence and usefulness. Perceiving and acting on reason is made possible by the study of computation. Artificial Intelligence differs from computer science and psychology in that it places focus on computing and an increased emphasis on observation, thinking, and action. It increases machine intelligence and utility. It operates with the aid of scientific theorems, which are if-then statements and logics, and Artificial Neural Networks (ANNs). The state of AI technology has progressed to the point where many of its applications are now producing real, practical benefits. Some of the primary areas of artificial intelligence include computer vision and scene identification, robotics and sensory systems, speech recognition, natural language processing, intelligent computer-aided instruction, expert systems, and neural computing. This expert system is the source of a rapidly developing technology that is significantly influencing various aspects of existence. Neural networks, fuzzy logic, evolutionary computing, computer-aided instruction, and hybrid artificial intelligence are some of the methods used in artificial intelligence.

Artificial Intelligence's Significance

Artificial Intelligence is the result of combining the terms I"artificial" and "intelligence." Artificial Intelligence is something that is "not real" or "natural," whereas intelligence is defined as " the ability to think, to generate fresh concepts, to observe, and to learn." The field of computer science known as artificial intelligence is largely concerned with building intelligent machines that have human-like behavior and thought processes. It is a combination of multiple tasks, including artificial intelligence design for computers, speech recognition, learning, and problem solving. A system that adapts to its environment is considered intelligent. The efficient utilization of scarce resources is the definition of artificial intelligence. Making computer programs that solve complicated problems in the same way that humans solve them is the definition of AI. It is therefore divided into two halves: the first focuses on machine-based complex issue solving, and the second is used to solve problems for people. The phrase "artificial intelligence" can also refer to a feature of programs or machines: the intelligence exhibited by the system. Combining science and engineering, artificial intelligence aims to create robots that exhibit intelligent behavior. It combines a number of disciplines, including computer science, psychology, and philosophy.

The ability of a software or machine to carry out tasks that typically require human intelligence is known as Artificial Intelligence (AI). At the vanguard of artificial intelligence research and engineering are the domains of speech recognition, visual perception, language translation, and decision-making. Artificial Intelligence (AI) is the computer, or more precisely, the computer system's imitation of human intellectual processes. Learning, thinking, planning, self-correction, and problem-solving are all necessary for this. The topic of Artificial Intelligence (AI) is controversial and often presented in a negative light. Although some believe that technology poses a threat to humanity's survival since it can subjugate and control people, in reality, AI has had a direct or indirect impact on our way of life and is influencing tomorrow's trends. Despite the indispensable applications of digital assistants on smartphones, driver assistance systems, chatbots, text and speech translators, and systems that help with personalized learning and product and service recommendations, Artificial Intelligence (AI) has already permeated every aspect of our daily lives and profoundly altered our way of life.

AI Types

One way to categorize artificial intelligence is through its features and capacities.

Based on capabilities, artificial intelligence can be divided into three categories:

Three types of AI:

- Narrow AI
- General AI
- Super AI

There are four categories of artificial intelligence under functionalities:

- Machines that React
- Self-awareness
- Theory of Mind
- Limited Theory

Using AI's Capabilities

1. Narrow: Weak AI or Narrow AI are other names for Narrow AI. AI that is narrowly focused is created and trained on a limited number of tasks. These AI systems, with limited scope, are purposefully created and trained. While these narrow systems accomplish their assigned objectives, their primary shortcoming is their inability to generalize tasks. Language translation tools, Examples include recommendation engines, image recognition software, and personal virtual assistants like Alexa or Siri.

2. General: We refer to it as Strong AI. It describes Artificial Intelligence (AI) systems with human intelligence and task-performance capabilities. Just as humans can adapt to different activities, systems are also capable of understanding, learning, and applying themselves to a wide range of tasks. AI is still mostly a theoretical idea, and no AI can currently reach this degree of intellect.

3. Super: Super-intelligent AI is the term for technology that outperforms humans in problem-solving, creativity, and general aptitude. Super AI acquires its own set of feelings, needs, wants, and beliefs. It possesses the ability to solve problems and make decisions on its own [1].

Considering AI's Functionality

1. Reactive Machines: IBM developed reactive machines in the mid-1980s. The most fundamental type of AI system is these devices. This implies that they are “Reactive” since they are unable to create memories or use the past to inform the present. Instead, they are only able to react to the circumstances that they find themselves in. A type of reactive machine currently in use is the supercomputer Deep Blue, which plays chess. This is the simplest kind of AI; it is capable of reacting to its surroundings, but is unable to create memories or make judgments based on past experiences. Simple rule-based systems, such as chess-playing software, are examples.

2. Limited Memory: This is made up of machine learning models from which the gadget learns new information based on events, stored data, and previously learned information. Limited memory, in contrast to Reactive machines, gains experience and knowledge by observing prior events or data provided to it.

3. Theory of Mind: This kind of AI can make decisions that are as good as those made by humans, but it does it through machines. Although some machines can already function like humans, such as voice assistants, none are totally capable of carrying on human-like conversations. AI systems with a theory of mind can comprehend and mimic the mental states of other agents. One aspect of human speech is the emotional capacity, or speaking and acting somewhat like a person would in ordinary discussions. Although still in development, this kind of AI is not yet useful.

4. Self-Awareness: With the help of this kind of AI, robots can now make decisions that are just as complex as those made by people. While some machines—like voice assistants—can already perform human-like tasks, none are fully capable of having human-like conversations. AI systems endowed with a theory of mind are capable of understanding and imitating other agents' mental states. The emotional capacity of human speech refers to the ability to speak and behave in a manner akin to that of an individual in casual conversations. This type of AI is still in its infancy and not yet very useful [2].

REALISTIC DOMAIN OF APPLICATION

Artificial neural networks have the potential to address a broad range of problems, including machine translation, computer vision, visualization, anomaly detection, clustering, dimension reduction, regression, structured prediction, and decision-making. Artificial neural networks also make it possible to model nonlinear processes. The application of artificial neural networks is made feasible by their broad range of capabilities. The vast application domain for artificial intelligence is being explored thanks to recent advancements in AI techniques, high processing capacity at progressively affordable prices, widespread accessibility of data with labels, and advancements in education methodologies. The predicted advancement of Artificial Intelligence is displayed in Fig. (**1**).

AI's projected advancement, as depicted in Fig. (**1**), represents a visual representation of artificial intelligence capabilities with a foreseen, expected capacity to evolve over time.

The McKinsey Global Institute predicts that by 2025, AI will have enabled automated knowledge work, advanced robots, and fully and partially autonomous vehicles. These will be worth between $5.2 and $6.77 trillion, $1.7 and $4.5 trillion, and $0.2 to $1.9 trillion, respectively 1. An Accenture study that looked at how AI could affect GDP growth found that by 2035, AI would raise the efficiency rates of workers in 12 countries by 11–37%.

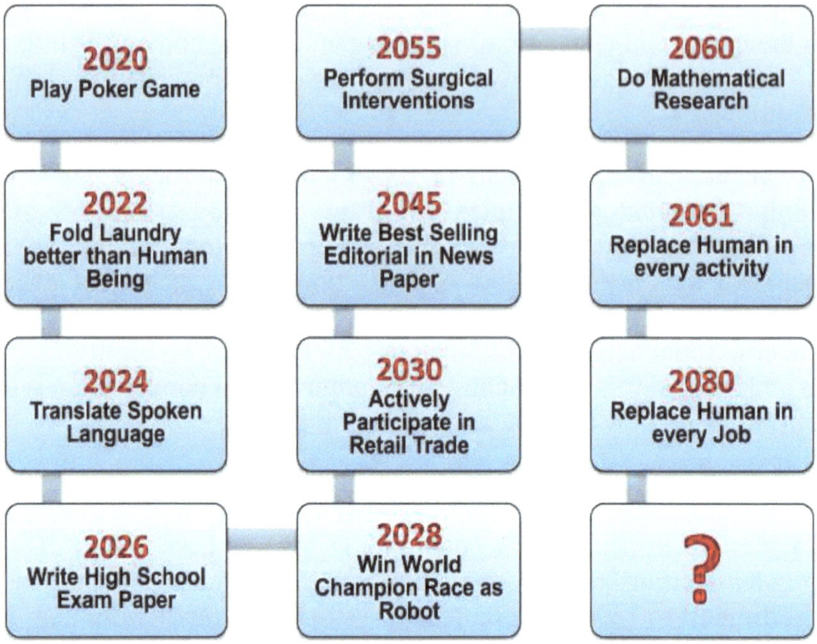

Fig. (1). : AI's projected advancement.

Additional Applications

Artificial Intelligence (AI) is being utilized across several businesses and sectors, encompassing healthcare, finance, transportation, and manufacturing.

Fig. (**2**) presents a generic representation of various areas where Artificial Intelligence (AI) is being extensively utilized. The figure aims to illustrate the broad scope of AI applications across diverse sectors.

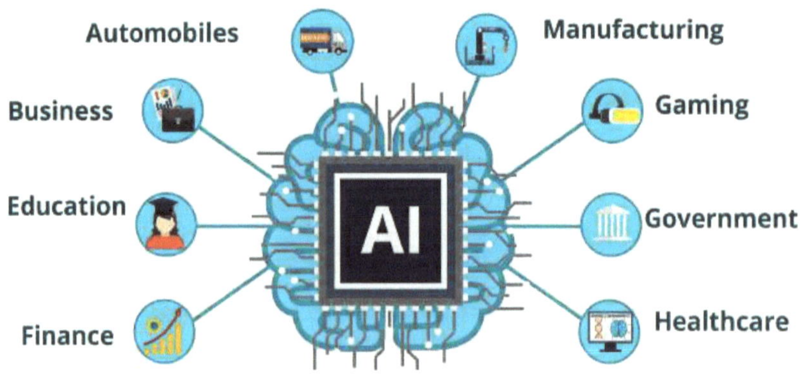

Fig. (2). Generic representation of areas, utilizing the AI extensively.

1. AI is employed in healthcare to do several tasks, including analysing images for diagnostics, processing natural language for electronic health records, and discovering new drugs.
2. Finance: AI is employed in the financial sector to do jobs such as identifying fraudulent activities, evaluating risks, and analyzing investments.
3. Transportation: Artificial Intelligence is employed in transportation to optimize traffic flow, enable autonomous vehicles, and enhance accident avoidance.
4. AI is employed in the manufacturing industry to enhance jobs such as process optimization, predictive maintenance, and quality control.
5. In the retail industry, Artificial Intelligence (AI) is employed for several purposes, including personalization, inventory management, and demand forecasting.
6. Agriculture: AI is employed in agriculture for activities such as farming, crop surveillance, and meteorological prediction.
7. AI is employed in the energy industry for predictive maintenance, demand forecasting, and grid optimization.
8. Cybersecurity uses Artificial Intelligence (AI) to carry out many activities, including identifying potential threats, responding to incidents, and managing vulnerabilities.
9. Artificial Intelligence is utilized in natural language processing for a range of tasks, including text-to-voice conversion, speech recognition, and language translation.
10. Robotics: Artificial Intelligence is employed in Robotics to perform functions such as perception, decision-making, and control.
11. Fraud detection. The financial services industry uses artificial intelligence in two different ways. The first step in the credit rating process utilizes AI to assess creditworthiness. Additionally, real-time tracking and identification of fraudulent credit card transactions are facilitated through the use of more sophisticated AI algorithms.
12. Virtual Customer Support (VCA) is available. Call centers use Virtual Customer Assistants (VCAs) to anticipate and respond to consumer requests when there is no human involvement. Voice recognition coupled with an artificial speech synthesizer is the initial point of contact for customer support inquiries. Higher-level inquiries are directed at specific people.
13. Medicine: A medical clinic can arrange beds, rotate staff, and give medical data by utilizing AI systems. AI is also applied to complex internal organ procedures, neurology (MRI), cardiology (CRG), and embryology (sonography).
14. Music: Scientists are trying to program a computer to replicate the movements of a skilled musician. The primary areas of focus for artificial intelligence and

music research are sound processing, performance, composition, and music theory. Orchestra, Chucks, Smart Music, *etc.*, are a few examples.

15. Antivirus: Artificial Intelligence (AI) methods are becoming increasingly important for identifying viruses. These techniques merge artificial intelligence and antivirus detection, promoting the creation of new artificial intelligence applications. It leverages artificial intelligence to enhance antivirus detection, promotes the development of new AI algorithms, and improves the functionality of antivirus detection systems [3].

USE OF ROBOTICS, AI, AND IOT IN AGRICULTURE

Precision farming also makes use of robotic AI. With 10 billion people expected to live on Earth by 2050, there will be considerable pressure on the agricultural sector to increase crop yields and productivity [4]. Precision farmers boost productivity and reduce waste while increasing yield through the use of tools and information. Robotic AI can analyze weather patterns, soil conditions, and moisture levels to help farmers choose the best times and places to plant crops. Increased crop yields and reduced waste could result in higher income for farmers.

The shortage of workers in the agricultural sector is something that robotic AI can help alleviate. Finding qualified workers has become increasingly difficult as the average age of farmers rises and younger generations leave rural areas. By automating previously labor-intensive tasks, such as planting and harvesting, robotic AI helps farmers save time and money.

Artificial intelligence robots can also help in making agriculture more sustainable. Farmers can lessen the adverse environmental impact by minimizing the use of toxic chemicals and increasing the efficiency with which they produce crops. Additionally, robotic AI can help reduce soil erosion and promote soil health by precisely targeting areas that require attention.

Extensive Use of AI in Digital Marketing

The application of Artificial Intelligence has become common in numerous businesses and human society. It has not only reduced human involvement in various procedures but also improved humans' efeciency in their work. Artificial intelligence and digital marketing are significantly correlated. There is a substantial need in the field of digital marketing to manage vast quantities of data. Artificial intelligence empowers digital marketers to accelerate data processing, thereby enhancing their ability to formulate digital plans with greater efficiency.

Artificial Intelligence (AI) has enormous potential in the world of digital marketing. Internet marketing is ranked at the highest position. Online advertising is a crucial element of digital marketing. It enables efficient communication between businesses and their target audience.

Programmatic Advertising, powered by Artificial Intelligence, efficiently manages the majority of modern web adverts through a complex delivery system.

The initiative facilitates the acquisition and disposal of advertising spaces. It enables the rapid buying and selling of advertising spots in auctions.

Before the emergence of AI, marketers had to conduct thorough research to choose the optimal platform for advertising their company. Currently, AI is tasked with conducting this research, thereby relieving marketers of the workload and allowing them to focus on other vital aspects of the digital strategy.

Furthermore, personalized user experience is delivered." Personalization has emerged as the most recent trend." According to the Average, 96% of marketers agree that customization is essential for delivering an outstanding customer experience.

AI facilitates the recognition of the preferences, behavioral patterns, interests, and activities of millions of individuals regularly. To accomplish this, it collects and analyses user data, considering criteria such as physiographic, demographic, device-related, geographic, and other pertinent information.

As the level of customization increases, the probability of conversion also increases. Moreover, AI also enables the advancement of improved consumer relationships.

The subject matter pertains to chatbots that are enhanced by artificial intelligence.

Frequently, there is a lack of clarity in distinguishing between a traditional Chatbot and an AI-driven Chatbot. AI-powered Chatbots are an improved version of traditional Chatbots.

AI-driven Chatbots engage in interactions with users in a manner that closely mimics human interaction, setting them apart from traditional Chatbots. Another advantage of these Chatbots is their capacity to maintain composure and patience when users inquire.

AI-powered chatbots possess the ability to handle several customer requests at the same time. The extensively tailored automated response possesses the capacity to convincingly influence any user to engage in the purchase of your products or services.

Predictive Analysis-AI is widely recognized for its proficiency in doing intricate computations and interpreting extensive datasets. Artificial Intelligence uses statistical models and software to predict a customer's future behaviors by analyzing their past behavior and characteristics.

Artificial Intelligence enables marketers to gather more comprehensive data about their customers, including their anticipated price preferences for specific products. Based on the data, Artificial Intelligence (AI) is capable of predicting the specific attributes that customers expect in a product upgrade.

PROJECTED ADVANCES IN ARTIFICIAL INTELLIGENCE

Artificial Intelligence (AI) improves people's lives by assisting with driving, providing personal care for the elderly and disabled, performing risky and difficult tasks, supporting decision-making, logically handling enormous volumes of data that might otherwise be difficult to understand, supporting translation, and enabling multilingual communication even in situations where language is not a barrier. AI is currently pervasive and is employed extensively in readily apparent ways. Several topics that are presently prioritized.

Collaborative Systems

Models and algorithms are studied in collaborative systems research to facilitate the creation of autonomous systems that can cooperate with humans and with one another.

In the rapidly developing field of machine perception, Natural Language Processing (NLP) is primarily focused on automatic voice recognition. It is much the same as teaching a computer program to understand spoken language. The creation of technologies that can converse with humans *via* dialogue as opposed to rote responses is the main objective of this field's study. Enterprise search, which involves the methodical retrieval of both structured and unstructured data within enterprises, can utilize these tools.

Von Neumann's architecture model is used by conventional computers, which employ neuromorphic computing. As a result of deep neural networks' success, more models—many of which draw inspiration from biological brain networks—are being created.

Reinforcement Learning: Pattern matching, Rule extraction, and mining have made ML an important tool. Reinforcement learning is used to enhance this tool with motivational decision-making capabilities. The use of reinforcement learning enhances AI's ability to manage challenging, dynamic real-world issues.

Robotics: The problem of robot navigation in static situations has been extensively studied and solved. These days, research focuses on how they can interact predictably in a dynamic, real-time context with the outside world.

THREATS OF ARTIFICIAL INTELLIGENCE

We now deal with a lot of AI-related concerns in our day-to-day lives. Certain concerns associated with AI are not as serious or worrisome as those posed by sentient AI or killer robots. Prominent dangers in contemporary times encompass issues such as infringement of customer privacy, programming that exhibits bias, threats to human safety, and ambiguous legal regulation [5]. The few core risk associated with AI are explained in the subsequent sections below:

Movement and Recovery Effects

Personnel working in the supply chain are impacted by measurement, equipment use, and the consequences of mechanical technology. As stated by the authors referenced in the citation, they argue that the replacement of jobs mostly drives the rise of this new phenomenon. As a result, the economy has seen substantial consequences. According to their claim, for the economy's profits to be long-lasting and for monetary reform to progress, it is essential to consider the extinction impact alongside all opposing forces, including the creation of new employment. A proficient labour force with remuneration that is both competitive and consistent is vital for achieving sustained financial progress. High levels of unemployment result in reduced consumer expenditure, thereby affecting businesses involved in the manufacturing of goods and the delivery of various services to workers. What prospective job prospects could arise in these conditions to compensate for the requirement to find employment? Artificial Intelligence (AI) has the potential to supplant specific technologies and computer-assisted endeavors created by humans, including confession, decision-making, communication, and power. As new nonprofit intelligence agencies emerge, they are distinguished by their complexity, discernment, learning based on relationships, innovative thinking, and a blend of practical work, empathy, and effective communication. Below are many illustrations of novel job designations: “Trainers” are individuals who provide instruction to the algorithm, “Interpreters” are responsible for uncovering non-technical intelligence findings, and “Sustainers” are tasked with evaluating the efficiency of artificial intelligence.

THE ACCOUNTABILITY AND DEPENDABILITY OF ARTIFICIAL INTELLIGENCE

Currently, AI systems operate within a largely unregulated environment, despite their significant advantages and growing influence a. An environment of climate change emerges when there is an absence of norms and when profitable commercial organizations are motivated to quickly develop cutting-edge technology, while disregarding the need to adequately test it to safeguard customers from harm and potential legal consequences [6]. Suppose the client suffers an injury as a result of using new equipment. In that case, the existence of a problematic guide hinders their ability to determine a legal solution or obtain protection from the supplier to ensure the equipment's proper functioning. If a self-regulating vehicle experiences a minor car accident or if a patient receives an inaccurate diagnosis due to faulty chemical therapy, how should a researcher behave? The limitations of artificial intelligence are clearly apparent in this scenario. Various ethical and practical recommendations have been put out in academic literature to address the challenges now faced. The purpose of these guidelines is to establish a framework for managing design businesses and to provide guidance for the development and use of products that contribute to the advancement of technology with improved quality. The results underscore the importance of clearly defined local criteria, as well as a thorough understanding and commitment to the entire network involved in developing artificial technology [6]. Most machine learning algorithms rely on neural connections to function, interpreting them as mysterious signals. These algorithms facilitate the examination of vast statistical data within massive databases to surpass the limitations of the model. Ultimately, they can collect or predict data based on a predetermined goal [7]. Although the design of an algorithm can be explained and validated, information enthusiasts frequently struggle to categorize the fundamental functions of artificial intelligence accurately. To address this issue, the General Data Protection Regulation was established by the European Union Parliament in 2016. Customers are permitted to challenge the determinations made by an automated system [7, 8].

Data Protection and Personalization

In order to guarantee that users interact with customized content and management, chains need to be able to gather, keep, and disseminate large volumes of personal data and include both organized data (such as name, address, and distinct identifiers) and unorganized data (such as tweets, posts, recordings, and images). To guarantee efficient data security and preservation, companies must actively participate in the information generation process. Chain merchants frequently reevaluate the viability of purchasing due to the financial implications involved in the transaction, and instead consider the possibility of forming partnerships with growing businesses. Small enterprises often require more cost-effective information repositories than their larger corporate counterparts.

The Influence of Robotics and Artificial Intelligence on Future Job Opportunities

There has been a notable worldwide partnership between robotics and AI to accomplish various objectives. The growing prominence and importance of robotics aid in the simplification of everyday tasks [9, 10]. Concurrently, when robots take over all roles in the industrial sector, there will be less labor performed by humans. Nonetheless, robots may increase production, but they could reduce job opportunities. Robots are replacing workers in blue-collar industries. The robots are progressively infiltrating professional occupations typically performed by office workers. Artificially engineered robots can perform mundane reduced social interaction, while offering the world's populace considerable comfort. According to [11], the growing presence of robots is resulting in a gradual increase in human-robot interaction, as they help improve convenience and comfort in people's lives.

Extensive Outlook for the Futuristic Use of AI and New Threats

The facility's cutting-edge technological capabilities, including mechanical systems and computational efficiency, appear to exceed the capacity to accommodate diverse aspects such as computer hardware, vehicles, and consumer electronics. This principle is also relevant to industries such as healthcare, advertising, education, law enforcement, housing, and finance [11]. These developments will offer businesses and clients a plethora of enticing and convenient alternatives, including increased efficiency, expanded customization, improved quality, and longer deadlines for completion. Nevertheless, individuals inevitably encounter obstacles that must be overcome throughout their lifetime. The difficulties in this situation include having human instructors assign tasks, developing safety protocols for both humans and robots at the same time, creating a framework to guarantee the reliability of robotic systems, and creating artificial insemination technologies to foster trust. The swift advancement of AI and technological enhancements require substantial changes, and institutions and testing organizations bear a vital obligation to adjust to such innovations. Typically, educational frameworks are implemented to foster the advancement of technology within a certain area. The implant's creative capabilities were evaluated by computer algorithms and in a real-world educational environment. Artificial Intelligence (AI) has gained significant value in the last twenty years, regardless of its specific attributes. The research [12] proposed that both cognitive and non-cognitive intelligence systems should surpass the restrictions imposed by scientific and design limitations in order to promote more inclusivity among individuals. Therefore, colleges must assume the responsibility of supervising this interdisciplinary approach, as businesses are in urgent need of individuals who possess both social and specialized skills and can efficiently collaborate in scientific teams comprising experts from various fields [12]. The integration of AI technology in workplaces has fundamentally revolutionized cognitive processes and job execution, empowering people with varied proficiencies to engage in collaborative efforts, exchange knowledge, and produce exceptional ideas and results. It is crucial to change people's views and ideas about AI, ML, and sophisticated technology devices, starting with the school system, particularly the way assessments are conducted. Therefore, the rapid progress of AI has made it an essential component in every corporate sector, and the advantages of AI in efficiently managing cybersecurity threats are readily evident [13].

Path modelling is a method that enables investigators to explore the causal associations between elements. The paradigm provides a comprehensive evaluation of both the immediate and long-term effects of several independent factors on a single dependent variable. The findings of the PLS-SEM analysis are presented in the Figure. The dependent variable is highly influenced by the benefits of cybersecurity, trust, and artificial intelligence among the five independent components. Trust and benefits negatively impact the dependent variable, but cybersecurity risk has a favorable impact. Respondents believe that the effects of AI are noticeable due to factors such as increased cybersecurity measures and perceived threats, as indicated by the statistics. In the future, there might be a decrease in career opportunities because of the extensive adoption of AI. Individuals who doubt AI's capacity to acquire human skills are more likely to hold a negative outlook on AI's role in the workplace. One possible explanation for this discrepancy could be the belief that AI is unable to equal the decision-making abilities of human management [14].

The PATH model of AI, as explained in Fig. (**3**) is based on the context-relevant summary.

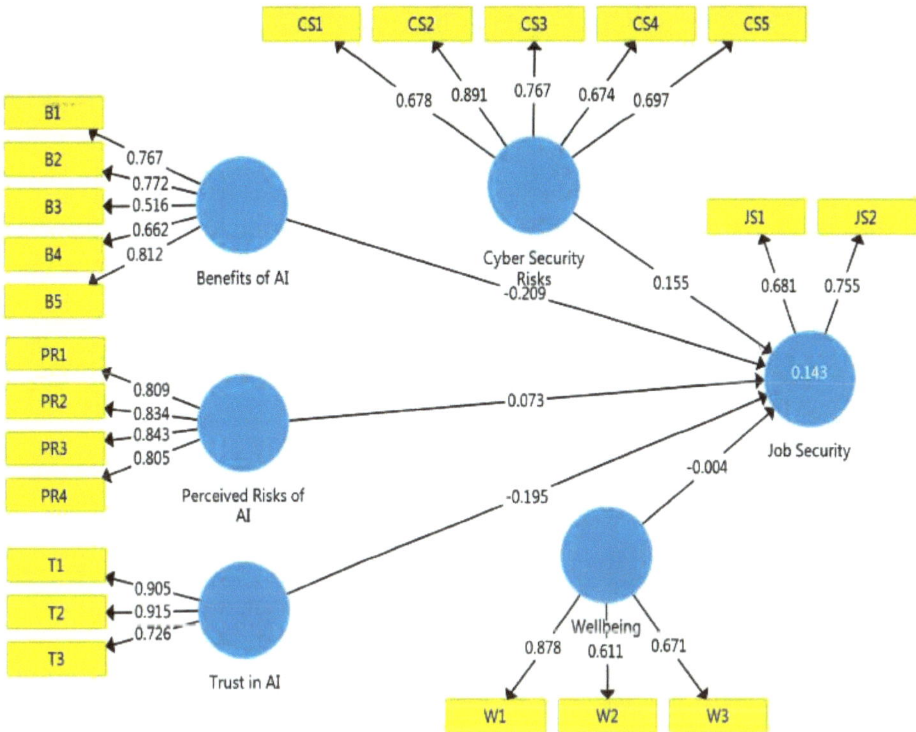

Fig. (3). PATH model of AI [14].

CHALLENGES WITH AI

Building trust: Most people lack knowledge about science, technology, or algorithms in Artificial Intelligence (AI), It makes their ability to trust the system challenging.

Artificial intelligence poses risks to fundamental rights and democratic principles. The outcomes of AI are influenced by its structure and the data it is fed. Architecture and data may demonstrate bias, whether deliberate or inadvertent. Numerical representation of intricate social networks in AI can lead to a misleading perception of precision and accuracy. This is occasionally called math washing.

Improper use of AI can result in biassed decisions based on factors including ethnicity, gender, and age in processes such as hiring, firing, loan approval, and legal matters.

The use of artificial intelligence can significantly impact the right to confidentiality and the security of data. It can be utilized in applications such as facial recognition software or for monitoring and creating biographies of individuals online. Furthermore, AI allows for the integration of data provided by an individual to provide novel insights that may be surprising to them.

AI poses a threat to democracy by fostering online echo chambers that cater to individual preferences rather than fostering a varied and inclusive environment for public discourse. It can also be utilized to produce extremely authentic fabricated video, audio, and images called deepfakes, which have the potential to pose financial dangers, damage reputation, and complicate decision-making. This situation could result in division and polarization in the general population realm, affecting electoral outcomes.

AI can impede the right to assembly and demonstration through tracking and profiling persons associated with specific views or acts.

AI-human Interaction: Given that data science and analytics are still in their infancy, there is a significant shortage of qualified personnel with these backgrounds who can be allocated to optimize AI's potential. As artificial intelligence advances rapidly, businesses are struggling to find competent employees who can effectively manage this technology.

1. **Investment:** With the plethora of opportunities that artificial intelligence presents, an increasing number of CEOs in India and around the world are prepared to spend money on the technology to grow their companies. According to the survey, generative AI is the top investment priority for organizations, as deemed by 66% of CEOs of Indian companies and 70% of CEOs of global corporations. The need for Artificial Intelligence (AI) intervention in business management has increased as a result of the growing demand for personalized content and the development of AI algorithms.
2. **Software Malfunction:** AI is controlled by machines and algorithms, which means that code-driven Black Box tools will always have the final say in decisions. It is challenging to determine the root cause of errors and malfunctions in automation. Furthermore, humans have little to no control over the system because they are unable to learn and comprehend how these tools operate. As automated systems become more widespread and advanced, the issue worsens.

AI has its limitations, just like any other technology; it cannot do all tasks. It will, however, because new job domains with distinct quality job profiles will emerge [15].

1. **High Standards:** A wide range of scientists and technologists with different goals, motivations, and interests engage in artificial intelligence research. The main goal of research is to unravel the basic principles of intelligence and cognition, with a focus on the mysteries of the human mind and mental processes. Some people may have very high expectations for artificial intelligence, and not everyone is aware of how it operates.
2. **Algorithm Bias:** Artificial Intelligence is based on data and algorithms, and the quality of AI's training and the use of actual, unbiased facts are the only factors that affect its capacity to make wise decisions. Important judgments will unavoidably have immoral and unfair effects if the training data incorporates biases related to race, gender, ethnicity, or community. Since most AI systems will likely still be taught on erroneous data, these biases will likely be more obvious.
3. **Data Scarcity:** The power and capabilities of Artificial Intelligence (AI) and its applications are significantly influenced by the quality and relevance of the supervised and labeled datasets used for training and learning. However, high-quality labeled data is often scarce.
4. **Illiterate:** AI is a nascent field, and many aspects of its fundamental operations remain unknown. This lack of knowledge could hinder the development of reliable and precise Artificial Intelligence (AI) systems [16].

CONCLUSION

Machine learning and Artificial Intelligence (AI) applications are changing at a speed that has never been seen before. Robotics and automation have come a long way thanks to Artificial Intelligence (AI). This has had a huge impact on many areas of business, especially in retail (marketing) services, healthcare, and education. Artificial Intelligence has a significant impact on various sectors of society and business, including healthcare, education, retail marketing, smart urban planning, transportation, and maintenance. Robots can think logically with the help of artificial intelligence, which applies ideas. In the last 20 years, methods for artificial intelligence have helped many fields a great deal. Artificial intelligence will become increasingly important in many fields. Based on the idea of artificial intelligence and how it is being used in many areas, especially in "the field of education," this article builds on that. This chapter provides a comprehensive review of Artificial Intelligence (AI) applications and explores the potential risks and opportunities that may arise in the future. We all know that artificial intelligence is a form of machine intelligence developed by experts.

No one needs to be told that AI has made our lives a lot easier in every way, from writing papers to playing games to making important decisions. Putting together several skilled minds can make any machine stronger than a single one. Multiple hard-to-do tasks can be done by one machine, and its best feature is that it never gets tired. Being able to make sensitive robots means that people will no longer be alone these days. But there's another aspect that might be unsafe for us. We might lose the drive to work for ourselves and become lazy if we rely too much on these machines, which could ruin our lives. Another thing is that it cannot evoke any emotions in people. Therefore, it is suggested to use tools only when necessary, as their overuse may prove to be harmful.

REFERENCES

[1] "Machine Learning - Types of Artificial Intelligence," GeeksforGeeks, Aug. 23, 2020. https://www.geeksforgeeks.org/machine-learning-types-of-artificial-intelligence/

[2] A. Bécue, I. Praça, and J. Gama, "Artificial intelligence, cyber-threats and Industry 4.0: challenges and opportunities", *Artif. Intell. Rev.,* vol. 54, no. 5, pp. 3849-3886, 2021. [http://dx.doi.org/10.1007/s10462-020-09942-2]

[3] D. F. Santos-Bustos, B. M. Nguyen, and H. E. Espitia, *Towards automated eye cancer classification via VGG and ResNet networks using transfer learning,* 2022. [http://dx.doi.org/10.1016/j.jestch.2022.101214]

[4] T. Davenport, and R. Ronanki, *Artificial Intelligence for the Real World,* 2018. https://blockqai.com/wp-content/uploads/2021/01/analytics-hbr-ai-for-the-real-world.pdf

[5] P.P. Groumpos, "Artificial intelligence: issues, challenges, opportunities and threats", *Commun. Comput. Inf. Sci.,* vol. 1083, pp. 19-33, 2019. [http://dx.doi.org/10.1007/978-3-030-29743-5_2]

[6] M. H. Jarrahi, D. Askay, A. Eshraghi, and P. Smith, *Artificial Intelligence and Knowledge management: a Partnership between Human and AI,* 2022.

[7] T. Panch, P. Szolovits, and R. Atun, "Artificial intelligence, machine learning and health systems", *J. Glob. Health,* vol. 8, no. 2, p. 020303, 2018. [http://dx.doi.org/10.7189/jogh.08.020303] [PMID: 30405904]

[8] B. Van Alsenoy, *"General Data Protection Regulation," Data Protection Law in the EU: Roles.* Responsibilities and Liability, 2019, pp. 279-324. [http://dx.doi.org/10.1017/9781780688459.021]

[9] A.O. Salau, S. Jain, and M. Sood, Computational intelligence and data sciences: paradigms in biomedical engineering. Book published by CRC Press, Taylor and Francis, pp. 1-272, 2022. eBook ISBN: 9781003224068. [http://dx.doi.org/10.1201/9781003224068]

[10] *The Rise Of Artificial Intelligence: Future Outlook And Emerging Risks About Allianz Global Corporate & Specialty,* 2018.

[11] J.F. Arinez, Q. Chang, R.X. Gao, C. Xu, and J. Zhang, "Artificial intelligence in advanced manufacturing: current status and future outlook", *J. Manuf. Sci. Eng.,* vol. 142, no. 11, p. 110804, 2020. [http://dx.doi.org/10.1115/1.4047855]

[12] M. Thomas, *7 Ways An Artificial Intelligence Future Will Change The World _ Built In.*

[13] M.U. Scherer, "Regulating artificial intelligence systems: risks, challenges, competencies, and strategies", *SSRN,* vol. 29, p. 353, 2015. https://heinonline.org/HOL/LandingPage?handle=hein.journals/hjlt29&div=15&id=&page=Rauf [http://dx.doi.org/10.2139/ssrn.2609777]

[14] M.A. Rauf, M. Ashfaq, R. Hasan, and M.A. Manju, "A comparative study on the impact of artificial intelligence on employment opportunities for university graduates in Germany and the Netherlands: AI opportunities and risks", *International Journal of Environment, Workplace and Employment,* vol. 6, no. 3, pp. 185-204, 2021. [http://dx.doi.org/10.1504/IJEWE.2021.119679]

[15] J. Manyika, M. Chui, J. Bughin, R. Dobbs, P. Bisson, and A. Marrs, *Disruptive technologies: Advances that will transform life, business, and the global economy.* vol. Vol. 180. McKinsey Global Institute: San Francisco, CA, 2013, pp. 17-21.

[16] Raich, M., Dolan, S.L., Cisullo, C., & Richley, B.A. Facts, fads and predictions about the joint venture of human mind and ai algorithms. European Business Review 2019.

CHAPTER 5

The Influence of AI-driven Digital Service Channels on Consumer Satisfaction

Neelu Tiwari[1], **Aashish Mehra**[2], **Sneha Rajput**[3,4,*], **Govind Soni**[5], **Serhat Ata**[6] and **Aman Sharma**[7]

[1] *Amity University, Noida, India*

[2] *School of Business, Galgotias University, Greater Noida, UP, India*

[3] *Prestige Institute of Management and Research, Gwalior (M.P.), India*

[4] *Centre for Peace Studies, Sammanthurai, Srilanka*

[5] *Sr. Faculty, Footwear Design and Development Institute, Chhindwara, (M.P.), India*

[6] *Duzce University, Uskubu Campus, Düzce, Turkey*

[7] *Symbiosis Institute of Business Management, Symbiosis International (Deemed University), Pune, Maharashtra, India*

Abstract: Consumer satisfaction and purchasing decisions made by consumers have always been a concern of marketers, taking into account these two aspects can encourage businesses to develop. The purpose of this study is to examine the relationship between AI-driven digital service channels and customer satisfaction, with a focus on the moderating effect of demographic variables. A survey of 189 consumers from Delhi NCR revealed that digital service channels—characterized by ease of use, convenience, and personalization—have a positive impact on customer satisfaction. Age, gender, and education have a moderating effect on the relationship. The existing literature has largely overlooked the role of demographic factors and lacks sufficient emphasis on digital service channels. The findings of this study can be used by businesses and the government to build more consumer/citizen-centric strategies.

Keywords: Customer satisfaction, Digital service channels, Demographics, Digital channels.

INTRODUCTION

The evolution of technology has provided businesses with new digital channels to communicate with consumers and influence their behavior [1]. 'Digital channels' are defined as digital shopping formats that are used by businesses to offer online

* **Corresponding author Sneha Rajput:** Prestige Institute of Management and Research, Gwalior, India; Centre for Peace Studies, Sammanthurai, Srilanka; E-mail: sneharajput19@gmail.com

Subir Gupta, Indrajit Ghosal, Keshav Kaushik & Monika Dandotiya (Eds.)

shopping opportunities to consumers [2]. It helps companies make shopping an emotional experience for consumers [3, 4]. Companies from a wide range of industries, sectors, and sizes are implementing innovative digital strategies to attract more customers and enhance their experience [5 - 7]. Top companies such as Amazon, Apple, Facebook, Microsoft, Tesla, Uber, Spotify, Adobe, and Slack utilize a range of digital channels, including email, social messaging, social media platforms, live chats and chatbots, virtual and augmented reality (VR/AR), voice agents, and mobile applications [8]. McKinsey revealed that in every country and region, the willingness to consider digital channels is more than 70% [9]. Thus, in today's interconnected world, the use of digital service channels is not a choice but a necessity for companies to enhance consumer experience and satisfaction.

One such digital transformation has been in the form of Artificial Intelligence (AI). AI has become an essential component for improving digital service channels. AI refers to the creation of computer systems capable of executing activities that would normally need human intelligence, including interpreting natural language, identifying patterns, and making judgments [10]. In the context of digital service channels, AI enables organizations to provide personalized suggestions, automate responses through chatbots, and effectively analyze consumer behavior [11]. The incorporation of AI-powered solutions improves the simplicity and efficiency of digital services, ultimately increasing customer satisfaction [12]. With advances in machine learning and data analytics, AI continues to play an important role in redefining how businesses interact with customers, creating a seamless experience.

Customer satisfaction is the attitude of the consumer that affects the purchase, which directly influences the repurchase intention of the person [13]. Faced with rapid technological innovations and increased regulatory constraints, companies must focus on customer satisfaction to build service loyalty relationships and improve service quality [14]. It also helps businesses increase their profitability while building consumer trust. However, over the years, the concept of consumer satisfaction has changed. Initially, good quality consumer service by salespersons was regarded as the means of satisfying consumers, but now the demands of consumers are more customized which are according to their lifestyles, needs, and tastes [15, 16]. The evolution of technology has enabled the provision of more customized services to customers, with Netflix and FedEx being primary examples [17].

One such digital transformation has been in form of Artificial Intelligence (AI). The AI technology enables more intelligent recognition and matching of consumers' preferences; consequently, consumers are more attracted to companies that utilize AI techniques [18]. To meet this need, companies utilize digital services like chatbots, which simulate human intelligence by responding to customer inquiries. The use of bots enables organizations to enhance digital service effectiveness and provide more satisfaction to consumers [19]. Thus, in digital service channels, AI integration is a powerful tool for increasing growth, improving efficiency, and driving loyalty [20].

In the literature, it was found that most studies connected either digital channels or demographic variables to customer satisfaction. However, given that the preferences of the consumers are affected by their needs, desires and lifestyles, demographics form a key component of the extent to which digital channels affect customer satisfaction. Moreover, there is extant literature examining "predetermined" factors such as customer loyalty [21] and brand image [22]. To bridge this gap, the study examines the effect of digital service channels on consumer satisfaction with the inclusion of demographical characteristics as moderators.

LITERATURE REVIEW AND HYPOTHESIS DEVELOPMENT

Relevance of AI-driven Digital Service Channels

The COVID-19 pandemic boosted the growth of internet-based businesses as a large number of consumers are now relying on the use of digital technologies. With this, organizations are compelled to explore digital technologies for value creation and consumer interaction [20, 23]. Nowadays, digital channels are used by companies for activities like rationalization, reaching target groups, automated document handling, process supervision, and delivery of services [24]. The usage of digital channels creates the ability to interact with customers, providing opportunities to reach new consumer segments, and increasing access to insights and data [24].

Digital channels allow organizations to communicate directly with their customers, resulting in more engaging and responsive partnerships. This direct communication allows firms to gather critical information, analyze consumer preferences, and create personalized experiences. Businesses can easily contact new customer groups that would otherwise be inaccessible by utilizing digital platforms such as social media, email, and chatbots. Furthermore, digital channels provide businesses with a wealth of data and insights into client behavior, allowing them to make better-informed decisions and change their strategies more effectively. This improved access to information increases consumer satisfaction and overall organizational success.

Digital service channels differ from traditional ones by offering real-time, interactive experiences rather than one-way, static communication [25]. Unlike conventional methods like print ads or in-store promotions, digital channels such as social media, email, and mobile apps enable direct, personalized engagement [26]. In today's digital business world, these channels are crucial for addressing consumers' growing need for convenience and speed [27]. They also enable businesses to gather valuable data and insights, leading to personalised experiences that traditional methods cannot provide. As a result, digital channels have increased consumer expectations for prompt responses, personalized services, and seamless interactions across all touchpoints [28].

Digital channel implementation is versatile and actionable for almost every industry, enabling more effective targeting of consumers. Banks are using digital service channels like mobile banking, internet banking, digital banking kiosks and ATMs to deliver the best quality services to consumers to reduce operating costs and raise profitability [29]. For SMEs, digital channels enable raising sales to existing customers, enhancing customer service, facilitating communication, facilitating advertising, and strengthening the brand [5]. For example, in the healthcare sector, digital channels are integrated to raise patient interaction opportunities with healthcare centre staff and caregivers [30].

Growing Complexity of Consumer Satisfaction

Consumer satisfaction is defined as the cognitive process wherein a consumer compares their expectations with the perceived value they receive from consumption. The favourable agreement between consumption and expectation leads to satisfaction among consumers [31]. In the new worldwide trend of Industry 4.0, the nature of consumers being less loyal to a single company, less forgiving towards the company's mistakes, and informed, results in raising the expectations of consumers from businesses [32].

Consumers expect quick responses from companies in the age of digital channels. The likelihood of a rise in response time indicates that companies are exerting less effort to resolve consumer issues, which can lead to feelings of dissatisfaction. They must design their strategies with the purpose of a quick response to the consumer [33].

Consumer satisfaction has evolved beyond the basic notion of meeting consumer needs; it now hinges on the overall experience offered across digital touchpoints. The expectations of modern consumers are not limited to just receiving a good product or service [34]. They increasingly want a seamless and personalized experience, regardless of the platform they utilize. Consumers today want brands to know them well, anticipate their requirements, and provide individualized services, whether they are reading a website, using an app, or participating on social media [26]. Personalization is no longer an option; it is a crucial driver of pleasure since it demonstrates that businesses appreciate their consumers as persons rather than data points.

Furthermore, responsiveness is a key factor in shaping consumer satisfaction. Quick and effective responses to questions and difficulties considerably improve a customer's view of a company's dedication to service [35]. Delays or a lack of clear communication quickly erode customer trust. Satisfaction now requires businesses to anticipate needs and provide a seamless digital experience that allows users to move effortlessly between different channels without any interruptions. Maintaining this continuity across platforms not only strengthens the brand's image but also encourages customer loyalty [36]. Thus, to keep customers satisfied today, companies need to provide a unified, responsive, and highly personalised experience across all digital service channels.

Although the modern consumer prefers the digital medium for making a purchase, the presence of uncertainty affects their rate of satisfaction [37]. The existence of consumer satisfaction creates a sense of repurchase, cooperation, and spread of positive word of mouth. However, sometimes there are exceptions. Even with the existence of a lower satisfaction level, the consumer tends to remain loyal to the company. This could be due to a lack of choice, experience, information or past costs [38]. Thus, consumer satisfaction is not something very straightforward. It's a complex procedure that involves the feelings of an individual and their prior experience. Quality and price are essential components, but the digital revolution has shifted consumers' priorities towards more innovative technology. Studies have identified that innovative virtual technologies serve as a means of communication for consumers and also influence their brand [39 - 41].

Therefore, companies need to work on creating more digital channels for engaging consumers and interacting with them. Hence, to address the growing complexity the investment in digital channels is a reasonable solution. To evaluate this solution's effectiveness, this study proposes the hypothesis that:

Hypothesis 1: Digital service channels affecting consumer satisfaction levels.

Demographics Affecting Digital Channels and Consumer Satisfaction

Demographics are an important referential variable that enables segmentation of consumer groups. The consumer demographics consist of elements like gender, age, income, education, and literacy [42]. In service marketing, consumer demographics are responsible for influencing consumer choices and decision-making. They contribute to affecting consumers' behavioural intentions and consumer decision-making [43]. Thus, demographic characteristics influence the behaviour of consumers and consequently the satisfaction level [44].

From an economic standpoint, demographics are critical for understanding market behavior. Consumer attributes such as age, income, and education significantly impact their purchasing power and demand for digital services [45]. Younger, tech-savvy consumers are more likely to purchase digital products, whereas elderly consumers tend to opt for traditional methods, which in turn influences corporate strategy [46]. These patterns vary dramatically among cultures, as different regions have varying amounts of technological availability and cultural attitudes toward digital services. Economically, demographic characteristics enable organizations to discover profitable consumer niches and personalize services to their specific needs [47].

Different demographic groups interact with digital media in various ways, which influences their degree of satisfaction. Younger, more tech-savvy consumers prefer and use digital services since they are more convenient and efficient [48]. On the other hand, older customers are less comfortable with digital platforms and prefer in-person interactions [49]. Their income level also influences the way people use digital services. Higher-income people often have more access to and benefit from current digital services [50]. This highlights the importance of making digital platforms user-friendly and accessible to all individuals, regardless of age or background, to enhance satisfaction across demographics.

Consumer demographics also influence the intent of consumers to adopt digital channels. For example, young and educated consumers are more likely to adopt digital channels like mobile banking applications in Jordon [51]. This has also been highlighted in other literature [52], which suggests that demographics are significant predictors of social media or technology adoption. For instance, an increase in age is associated with a decrease in the probability of using social media. Similarly, the literature suggests that demographics influence the adoption of online banking, as consumer perspectives vary by gender. Therefore, with the change in demographics, the preference and adoption of digital channels vary. Accordingly, the below-stated hypothesis is proposed [53]:

Hypothesis 2: The demographics of a consumer have a moderating role in influencing the link between digital channels and consumer satisfaction.

Empirical Review: Impact of Digital Service Channels on Consumer Satisfaction

Many studies have explored the relationship between digital channels and consumer satisfaction. Literature explored cultural differences and found that social presence and perceived media richness have an impact on customer satisfaction [54]. Social presence is the sense of engaging with others *via* digital channels, whereas perceived media richness refers to how well a communication medium delivers information. Both factors contribute to customer satisfaction by increasing engagement, trust, and understanding, resulting in more personal and meaningful encounters and hence higher overall satisfaction. The impact of digital marketing on consumer behaviour using 14 millennial consumers of the Gauteng region, and found that millennial consumers consider digital marketing as an effective means for affecting their intentions [55].

Millennial customers view digital marketing as a powerful tool for influencing their purchasing decisions. This technologically savvy demographic is affected by online marketing, social media campaigns, and targeted digital interactions. These marketing methods increase brand exposure and trust, guiding millennials to make informed purchasing decisions. Thus, digital marketing is crucial in their purchasing process.

Extending the consumer behaviour scope to satisfaction [40], with an exploration of 315 consumers' perception revealed that social media and mobile marketing contribute to having a positive influence on customer satisfaction by providing businesses with a direct, personalized, and easily accessible contact channel. These solutions enable companies to engage with their customers in real time while adapting material to different cultural preferences. This cross-cultural strategy enables businesses to meet a wide range of consumer needs while promoting trust, loyalty, and a pleasant overall customer experience. The area was further explored by including mediating variables. An examination of 100 participants' perceptions, conducted through qualitative analysis, revealed that online advertisements facilitate the creation of brand recognition and increase knowledge about the brand and its services [56]. This enables building consumer confidence, leading to a rise in customer satisfaction.

There is also a mediating impact by including purchase decisions as a mediating variable [57]. The analysis of 100 respondents' perceptions using SEM revealed that digital marketing has an impact on the purchasing decision of the consumer and customer satisfaction by providing targeted and personalized experiences. Businesses engage clients through digital platforms by offering targeted promos, product recommendations, and quick purchasing alternatives. This builds consumer trust and happiness, which drives purchase decisions. The interactive element of digital marketing increases the bond between firms and consumers, hence increasing loyalty.

The examination of 125 consumer behaviours using one-way ANOVA shows that gender has no impact on selecting the channels for digital marketing [58]. A new technique, *i.e.*, Chat GPT's impact on customer experience, is analyzed using 394 clients' perceptions, as analyzed by SPSS. The analysis, which included demographics as a moderating variable, revealed that all demographics except gender play a moderating role in influencing the linkage between customer experience with ChatGPT and overall satisfaction with digital marketing [59]. With this, the conceptual framework in Fig. (**1**) for this study can be understood as follows:

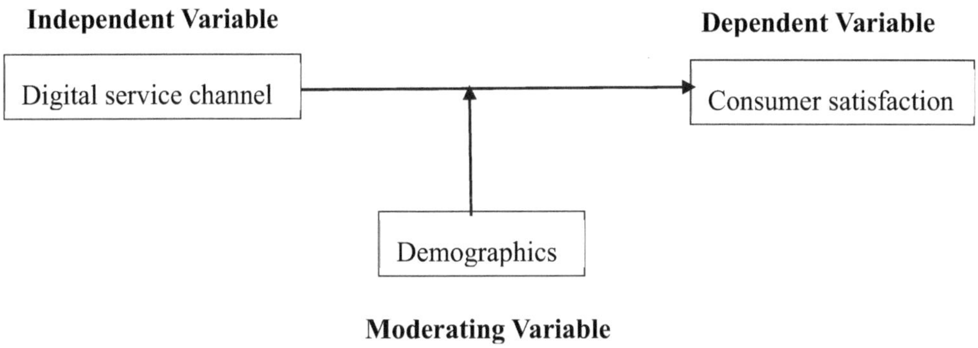

Fig. (1). Proposed model (Source: Synthesized by the author).

RESEARCH METHODOLOGY

Data Collection

The study employed a quantitative research approach, along with an interpretivist paradigm, for testing the research hypothesis. For this, we used a sample of 200 consumers who use digital channels in the Delhi NCR region of India. The survey was used for the collection of data on consumers. Herein, a closed-ended questionnaire was used as the main instrument for the collection of sample data. Among the selected sample, young consumers are the most relevant sample group for the study as they are mainly the ones using digital channels and are more demanding towards personalization of products [60]. The questionnaire is also formulated using existing verified responses for each variable, specifically consumer satisfaction and digital service channels. The respondents were contacted *via* phone, and once their consent was obtained, the questionnaire was shared using Google Forms.

Common Method Biasness (CMB)

To ensure that bias is not present, the test "Harman Single Factor" method [45, 61] was incorporated. The total variance value was below the threshold value of 40%. Thus, the data was found to be free from any bias.

Sample Characteristics

A sample of approximately 110 respondents was derived post-first follow-up, while the remaining 90 respondents' data were collected post-second follow-up. The demographic details of the collected sample are stated below.

The researchers maintained regular contact with respondents *via* email to ensure the study's aim and purpose were understood by the sample and to address any questions they had about the questionnaire. Among 200 questionnaires, approximately 11 were excluded due to insufficient information or incomplete responses; thus, the statistical analysis was applied to 189 questionnaires. After creating an Excel sheet of collected data using MS Excel and importing the data into IBM SPSS 23, the following statistical tests were applied to the data (Table **1**).

Table 1. Demographics of the sample (Source: Researcher).

Demographic	Characteristics	Frequency	Percent
Age	18-25 years	19.00	10.05
	25-35 years	75.00	39.68
	35-45 years	53.00	28.04
	45-55 years	24.00	12.70
	More than 55 years	18.00	9.52
Gender	Male	82.00	43.39
	Female	95.00	50.26
	Don't want to say	12.00	6.35
Marital status	Married	66.00	34.92
	Unmarried	71.00	37.57
	Divorced	44.00	23.28
	Widow/Widower	8.00	4.23
Monthly Income	Below Rs 20000	16.00	8.47
	Rs 20000 - 40000	25.00	13.23
	Rs 40000- 60000	36.00	19.05
	Rs 60000-80000	65.00	34.39
	Rs 80000-100000	31.00	16.40
	Above Rs 100000	16.00	8.47

(Table 1) cont.....

Demographic	Characteristics	Frequency	Percent
Education	Graduate	65.00	34.39
	Postgraduate	54.00	28.57
	Diploma	16.00	8.47
	Professional Degree	15.00	7.94
	Others	39.00	20.63
Occupation	Student	48.00	25.40
	Businessman	54.00	28.57
	Employed	21.00	11.11
	Prefer not to say	66.00	34.92

- Descriptive analysis of background information.
- The scale reliability was examined using the Cronbach alpha test with a required level of 0.7.
- Pearson correlation analysis for testing the linkage between digital service channels and customer satisfaction.
- The regression analysis aims to determine the impact of a moderator (demographic variable) on the relationship between digital service channels and customer satisfaction.

Measures

Digital service channels -The features of digital service channels are used as statements. Herein, a 5-point Likert scale is used to represent the statements. Based on a study [57], the features included are better communication facilities, easy-to-use features, clear information availability, more convenience features, and personalized services.

Demographics – The demographic is the moderating variable in the study. Generally, the essential demographical characteristics of an individual [59] are age, gender, and education. Thus, these variables are included in the questionnaire.

Customer satisfaction – Customer satisfaction is the dependent variable in the study, and thus, a single question is used to assess the impact of digital channels on customer satisfaction.

Data Analysis

The present study uses IBM SPSS 25 to state the model for assessing the relationship between variables. The tool is widely used in social science and business studies for estimating the indirect and direct effects of mediating variables, the interactions in the form of moderation, and the combination of mediating and moderating variables. In this study, the purpose was to examine the impact of digital service channels on consumer satisfaction, with demographics moderating. Therefore, regression analysis with the interaction effect of the moderating variable was implemented to test the hypothesis.

Ethical Consideration

The researcher addressed the ethical issues in the study by maintaining the confidentiality and security of the sample's personal information, which was stored on password-protected devices.

DATA ANALYSIS AND FINDINGS

Descriptive Analysis

Descriptive analysis is a method for evaluating responses to gain an overview of the data. Herein, the background information is collected to know about consumers' perceptions of digital channels and customer satisfaction (Table **2**).

Table 2. Descriptive statistics of background knowledge (Source: SPSS Output).

-	N	Minimum	Maximum	Mean	Std. Deviation
Meaning	189	1	3	1.80	0.87
Factors	189	1	5	3.28	1.10
Usage	189	1	5	2.65	1.16
Type	189	1	9	5.44	2.70
Device	189	1	5	2.71	1.24
Channel	189	1	9	4.25	2.55
Important	189	1	10	5.32	2.92
Expertise	189	1	5	2.78	1.28

The findings reveal that the meaning value is approximately 2, showing that most people consider customer satisfaction as the degree to which expectations are met. Regarding the factors of price, convenience, and customer service, these are important. The data shows that most people primarily use digital service channels, such as monthly or weekly. The most common use of digital service channels is for shopping, healthcare services, banking, entertainment, and communication. Digital service channels are most used *via* smartphones, laptops/PCs, and voice assistants. The commonly used digital service channels are chatbots, self-service,

SMS, social media, and live chat. About the importance of digital service channels, speed, convenience, data security, ease of use, and consistency are the most relevant features for customers. Lastly, the respondents considered for the study are highly advanced in their technology usage, but have expertise in using digital service channels. Thus, the background information reveals that the respondents are aware of relevant concepts, familiar with digital channels, and also use them, making them suitable for study.

Reliability of the Scale

The reliability of the digital channel scale was evaluated using the Cronbach's alpha test. The value for the 5 statements was 0.94, which exceeds the required level of 0.7. Thus, the total Cronbach alpha value is good and is also above the minimum acceptable value [62, 63].

CORRELATION

The essential step in the model-building procedure is to test the linkage between the variables. The Pearson correlation analysis is employed for this purpose.

The analysis reveals that for each of the variables, the value is significant at a 5% level of significance with a Pearson correlation magnitude of more than 0.5. Although there is a possibility of multicollinearity between independent variables due to significant values, the independent variables are included to compute the interaction effect, so the problem of multicollinearity can be addressed. This reveals that digital channels and customer satisfaction are related, and the hypothesis can be tested to assess their linkage and the moderating effect of demographic variables (Table **3**).

Table 3. Correlation analysis (Source: SPSS output).

-	Customer Satisfaction	Communicate	Easy to Use	Insights	Convenience	Personalized
Customer satisfaction	1.00	-	-	-	-	-
Communicate	0.79*	1.00	-	-	-	-
Easy to use	0.83*	0.83*	1.00	-	-	-
Insights	0.75*	0.76*	0.74*	1.00	-	-
Convenience	0.90*	0.71*	0.75*	0.71*	1.00	-
Personalized	0.83*	0.80*	0.77*	0.89*	0.75*	1.00

Regression

In the model for assessing the main effect between variables, the value of the coefficient and its significance are examined. The regression results for Hypothesis 1 are presented below.

The table shows the model is effective with an R-squared and adjusted R-squared value of 0.89, indicating 89% of variation in customer satisfaction. The F value of the model is 306.31 with a significance of 0.00, indicating that the model is statistically significant. The coefficient values for easy-to-use, insights, convenience, and personalized services are statistically significant, with p-values of less than 0.01. Recalling hypothesis 1, it can be stated that digital service channels contribute to affecting customer satisfaction. The shown coefficient value represents a rise in customer satisfaction of 0.21%, 0.152%, and 0.33% with a 1% increase in digital service channels integration, offering easy-to-use, convenient, and personalized services (Table **4**).

Table 4. Regression analysis output (Source: SPSS output complied by authors).

Variables	Model 1
R square	0.89
Adjusted R square	0.89
F	306.31
N	189
Constant	0.14
Independent variables	-
Communicate	0.08
Easy to use	0.21****
Insights	-0.15***
Convenience	0.52****
Personalized	0.33****
-	-
Notes	*p≤ 0.10, **p ≤ 0.05, ***p ≤ 0.01, ****p≤0.001

Testing the Moderation Effect

To test the moderating effect, as hypothesized in hypothesis 2, thc impact of demographic variables on the relationship between digital service channels and customer satisfaction is examined.

As for the results, the model is significant, with R-squared and adjusted R-squared values of 0.89 and 0.94, respectively, without an interaction effect, and 0.93 and 0.93, respectively, with an interaction effect. Even the F-values of both models are 189.45 and 104.61, with a significance of 0.00. The findings indicate that the inclusion of the interaction effect has increased the interpretive power of the regression model, as evidenced by a higher adjusted R-squared value. The results show no direct effect of demographic variables on customer satisfaction. However, when considering interaction effects, the following combinations have an impact on customer satisfaction: "age and insight", "age and convenience", "gender and insight", "gender and convenience", "gender and personalized", "education and easy to use", and "education and convenience". Thus, it reveals that demographics have an impact on assessing the linkage between digital service channels and customer satisfaction, revealing rejection of hypothesis 2 (Table **5**).

Table 5. Regression model with interaction effect (Source: SPSS Output).

Variables	Model 1	Model 2
R square	0.89	0.94
Adjusted R square	0.89	0.93
F	189.45	104.61
N	189	189
Constant	0.22	0.11
Independent variables	-	-
Communicate	0.09 (0.10)	0.06
Easy to use	0.21****	0.28****
Insights	-0.16***	-0.32****
Convenience	0.52****	0.58****
Personalized	0.33****	0.40****
Demographic variables	-	-
Age	-0.01	0.01
Gender	0.00	-0.02
Education	-0.02	-0.02
Interaction effect	-	-
age*communicate	-	0.04
age*easy to use	-	0.04
age*insights	-	-0.25***
age*convenience	-	0.15***
age*personalized	-	0.01

(Table 5) cont.....

Variables	Model 1	Model 2
gender*communicate	-	0.09
gender* easy to use	-	0.08
gender*insights	-	-0.46****
gender*convenience	-	-0.17***
gender*personalized	-	0.44****
education*communicate	-	-0.1
education*easy to use	-	-0.12**
education*insights	-	-0.15*
education*convenience	-	0.25****
education*personalized	-	0.15*
-	-	-
Notes:	*p≤ 0.10, **p ≤ 0.05, ***p ≤ 0.01, ****p≤0.001	

DISCUSSION

With the outbreak of COVID-19, digital service channels have been recognized as the means of connecting businesses with consumers by understanding their needs and demands. A growing number of companies are adopting digital service channels to target specific groups, improve service delivery, interact with customers, enhance customer service, and facilitate communication and advertising (Heinonen and Michelsson, 2010; Taiminen and Karjaluoto, 2015). However, despite adopting new technology to provide a better experience to consumers, maximizing consumer satisfaction has remained a challenge for companies.

The digital revolution has prompted consumers to gravitate towards using innovative technology for an easy experience and providing effective means of communication [39 - 41]. Therefore, there is constant pressure on companies to innovate and understand consumer preferences. Demographics in this regard is identified as the measure of identifying aspects affecting consumers' behavioural intention [43]. Thus, while working on consumer satisfaction, consideration of demographics is essential [44]. Existing studies [40, 54 - 56] examined different digital service channels and their role in influencing consumer satisfaction. However, there is limited information available on the role of demographics. This study bridged this gap by assessing the role of age, gender and education. The examination of consumer perception confirmed that individual demographics do not have a significant contribution, but when included as a moderating variable, consumer satisfaction is affected. Hence, the study's findings have contributed to extending the existing research in the field of digital service channels and consumer satisfaction by defining demographics as an important means of influencing the contribution of digital service channels to consumer satisfaction.

Suggestions and Implications

The research highlighted the significant role of demographics in enhancing the impact of digital service channels on consumer satisfaction. Though businesses are focusing on innovating technologies while still providing better experiences to consumers, some of the changes could be implemented, such as:

- The user-centric designs could be used by businesses to make digital interfaces more user-friendly. This could be achieved through user testing based on demographics, incorporating feedback to refine the interface.
- The digital experience could be tailored based on preferences and demographics, such as the use of personalized algorithms for giving customized recommendations. This enhances the satisfaction of consumers.
- The communication facility should be tailored to the demographics of consumers, offering options such as preferred language choice, customized notifications, and 24/7 customer support to ensure effective communication resonance.
- Emphasize privacy policies and strong security measures to protect the interests of consumers. Clear communication about privacy features can help build consumer trust and enhance satisfaction.

Thus, the study's findings motivate businesses to enhance their digital service channels by catering to diverse demographics, thereby meeting user expectations and needs and achieving improved satisfaction.

In addition to providing recommendations for businesses, the study's findings are also relevant to academia. These findings could be used to expand the scope of available literature on digitalization and customer satisfaction, highlighting the significant role academics play in studying consumer satisfaction.

For businesses, this study enlightens that there is no direct connection between customers and services. There are always many external or internal aspects that affect consumer choice. Therefore, when designing customer-centric strategies, considering the characteristics of the consumer and their demographics is essential.

CONCLUSION

The growth in familiarity with digitalized services has motivated companies to shift to digital channels, enabling them to connect with more customers and provide them with more customized services. The existing literature has focused on exploring the link between digital channels and customer satisfaction; however, the present study argues that the relationship between digital service channels and consumer satisfaction is further complicated by the inclusion of an important moderating variable: demographic factors. Consequently, this study included age, gender and education as moderating variables and verified that demographic variables have a moderating role in influencing digital service channels and consumer satisfaction relationships. The study's findings can be applied in academic settings to expand the scope of literature on digitalization and customer satisfaction, and to inform students about the significant role academics play in consumer satisfaction studies. Furthermore, the study's findings have implications for businesses, as they reveal that there is no direct connection between customers and services. Moreover, the study is beneficial for the government, as it suggests that government services, new initiatives, and campaign launches should prioritize integrating digital service channels, considering demographics. This approach would enhance the delivery of messages to consumers and foster greater citizen satisfaction. Hence, the study has many practical implications, which make its findings significant.

Although the relationship between demographics, digital service channels, and customer satisfaction has been established, the study's scope is limited by time and resources, and it considers only age, gender, and education as demographics. Since many elements, such as income, marital status, or occupation, are not included, and the study's scope is limited to the Delhi NCR region, future studies could expand the study and integrate these aspects as well. Additionally, the studies could focus on determining the contribution of each digital service channel, enabling the identification of the most effective service channel for customer targeting.

REFERENCES

[1] P.B. Pires, J.D. Santos, P.Q. Brito, and D.N. Marques, "Connecting digital channels to consumers' purchase Decision-Making process in online stores", *Sustainability (Basel),* vol. 14, no. 21, p. 14392, 2022. [http://dx.doi.org/10.3390/su142114392]

[2] G. Wagner, H. Schramm-Klein, and S. Steinmann, "Online retailing across e-channels and e-channel touchpoints: Empirical studies of consumer behavior in the multichannel e-commerce environment", *J. Bus. Res.,* vol. 107, pp. 256-270, 2020. [http://dx.doi.org/10.1016/j.jbusres.2018.10.048]

[3] K. Straker, and C. Wrigley, "Designing an emotional strategy: Strengthening digital channel engagements", *Bus. Horiz.,* vol. 59, no. 3, pp. 339-346, 2016. [http://dx.doi.org/10.1016/j.bushor.2016.01.010]

[4] R.K. Behera, A. Gunasekaran, S. Gupta, S. Kamboj, and P.K. Bala, "Personalized digital marketing recommender engine", *J. Retailing Consum. Serv.,* vol. 53, p. 101799, 2020. [http://dx.doi.org/10.1016/j.jretconser.2019.03.026]

[5] H.M. Taiminen, and H. Karjaluoto, "The usage of digital marketing channels in SMEs", *J. Small Bus. Enterprise Dev.,* vol. 22, no. 4, pp. 633-651, 2015. [http://dx.doi.org/10.1108/JSBED-05-2013-0073]

[6] M. Ardolino, M. Rapaccini, N. Saccani, P. Gaiardelli, G. Crespi, and C. Ruggeri, "The role of digital technologies for the service transformation of industrial companies", *Int. J. Prod. Res.,* vol. 56, no. 6, pp. 2116-2132, 2018. [http://dx.doi.org/10.1080/00207543.2017.1324224]

[7] M.E. Styvén, and Å. Wallström, "Benefits and barriers for the use of digital channels among small tourism companies", *Scand. J. Hosp. Tour.,* vol. 19, no. 1, pp. 27-46, 2019. [http://dx.doi.org/10.1080/15022250.2017.1379434]

[8] S. Ramachandran, H. Jenkač, N. Clark, and P-M. Despontin, *Four ways to improve digital customer service,* 2022. https://www.bcg.com/publications/2017/four-ways-improve-digital-customer-service

[9] S. Khon, A. Nizam, D. Tan, and Z. Taraporevala, *Best of both worlds: Balancing digital and physical channels in retail banking,* 2022. https://www.mckinsey.com/industries/financial-services/ou--insights/best-of-both-worlds-balancing-digital-and-physical-channels-in-retail-banking#/

[10] M.H. Kryger, "Artificial intelligence in sleep and art", *Sleep Health,* vol. 9, no. 4, pp. 387-388, 2023. [http://dx.doi.org/10.1016/j.sleh.2023.07.005] [PMID: 37460378]

[11] D. Aggarwal, D. Sharma, and A. B. Saxena, *Enhancing the online shopping experience of consumers through Artificial Intelligence,* 2024. [http://dx.doi.org/10.55529/ijitc.42.1.5]

[12] Y. Chen, and C. Prentice, "Integrating artificial intelligence and customer experience", *Australas. Mark. J.,* no. May, 2024. [http://dx.doi.org/10.1177/14413582241252904]

[13] B. Bilgili, and E. Ozkul, "Brand awareness, brand personality, brand loyalty and consumer satisfaction relations in brand positioning strategies (a Torku brand sample)", *Journal of Global Strategic Management,* vol. 2, no. 9, p. 89, 2015. [http://dx.doi.org/10.20460/JGSM.2015915576]

[14] G. Dash, K. Kiefer, and J. Paul, "Marketing-to-Millennials: Marketing 4.0, customer satisfaction and purchase intention", *J. Bus. Res.,* vol. 122, pp. 608-620, 2021. [http://dx.doi.org/10.1016/j.jbusres.2020.10.016]

[15] S.M. Lee, "Innovation: from small "i" to large "I"", *International Journal of Quality Innovation,* vol. 4, no. 1, p. 2, 2018. [http://dx.doi.org/10.1186/s40887-018-0022-4]

[16] *Living Innovation by Sang M. Lee | Open Library,* 2018. https://openlibrary.org/books/OL28700947M/Living_Innovation

[17] S.M. Lee, and D. Lee, ""Untact": a new customer service strategy in the digital age", *Serv. Bus.,* vol. 14, no. 1, pp. 1-22, 2020. [http://dx.doi.org/10.1007/s11628-019-00408-2]

[18] B. Li, P. Qi, B. Liu, S. Di, J. Liu, J. Pei, J. Yi, and B. Zhou, "Trustworthy AI: From principles to practices", *ACM Comput. Surv.,* vol. 55, no. 9, pp. 1-46, 2023. [http://dx.doi.org/10.1145/3555803]

[19] M. Alkhayyat, A. M. Ahmed, and School of Business, Society & Engineering, "The impact of artificial intelligence in digital marketing," Thesis, Jun. 2022. [Online]. Available: https://www.diva-portal.org/smash/get/diva2:1663148/FULLTEXT01.pdf

[20] J. Holmström, "From AI to digital transformation: The AI readiness framework", *Bus. Horiz.,* vol. 65, no. 3, pp. 329-339, 2022. [http://dx.doi.org/10.1016/j.bushor.2021.03.006]

[21] O. John, "Analysing the moderating effect of customer loyalty on long run repurchase intentions", *Afr. J. Mark. Manage.,* vol. 9, no. 3, pp. 25-34, 2017. [http://dx.doi.org/10.5897/AJMM2016.0505]

[22] V. Dhingra, M. Sainy, and P.N. Mishra, "Effect of customer satisfaction on customer loyalty with the moderation of brand image", *Journal of Media and Communication,* vol. 3, no. 1, pp. 17-28, 2017.

[23] S.I. Dubbelink, C. Herrando, and E. Constantinides, "Social media marketing as a branding strategy in extraordinary times: lessons from the COVID-19 pandemic", *Sustainability (Basel),* vol. 13, no. 18, p. 10310, 2021. [http://dx.doi.org/10.3390/su131810310]

[24] K. Heinonen, and T. Michelsson, "The use of digital channels to create customer relationships", *Int. J. Internet Mark. Advert.,* vol. 6, no. 1, p. 30430, 2010. [http://dx.doi.org/10.1504/IJIMA.2010.030430]

[25] M.W.M. Al-Quran, "Traditional media *versus* social media: challenges and opportunities", *Technium,* vol. 4, no. 10, pp. 145-160, 2022. [http://dx.doi.org/10.47577/technium.v4i10.8012]

[26] Y.K. Dwivedi, E. Ismagilova, D.L. Hughes, J. Carlson, R. Filieri, J. Jacobson, V. Jain, H. Karjaluoto, H. Kefi, A.S. Krishen, V. Kumar, M.M. Rahman, R. Raman, P.A. Rauschnabel, J. Rowley, J. Salo, G.A. Tran, and Y. Wang, "Setting the future of digital and social media marketing research: Perspectives and research propositions", *Int. J. Inf. Manage.,* vol. 59, no. 1, p. 102168, 2021. [http://dx.doi.org/10.1016/j.ijinfomgt.2020.102168]

[27] P.B. Pires, J.D. Santos, P.Q. Brito, and D.N. Marques, "Connecting digital channels to consumers' purchase decision-making process in online stores", *Sustainability (Basel),* vol. 14, no. 21, p. 14392, 2022. [http://dx.doi.org/10.3390/su142114392]

[28] A. Muthaffar, S. Vilches-Montero, and R. Bravo-Olavarria, "From digital touchpoints to digital journeys: How shopping mindsets influence appraisal of omnichannel journeys", *Int. J. Inf. Manage.,* vol. 77, p. 102778, 2024. [http://dx.doi.org/10.1016/j.ijinfomgt.2024.102778]

[29] S.J. Kaur, L. Ali, M.K. Hassan, and M. Al-Emran, "Adoption of digital banking channels in an emerging economy: exploring the role of in-branch efforts", *J. Financ. Serv. Mark.,* vol. 26, no. 2, pp. 107-121, 2021. [http://dx.doi.org/10.1057/s41264-020-00082-w]

[30] J.W. Ross, I.M. Sebastian, C.M. Beath, M. Mocker, K. Moloney, and N.O. Fonstad, "Designing and Executing Digital Strategies", *7th International Conference on Information Systems,* 2001 Dublin.

[31] D.C. Ahrholdt, S.P. Gudergan, and C.M. Ringle, "Enhancing loyalty: When improving consumer satisfaction and delight matters", *J. Bus. Res.,* vol. 94, pp. 18-27, 2019. [http://dx.doi.org/10.1016/j.jbusres.2018.08.040]

[32] T. von Leipzig, M. Gamp, D. Manz, K. Schöttle, P. Ohlhausen, G. Oosthuizen, D. Palm, and K. von Leipzig, "Initialising customer-orientated digital transformation in enterprises", *Procedia Manuf.,* vol. 8, pp. 517-524, 2017. [http://dx.doi.org/10.1016/j.promfg.2017.02.066]

[33] D. Istanbulluoglu, "Complaint handling on social media: The impact of multiple response times on consumer satisfaction", *Comput. Human Behav.,* vol. 74, pp. 72-82, 2017. [http://dx.doi.org/10.1016/j.chb.2017.04.016]

[34] D. Patil, and N. Rane, "Customer experience and satisfaction: Importance of customer reviews and customer value on buying preference", *International Research Journal of Modernization in Engineering Technology and Science,* vol. 5, no. 3, pp. 3437-3447, 2023. [http://dx.doi.org/10.56726/IRJMETS36460]

[35] N.A. Saad, S. Elgazzar, and S. Mlaker Kac, "Investigating the impact of resilience, responsiveness, and quality on customer loyalty of MSMEs: empirical evidence", *Sustainability (Basel),* vol. 14, no. 9, p. 5011, 2022.
[http://dx.doi.org/10.3390/su14095011]

[36] K. Chung, K.W. Oh, and M. Kim, "Cross-channel integration and customer experience in omnichannel retail services", *Serv. Sci.,* vol. 14, no. 4, pp. 307-317, 2022.
[http://dx.doi.org/10.1287/serv.2022.0308]

[37] Y. Rao, A. Saleem, W. Saeed, and J. Ul Haq, "Online consumer satisfaction during COVID-19: perspective of a developing country", *Front. Psychol.,* vol. 12, p. 751854, 2021.
[http://dx.doi.org/10.3389/fpsyg.2021.751854] [PMID: 34659069]

[38] S.S. Demtsura, "Analysis of customer satisfaction of the quality and price of services", *Espacios,* vol. 38, no. 55, 2017.

[39] K.N. Lemon, and P.C. Verhoef, "Understanding customer experience throughout the customer journey", *J. Mark.,* vol. 80, no. 6, pp. 69-96, 2016.
[http://dx.doi.org/10.1509/jm.15.0420]

[40] M. Alwan, and M. Alshurideh, "The effect of digital marketing on value creation and customer satisfaction", *International Journal of Data and Network Science,* vol. 6, no. 4, pp. 1557-1566, 2022.
[http://dx.doi.org/10.5267/j.ijdns.2022.4.021]

[41] P. Pfister, and C. Lehmann, "Measuring the success of digital transformation in German SMEs", *Journal of Small Business Strategy,* vol. 33, no. 1, 2023.
[http://dx.doi.org/10.53703/001c.39679]

[42] S. H. Wang, and Y.L. Pang, "Demographics and customer satisfaction", *Int. J. Environ. Econ. Commer. Educ. Manag. J.,* vol. 7, pp. 1-6, .
[http://dx.doi.org/10.36713/epra0414]

[43] W. Manyanga, C. Makanyeza, and Z. Muranda, "The effect of customer experience, customer satisfaction and word of mouth intention on customer loyalty: The moderating role of consumer demographics", *Cogent Business & Management,* vol. 9, no. 1, p. 2082015, 2022.
[http://dx.doi.org/10.1080/23311975.2022.2082015]

[44] R.M. Juneja, and P. Mehta, "Customer satisfaction towards online shopping in Surat city", *Int. J. Acad. Res. Dev.,* vol. 2, no. 6, pp. 713 717, 2017.

[45] A. Azwardi, S. Andaiyani, and A. Mahdi Igamo, "Digital entrepreneurship: Socio-demographics and consumer behavior in Indonesia", *Probl. Perspect. Manag.,* vol. 21, no. 3, pp. 290-299, 2023.
[http://dx.doi.org/10.21511/ppm.21(3).2023.23]

[46] E. Frąckiewicz, "Information and communication technologies as a source of customer value in the context of balancing the positions of younger and older consumers", *Sustainability (Basel),* vol. 13, no. 9, p. 4722, 2021.
[http://dx.doi.org/10.3390/su13094722]

[47] S. Ha, M. Childs, C.T. Sneed, and A. Berry, "Consumer sustainable shopping practices for small business during COVID-19", *Sustainability (Basel),* vol. 13, no. 22, p. 12451, 2021.
[http://dx.doi.org/10.3390/su132212451]

[48] C.V. Priporas, N. Stylos, and A.K. Fotiadis, "Generation Z consumers' expectations of interactions in smart retailing: A future agenda", *Comput. Human Behav.,* vol. 77, no. 1, pp. 374-381, 2017.
[http://dx.doi.org/10.1016/j.chb.2017.01.058]

[49] A. Seifert, and N. Charness, "Digital transformation of everyday lives of older Swiss adults: use of and attitudes toward current and future digital services", *Eur. J. Ageing,* vol. 19, no. 3, pp. 729-739, 2022.
[http://dx.doi.org/10.1007/s10433-021-00677-9] [PMID: 35035340]

[50] I. Ucar, M. Gramaglia, M. Fiore, Z. Smoreda, and E. Moro, "News or social media? Socio-economic

divide of mobile service consumption", *J. R. Soc. Interface,* vol. 18, no. 185, p. 20210350, 2021. [http://dx.doi.org/10.1098/rsif.2021.0350] [PMID: 34847793]

[51] M. Alafeef, D. Singh, and K. Ahmad, "Influence of demographic factors on the adoption level of mobile banking applications in Jordan", *Journal of Convergence Information Technology,* vol. 6, no. 12, pp. 107-113, 2011. [http://dx.doi.org/10.4156/jcit.vol6.issue12.14]

[52] K.A. Gazal, I. Montague, and J. Wiedenbeck, "Factors affecting social media adoption among wood products consumers in the United States", *BioProducts Business,* vol. 4, no. 5, 2019. [http://dx.doi.org/10.22382/bpb-2019-005]

[53] D. Yannacopoulos, *Evaluating Websites and Web Services: Interdisciplinary Perspectives on User satisfaction,* 2014. https://www.researchgate.net/profile/Luc_Honore_Petnji_Yaya/publication/259580302_Customer_Satisfaction_and_the_Role_of_Demographic_Characteristics_in_Online_Banking/links/54117a830cf29e4a23296542.pdf [http://dx.doi.org/10.4018/978-1-4666-5129-6]

[54] H. Gimpel, J.B. Huber, and S. Sarikaya, *Customer satisfaction in digital service encounters: The role of media richness, social presence, and cultural distance.* https://aisel.aisnet.org/cgi/viewcontent.cgi?article=1103&context=ecis2016_rp

[55] F. Schutte, and T. Chauke, "The impact of digital marketing on consumer behaviour: a case study of millennials in South Africa", *DOAJ (DOAJ: Directory of Open Access Journals),* 2022. [http://dx.doi.org/10.46222/ajhtl.19770720.263]

[56] A.A. Salameh, M. Ijaz, A.B. Omar, and H.M. Zia ul Haq, Ijaz, A. B. Omar, and H. M. Z. U. Haq, "Impact of online advertisement on customer satisfaction with the mediating effect of brand knowledge", *Front. Psychol.,* vol. 13, p. 919656, 2022. [http://dx.doi.org/10.3389/fpsyg.2022.919656] [PMID: 35846604]

[57] S. Bachri, S.M. Putra, E.S. Farid, D. Darman, and A.G. Mayapada, "The digital marketing to influence customer satisfaction mediated by purchase decision", *Jurnal Aplikasi Manajemen,* vol. 21, no. 3, 2023. [http://dx.doi.org/10.21776/ub.jam.2023.021.03.03]

[58] M.R. Chandrasekar, and S.D. Janani, "The impact of digital marketing on consumer buying behaviour on electronic goods in Coimbatore city", *International Journal of Multidisciplinary Research and Development,* vol. 10, no. 7, pp. 78-8, 2023.

[59] O.A. Abdelkader, "ChatGPT's influence on customer experience in digital marketing: Investigating the moderating roles", *Heliyon,* vol. 9, no. 8, p. e18770, 2023. [http://dx.doi.org/10.1016/j.heliyon.2023.e18770] [PMID: 37576290]

[60] R.R. Ahmed, D. Streimikiene, G. Berchtold, J. Vveinhardt, Z.A. Channar, and R.H. Soomro, "Effectiveness of online digital media advertising as a strategic tool for building brand sustainability: evidence from FMCGs and services sectors of pakistan", *Sustainability (Basel),* vol. 11, no. 12, p. 3436, 2019. [http://dx.doi.org/10.3390/su11123436]

[61] P.M. Podsakoff, S.B. MacKenzie, J.Y. Lee, and N.P. Podsakoff, "Common method biases in behavioral research: A critical review of the literature and recommended remedies", *J. Appl. Psychol.,* vol. 88, no. 5, pp. 879-903, 2003. [http://dx.doi.org/10.1037/0021-9010.88.5.879] [PMID: 14516251]

[62] J.C. Nunnally, *Psychometric theory.* 2nd ed. Mcgraw-Hill College: New York, 1978.

[63] S. Rajput, F. Ali, and R.P.S. Kaurav, "Structural equation modelling (SEM)", *Encyclopedia of Tourism Management and Marketing.,* Edward Elgar Publishing: Cheltenham, pp. 277-280, 2022. [http://dx.doi.org/10.4337/9781800377486.structural.equation.modelling]

CHAPTER 6

Effects of News on the Stock Prices Using Machine Learning: A Comparative Study

Sapna Jain[1,*] and **Saurabh Mukherjee**[2]

[1] *Banasthali Vidyapith, Rajasthan, India*

[2] *Computer Science Department, Banasthali Vidyapith, Rajasthan, India*

Abstract: With the advent of technology, it has become an area of interest to forecast stock prices based on the news. Important "new news" is most likely to affect the stock price. The growth of social media platforms has enabled users to express their views on commonplace issues. Hence, the feedback from the public and customers is important. Sentiment analysis, also known as opinion mining, is a popular pre-planning exercise for conversations that seek to identify the underlying feelings associated with various text types. Moreover, public opinion research can provide us useful information. Sentiment analysis is a powerful tool with numerous applications. It can be used to understand user attitudes on social media sites such as Facebook and Twitter.

This sentiment analysis helps determine the customer's inclination, which in turn affects market trends. These trends often indicate a shift in stock prices in response to major announcements and significant news. With the aid of machine learning algorithms, suitably training and testing the data, this effect has been studied, and significant price movements have been observed. This paper employs sentiment analysis, machine learning, and deep learning techniques to examine the influence of news on market prediction, diverging from traditional stock structured data analysis.

However, the efficacy and accuracy of sentiment analysis are being hampered by issues with Natural Language Processing (NLP). Recent studies have shown that deep learning models offer a promising approach to addressing the challenges in natural language processing.

Keywords: Deep learning, Machine learning, Natural language processing, Neural network, News-based stock price prediction, Sentiment analysis.

INTRODUCTION

Shares, or stocks, deal with fragmented ownership in a company, asset, or security. The stock market provides a venue for investors to buy and sell

* **Corresponding author Sapna Jain:** Banasthali Vidyapith, Rajasthan, India; E-mail: rite2sapna@gmail.com

Subir Gupta, Indrajit Ghosal, Keshav Kaushik & Monika Dandotiya (Eds.)

ownership of investable assets or offers [1]. Market participants are individuals who engage in the trading of stocks and assets.

An organization can go public and issue stocks, which are then exchanged in secondary markets, or stock exchanges, as a means of raising capital for debt repayment or corporate expansion. By offering shares rather than taking out a cash loan, the company can reduce the risk of losses, debt, and interest payments. Another reason to issue stock is to generate income and profits for the stockholders. These individuals, also known as shareholders, may profit from businesses whose stocks consistently yield dividends or by selling their shares when the company's stock price exceeds the initial investment [2]. Therefore, individuals engaged in stock trading exhibit a significant interest in predicting the market value of these financial assets.

Stock market prediction is the process of estimating a stock's, market segments, or even the market's future value. Numerous individuals have focused their attention on this topic, including corporations, traders, market stakeholders, data analysts, and computer scientists specializing in Machine Learning (ML) and Artificial Intelligence (AI), among others. Since the value of a company's shares is several. It can fluctuate based on a number of variables, primarily determined by its performance and earnings in the market. Investing in it entails several risks. The value can fluctuate based on various factors such as supply and demand, government regulations, and microeconomic indicators. ML, Deep Learning, Neural Networks, AI, and other techniques are investigated to produce software and algorithms based on these market variations [3].

The advent of Web 2.0 has enabled people to discuss and share their thoughts on any subject through blogs, forums, and online social networks. They might discuss current events, air grievances about a recent purchase, or share their political opinions [4]. This platform offers a medium for individuals to express their viewpoints and opinions, often in a casual and informal manner. The open and easy availability of news and events significantly influences the user's perception of the market. The user actively or passively absorbs the market's emotion and tends to make decisions accordingly. Sentiment analysis on social media platforms has numerous applications and hasevolved into a powerful tool for gaining insight into user perspectives.

Although news influences the stock market, public sentiment and mood also play an equally important role. It is evident from psychological research that emotions and information together play a pivotal role in human decision-making [5]. Behavioural finance supports the notion that financial decisions are largely driven by emotion and mood. Thus, it seems valid to believe that attitude and public mood might influence stock market values just as much as news.

Financial economists have been interested in the dissemination of news and events into financial assets in recent years. Numerous studies have examined how different types of information (political, macroeconomic, and earnings announcements, among others) affect the pricing of financial assets, thereby capturing the correct user sentiment, which is often an important aspect that requires study.

However, the difficulties in using Natural Language Processing (NLP) are impeding the effectiveness and accuracy of sentiment analysis. Furthermore, these platforms provide people with access to worldwide news, enabling them to formulate opinions and engage with global news. In this case, we are specifically concerned with the impact of any political news that undoubtedly stimulates. Many applications depend on users utilizing this information to function properly [6].

According to several studies, stock values might fluctuate for several months following significant business events [7]. This implies that to some extent, the drift is caused by an information-related reaction (either over- or under). Previous research has shown that news has a significant impact on market trends [8]. In the era of widespread machine learning applications, utilizing news for stock forecasts is uncommon due to the difficulty in using news as input, which hinders its application in stock predictions. This issue will be resolved with the advancement of technology like Natural Language Processing (NLP) [9].

SENTIMENT CLASSIFICATION METHODOLOGY

Sentiment classification methodologies encompass two primary approaches: the Machine Learning approach and the Lexicon-based approach [6]. The subsequent section will elaborate on these categorizations as given in Fig. (**1**).

Machine Learning Approach

The methodologies employed in sentiment analysis encompass a combination of unsupervised and supervised machine learning techniques. The following section outlines these methodologies:

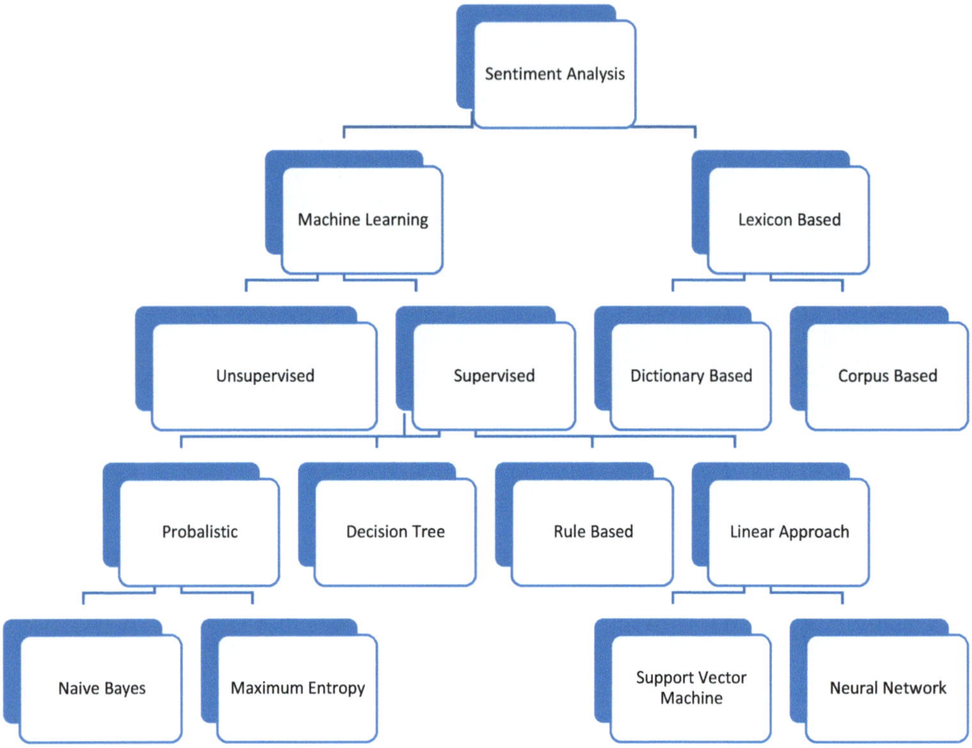

Fig. (1). Sentiment classification techniques.

Unsupervised Learning

This is a form of learning by observation that lacks a clear intended output, similar to onethat lacks a clear intended output linked to the input. The idea is to let the machine learn on its own without explicit guidance. Clustering is a well-known unsupervised learning technique that finds similarities between items in the training data. Euclidean distance and other metrics are used to define the cluster similarity parameter. Among the clustering techniques are Hierarchical, K-means, Hidden Markov models, Gaussian mixture models, and Self-organizing maps [10].

Supervised Learning

Utilizing a known dataset to anticipate the outcome is known as supervised learning. Two collections of documents are required for supervised learning: a training set and a test set. The training set is used to acquire knowledge of different document characteristics, while the test set is employed to evaluate the classifier's effectiveness. The subsequent section delves into several supervised learning methodologies as illustrations.

Probabilistic Classifiers

In many applications, it is crucial to consider both user preferences and the context of the content. This necessitates more investigation into context-based sentiment analysis. The prediction of the input given the probability distribution is the foundation of a probabilistic classifier. Herein, two of the most significant probabilistic classifiers are examined:

- *Naïve Bayes classifier*: Naive Bayes is a probabilistic algorithm that is used for classification problems. It is based on Bayes' theorem of probability and assumes that the features are conditionally independent of each other given the class. It is used to calculate the probability of a given sample belonging to a particular class. Here, the likelihood of a sentence is determined by classifying it as negative or positive.
- *Maximum Entropy classifier*: This classifier, belonging to the exponential model class, exhibits a probabilistic nature [11]. It parameterizes the model to attain the highest possible categorical entropy, subject to the requirement that the model's resultant probability on the training data equals the real distribution. Unlike the Naive Bayes classifier, it does not make the assumption that the characteristics are conditionally independent of one another.

Decision Tree Classifier

It partitions training data according to the condition of attribute values using a hierarchical decomposition method. Generally, the presence or lack of words determines whether the divide is made. Each leaf node has a corresponding positive or negative classification value, and each non-leaf node has a corresponding attribute feature. In other words, each internal node in this structure, which resembles a flowchart, represents a choice made based on an attribute; each branch shows the decision's result; and each leaf node shows a class label or a continuous value.

Rule-based Classifier

The rule controlling the occurrences of emotions in the text serves as the foundation for a rule-based classifier. These classifiers are typically used to create descriptive models because these principles are simple to understand. A term is seen as positive if it conveys positive feelings, and as negative if it conveys negative feelings. Rule-based classifiers are comparable to fuzzy logic systems in that they enable the definition of intermediate values between binary classifications, such as true or false, yes or no, high or low, *etc.*

Linear Classifier

It uses a line to divide a set of objects into their corresponding domains; a curve-based partitioning method is known as a hyperplane. The principal methodologies for linear classification are presented as follows:

- *Support Vector Machine (SVM):* Specializing in textual elements that are indicative of the overall tone of a text might be a challenging task when performing sentiment analysis. A popular supervised learning classifier for regression analysis and classification is SVM. The primary concept behind Support Vector Machines (SVM) involves identifying a hyperplane within the feature space that effectively separates distinct classes.
- *Neural Network:* It is based on the concepts of neurons. In order to create non-linear boundaries for enclosed areas of a specific kind, multilayer neural networks are utilized. Artificial neural networks aggregate neuronal input in a linear fashion with varying weights. Following this combination, the output is sent into a non-linear activation unit, which is essentially a threshold unit. Neural networks provide fault tolerance, adaptability, input-output mapping, and nonlinearity. The network's high connectedness makes sure that errors will only have a minor impact, which ideally results in a high fault tolerance.

Lexicon-based Approach

Lexicon-based sentiment analysis techniques are robust and produce strong cross-domain results. Contextual sentiment orientation is the cornerstone of this approach. There are two more categories for this approach, which are covered below:

- *Dictionary-Based Approach:* This methodology utilizes a predetermined lexicon, where each term is linked to a specific level of sentiment polarity. A person's emotional state, such as happiness, sadness, or depression, can be ascertained by cross-referencing words with dictionary definitions.
- *Corpus-based approach*: A corpus-based method looks for word co-occurrence patterns to infer attitudes. This methodology commences by establishing a foundational list of subjective terms and subsequently endeavours to identify additional subjective vocabulary within comparable contexts. Using this technique, words are assigned a happiness score based on how frequently they appear in “happy” or “sad” blog posts.

LITERATURE REVIEW

The literature has been divided into two categories: machine learning is used to predict stock prices, and sentiment analysis is used to gather the market sentiment. These studies are usually derived from stock market research, where "any" news used to influence stock prices in the past. This concept, in which the machine learns and forecasts stock prices, has been advanced.

Machine Learning for Stock Prediction

Stock forecasting has traditionally been seen as difficult. But people have long wanted to be able to predict the path of equities more accurately. Just 10% of people actively participate in the stock market in any given country because of its unpredictable character. One common fallacy regarding the stock market is the belief that "investing in or selling shares is an act of gambling" [12]. Therefore, changing people's perception of this can be accomplished by raising awareness of it. Stock market prediction techniques can be quite helpful in attracting new and current investors to one location. Among the techniques employed, machine learning techniques are particularly well-liked due to their ability to identify stock trends from large datasets that represent the underlying dynamics of stock prices.

The paper [13] forecasts shifts in the market trend by examining the impact of non-quantifiable data (news articles). Based on the Efficient Markets Hypothesis, the authors examine the news articles' direct influence on the time series (EMH). To find trends in the time series, a novel piecewise segmentation approach based on statistics is proposed. Based on the slope and coefficient of determination of the segmented trends, two clusters are identified: Rise and Drop. Using the clusters that they have gathered from trends, a novel method known as guided clustering is presented to filter news stories. Additionally, they propose a novel differentiated weighting technique that assigns features greater weights if they appear in the news-article cluster labelled as Rise (Drop) but not in its opposite, Drop (Rise).

In a study [14], the authors elucidate how experimental psychology research indicates that most people tend to "overreact" to sudden and dramatic occurrences in news, defying Bayes' rule. This market efficiency study examines whether stock prices are influenced by such behavior. The overreaction theory is supported by the empirical data (based on CRSP monthly return data). The efficient-market hypothesis, or EMH, is a crucial stock market theory. It contends that in a stock market with robust regulations, appropriate procedures, a high degree of openness, and enough competition, the stock price appropriately and promptly reflects all relevant information. More people will earn from the stock market if the prognosis is more accurate.

Early on, there was a strong desire to forecast stock movements using conventional machine learning techniques. In this paper [15], an innovative technique for predicting the behaviour of financial markets is the proposal of a Bayesian regularized artificial neural network. The daily market prices and financial technical indicators are utilized as inputs to predict the closing price of particular stocks one day ahead in the future. Enhancing stock profits for investors may depend on one's ability to forecast stock price fluctuations. Predicting these patterns is challenging due to the noise and volatility inherent in the daily movement of stock prices. The Bayesian regularised network gives the network's weights a probabilistic quality, which facilitates the network in automatically and appropriately penalizing models that are overly complex. By lowering the likelihood of overfitting and overtraining, the suggested method enhances the network's generalization and prediction quality. The model's efficacy was tested using Microsoft Corp. and Goldman Sachs Group Inc. stock through experiments. The findings suggest that the recommended model achieves comparable performance to more advanced models, eliminating the need for data preprocessing, seasonality assessment, or cycle analysis.

In anotherpaper [16], the author examines the impact of daily announcements on the discount rate, real economic activity, inflation, and money supply on stock prices. The surprise element of the announcements is ascertained using survey data on market participants' expectations of these announcements, in addition to the discount rate. In an effort to verify the efficient markets hypothesis, which posits that the unexpected or surprising part of announcements solely influences the stock prices. The empirical results support this idea and demonstrate that monetary policy surprises significantly impact stock prices.

In a paper [8], the author examines monthly returns following public news and utilizes an extensive database of headlines about specific companies. He contrasts them with equities that have comparable returns but no noteworthy news releases. The two sets differ from one another. a sharp decline following negative news. Investor response to this information appears to be sluggish. Reversals are also observed following strong price swings that are not supported by the media. Even after controlling for other variables and risk exposure, distinct patterns still show up. Nonetheless, they are primarily observed in smaller, less liquid stocks. These findings support several comprehensive theories of investor over- and underreaction.

In a paper [17], the authors propose a stock market prediction methodology driven by events and rooted in deep learning. Initially, events are identified in textual news through an innovative neural tensor network and subsequently encoded as compact vectors for training. Subsequently, the impact of events, both immediate (short-term) and prolonged (long-term), on fluctuations in stock values is analyzed through the application of a complex convolutional neural network.

Analysing this enormous volume of transactions has become possible in today's financial markets, where the majority of deals are executed entirely electronically and a significant portion are fully automated. Investors can analyse the generated data to identify recurring trends in price fluctuations, as every transaction is meticulously documented. Being able to anticipate them enables individuals to take advantage of favourable opportunities or steer clear of unusual occurrences in the financial markets. In this paper [18], the authors introduced a deep learning methodology that relies on Convolutional Neural Networks (CNNs) for forecasting stock price variations. This approach employs extensive, high-frequency time-series data sourced from the order books of financial markets. Nevertheless, few studies have enhanced the CNN model to make it more appropriate for prediction, even though it is frequently used directly for prediction.

Sentiment Analysis

In a paper [6], the author examines the consequences of user opinion. To predict stock prices, sentiment analysis has been applied to news articles from online newspaper websites, examining the behavior exhibited by the SENSEX and NIFTY50 indices. This study emphasizes the importance of sentiment analysis about stock market indicators like Sensex and Nifty.

In another paper [19], the authors propose several methods to forecast an asset's behavior in the stock market using existing data. These methods simply take into account statistical data; they do not take into account public sentiment. To forecast active behaviour, this article first uses Natural Language Processing methods (NLP) to ascertain the overall mood of public. Then, it employs the SVM algorithm to extract patterns. By taking into account an attribute representing the general public's mood, they were able to predict market trends more accurately using SVM. A day where the quantity of tweets expressing gratitude over those expressing disapproval is suggestive of an all-around favourable public perception of the stock.

In a paper [5], the authors developed a novel sentiment analysis framework, utilizing the Profile of Mood States (POMS) questionnaire to evaluate collective mood. Utilizing readings of the Dow Jones Industrial Average (DJIA) Index from the preceding day, along with their corresponding results, a Self-Organizing Fuzzy Neural Network (SOFNN) was trained for forecasting market fluctuations.

In a paper [20], some researchers experimented with representing tweets for sentiment analysis using Word2Vec and N-gram bases. They found a significant relationship between the public's perception and changes in DJIA prices. They have analysed the relationship between a company's stock market movements and sentiments in tweets by applying supervised machine learning concepts and sentiment analysis to the tweets that were taken from Twitter. In a more complex sense, positive news and social media posts about a firm, would undoubtedly motivate people to buy its stocks, which would raise the valuation of the company's shares in the financial market. The paper's conclusion demonstrates the substantial relationship between changes in stock values and changes in public opinion in tweets.

In the paper [21] the authors assert that stock market values are impacted by sentiment analysis of RSS news streams. For a certain amount of time, data from RSS news feeds is gathered in addition to stock market investment data. They establish the association between stock market prices and sentiments in RSS news streams using their sentiment analysis technique. With the help of Really Simple Syndication news streams and this trained model, SENSEX points are analysed and stock market rates are forecast. They used companies listed on the Amman Stock Exchange (ASE) to enhance projections using their decision tree-based algorithms, such as ID3 and C4.5.

In a paper [22], the researchers create a system that gathers historical tweets, analyzes them further, and assesses whether several machine learning methods, such as Support Vector Machine (SVM) and Naive Bayes Bernoulli classification, are effective at identifying positive or negative sentiment in the corpus of tweets. We then use the same machine learning algorithms to examine the relationship between tweets and the movements of stock prices. They compare the output of their algorithm with the actual close price of the following day to assess the mistake in their prediction. Ultimately, this project's objective is to use sentiment analysis on a collection of tweets from the previous few days to predict future market behaviour and determine whether the contrarian investing theory applies in this case. The final findings indicate a positive link between stock prices and tweet sentiment.

COMPARATIVE ANALYSIS

This section compares the various research works carried out in the related area based on Machine Learning and sentiment analysis (Table **1**) for the stock market predictions.

Table 1. Comparative analysis.

Author/Year	Methodology	Conclusion
[14], 1985	The Overreaction Hypothesis states that people frequently "overreact" to spectacular or unexpected news occurrences.	Consistent with the overreaction hypothesis.
[16], 1985	Daily response of stock prices to announcements as per the efficient market hypothesis.	The empirical findings confirm this theory and show that monetary policy surprises have a big impact on stock prices.
[17], 2002	The fluctuations due to events in stock values are analysed through the application of a complex convolutional neural network.	Improvements in index prediction and individual stock prediction.
[13], 2002	Trends are identified and labeled using, an agglomerative hierarchical clustering method and a piecewise segmentation approach based on the t-test.	A novel weighting system and directed clustering are two of the new methods that are presented. The incremental K-means algorithm is used to construct the guided clustering. Article-trend alignment and article filtering are two uses for it. The goal of the new weighting scheme is to highlight the key elements in the collection of articles.
[8], 2003	Examined monthly stock returns after news releases.	Reversal following extreme price fluctuations is unaccompanied by a strong drift following bad news.
[15], 2013	A Bayesian regularized artificial neural network is proposed to forecast market behavior.	By lowering the likelihood of overfitting and overtraining, the suggested method enhances the network's generalization and prediction quality. The model's efficacy was tested using Microsoft Corp. and Goldman Sachs Group Inc. stock through experiments.
[6], 2015	The price of stocks has been predicted by sentiment analysis of stock market indicators.	The stock market status was predicted using real-time server data values at various time intervals.
[19], 2016	Employed SVM, Naïve-Bayes and natural language processing methods (NLP) to ascertain the overall mood.	SVM produced a significant gain in the correct classification of instances.
[21], 2017	Sensex points and Really Simple Syndication (RSS) feeds have an impact on stock market values and together provide an accurate stock price prediction.	Compared to the usual algorithms of ID3, C4.5, and the moving average stock level indicator, there was an improvement of 14.43% in prediction accuracy.

(Table 1) cont.....

Author/Year	Methodology	Conclusion
[20], 2017	Used supervised machine learning techniques and sentiment analysis to examine the correlation between a company's stock market movements and the sentiments conveyed in the tweets that were pulled from Twitter.	There is a direct correlation between shifts in stock prices and public sentiment expressed in tweets.
[18], 2017	A deep learning approach using CNNs (convolutional neural networks) predicts the price movements of stocks.	Multilayer neural networks and support vector machines are less suitable for price prediction than CNNs.
[12], 2018	Make use of Random Forest, Naive Bayes, K-Nearest Neighbor (KNN), Support Vector Machine (SVM), and Softmax.	For large datasets, the Random Forest method works best, and for small datasets, the Naive Bayesian Classifier performs best.
[23], 2019	Twitter postings with hashtags particular to a company are categorized as positive or negative using a trained Word2Vec model, and an ensemble model is suggested.	The ensemble model is more dependent on the kind and volume of training data than the individual models, yet it still performs better overall.
[5], unpublished	Compared to the individual models, the ensemble model is more sensitive to the type and quantity of training data, although it still performs better overall.	Self-organizing fuzzy neural networks (SOFNN) are used in a novel cross-validation technique for financial data, yielding an accuracy of 75.56% on Twitter feeds.

CHALLENGES IN EXISTING MECHANISMS

This section outlines some of the research constraints identified when examining various methodologies for stock market predictions.

The authors [3] assert that machine learning is not as accurate as deep learning. This does not imply, however, that deep learning techniques will be used to stock predictions. In a long-term investigation, certain machine learning techniques have developed reliable structures and methodologies that might be more reliable in stock prediction. Models for deep learning are more intricate and flexible. Different approaches may produce significantly different outcomes by altering the model's structure and the number of its parameters.

Unlike traditional systems [1], the construction of contemporary stock markets makes use of numerous linked technologies, including big data, expert systems, and machine learning, which allow for better decision-making. The stock market is now more susceptible to damaging attacks, less stable due to changing news, and sensitive to user opinions due to the widespread internet access of users. Here is where more research can be quite beneficial in establishing the foundation for upcoming stock market analysis and fortifying it.

According to the author [24], the suggested method can only handle English-language tweets. This is a drawback because a lot of news and information is available in other languages, which means that more effort needs to be made on other language recognition.

Further studies [19] point out that the genuine feeling toward a specific asset of any firm is not always reflected in the collective mood. The company's assets could be devalued by an unfavourable political development, which would impact share prices.

There is a possibility that the news is deliberately circulated to cover up another major event (which may not be true), making it challenging for algorithms to identify as false news or less important news.

The research is ongoing in the field to fill the gaps, thereby offering a more reliable and accurate solution to study and explore market behavior in advance.

CONCLUSION AND FUTURE SCOPE

The distinctive platform of the financial markets facilitates trading and investment, enabling transactions to be carried out from any device with an Internet connection. Since the creation of stock markets, investors have had more opportunities to increase their capital. Online trading platforms have completely transformed the way consumers buy and sell stocks. The world's financial markets have evolved rapidly into a powerful, interconnected economy. These developments open up new possibilities, and data science methods have numerous benefits, but they also present a host of new difficulties. These days, news sources, blogs, and microblogs are all commonly used in SA. The information in the media greatly contributes to the expression of people's thoughts and feelings around a certain subject or item. Further research is still needed on the use of social networking sites and microblogging platforms as data sources. In many apps, it is essential to consider both the context of the content and the user's choices. This calls for additional research on context-based sentiment analysis.

An additional development in the industry is chatbot applications, which enable inexperienced traders to make informed buy and sell decisions. Aggregating positive and negative tweet counts, considering a tweet's half-life, may yield better findings because earlier tweets will have less of an impact on the current price.

Furthermore, the majority of the job is done using news that is shared on Twitter, which occasionally contains biased content as well. Thus, it is also possible to think about other platforms that maintain a wide range of "any" news that could potentially impact stock values. There is no control mechanism to check for biased or less important news, which can impact stock prices.

REFERENCES

[1] D. Shah, H. Isah, and F. Zulkernine, "Stock market analysis: A review and taxonomy of prediction techniques", *International Journal of Financial Studies,* vol. 7, no. 2, p. 26, 2019. [http://dx.doi.org/10.3390/ijfs7020026]

[2] O. Bustos, and A. Pomares-Quimbaya, "Stock market movement forecast: A Systematic review", *Expert Syst. Appl.,* vol. 156, p. 113464, 2020. [http://dx.doi.org/10.1016/j.eswa.2020.113464]

[3] J. Guo, and B. Tuckfield, "News-based machine learning and deep learning methods for stock prediction", *J. Phys. Conf. Ser.,* vol. 1642, no. 1, p. 012014, 2020. [http://dx.doi.org/10.1088/1742-6596/1642/1/012014]

[4] A. Chamekh, M. Mahfoudh, and G. Forestier, "Sentiment analysis based on deep learning in e-commerce", In: *Lect. Notes Comput. Sci. (including Subser. Lect. Notes Artif. Intell. Lect. Notes Bioinformatics)* vol. 13369. , 2022, pp. 489-507. [http://dx.doi.org/10.1007/978-3-031-10986-7_40]

[5] A. Goel, and A. Mittal, *Stock prediction using twitter sentiment analysis. Standford University, CS229,* 2012. http://cs229.stanford.edu/proj2011/GoelMittal-StockMarketPredictionUsingTwitterSentimentAnalysis.pdf

[6] A. Bhardwaj, Y. Narayan, Vanraj, Pawan, and M. Dutta, "Sentiment analysis for indian stock market prediction using sensex and nifty", *Procedia Comput. Sci.,* vol. 70, pp. 85-91, 2015. [http://dx.doi.org/10.1016/j.procs.2015.10.043]

[7] E.F. Fama, "Market efficiency, long-term returns, and behavioral finance", *J. Financ. Econ.,* vol. 49, no. 3, pp. 283-306, 1998. [http://dx.doi.org/10.1016/S0304-405X(98)00026-9]

[8] W.S. Chan, "Stock price reaction to news and no-news: drift and reversal after headlines", *J. Financ. Econ.,* vol. 70, no. 2, pp. 223-260, 2003. [http://dx.doi.org/10.1016/S0304-405X(03)00146-6]

[9] C.D. Manning, M. Surdeanu, J. Bauer, J. Finkel, S.J. Bethard, and D. McClosky, "The stanford CoreNLP natural language processing toolkit", *Proc. Annu. Meet. Assoc. Comput. Linguist.,* 2014, pp. 55-60. [http://dx.doi.org/10.3115/v1/P14-5010]

[10] R. Batool, A. M. Khattak, J. Maqbool, and S. Lee, "Precise tweet classification and sentiment analysis," *2013 IEEE/ACIS 12th Int. Conf. Comput. Inf. Sci. ICIS 2013 - Proc.,* pp. 461–466, 2013. [http://dx.doi.org/10.1109/ICIS.2013.6607883]

[11] Y. Luo, M. Fan, and X. Zhou, "The design and implementation of Feature-Grading recommendation system for e-commerce", *2011 IEEE Int. Conf. Inf. Autom. ICIA 2011,* pp. 236-241, 2011. [http://dx.doi.org/10.1109/ICINFA.2011.5948994]

[12] I. Kumar, K. Dogra, C. Utreja, and P. Yadav, "A comparative study of supervised machine learning algorithms for stock market trend prediction", *Proc. Int. Conf. Inven. Commun. Comput. Technol. ICICCT 2018,* pp. 1003-1007, 2018. [http://dx.doi.org/10.1109/ICICCT.2018.8473214]

[13] G.P.C. Fung, J.X. Yu, and W. Lam, "News sensitive stock trend prediction", In: *Lect. Notes Comput. Sci. (including Subser. Lect. Notes Artif. Intell. Lect. Notes Bioinformatics)* vol. 2336. , 2002, pp. 481-493. [http://dx.doi.org/10.1007/3-540-47887-6_48]

[14] W.F.M. De BONDT, and R. Thaler, "Does the stock market overreact?", *J. Finance,* vol. 40, no. 3, pp. 793-805, 1985. [http://dx.doi.org/10.1111/j.1540-6261.1985.tb05004.x]

[15] J.L. Ticknor, "A Bayesian regularized artificial neural network for stock market forecasting", *Expert Syst. Appl.,* vol. 40, no. 14, pp. 5501-5506, 2013. [http://dx.doi.org/10.1016/j.eswa.2013.04.013]

[16] D.K. Pearce, and V.V. Roley, "Stock prices and economic news", *J. Bus.,* vol. 58, no. 1, p. 49, 1985. [http://dx.doi.org/10.1086/296282]

[17] A.M. El-Masry, M.F. Ghaly, M.A. Khalafallah, and Y.A. El-Fayed, "Deep learning for event-driven stock prediction xiao", *J. Sci. Ind. Res. (India),* vol. 61, no. 9, pp. 719-725, 2002.

[18] A. Tsantekidis, N. Passalis, A. Tefas, J. Kanniainen, M. Gabbouj, and A. Iosifidis, "Forecasting stock prices from the limit order book using convolutional neural networks", *Proc. - 2017 IEEE 19th Conf. Bus. Informatics, CBI,* vol. 1, pp. 7-12, 2017. [http://dx.doi.org/10.1109/CBI.2017.23]

[19] M.L. Lima, "Using sentiment analysis for stock exchange prediction", *Int. J. Artif. Intell. Appl.,* vol. 7, no. 1, pp. 59-67, 2016. [http://dx.doi.org/10.5121/ijaia.2016.7106]

[20] V.S. Pagolu, K.N. Reddy, G. Panda, and B. Majhi, "Sentiment analysis of Twitter data for predicting stock market movements", *Int. Conf. Signal Process. Commun. Power Embed. Syst. SCOPES 2016 - Proc.,* pp. 1345-1350, 2017. [http://dx.doi.org/10.1109/SCOPES.2016.7955659]

[21] S. Bharathi, and A. Geetha, "Sentiment analysis for effective stock market prediction", *International Journal of Intelligent Engineering and Systems,* vol. 10, no. 3, pp. 146-154, 2017. [http://dx.doi.org/10.22266/ijies2017.0630.16]

[22] J. Kordonis, S. Symeonidis, and A. Arampatzis, "Stock price forecasting *via* sentiment analysis on Twitter", *ACM Int. Conf. Proceeding Ser,* 2016. [http://dx.doi.org/10.1145/3003733.3003787]

[23] U. Pasupulety, A. Abdullah Anees, S. Anmol, and B.R. Mohan, "Predicting stock prices using ensemble learning and sentiment analysis", *Proc. - IEEE 2nd Int. Conf. Artif. Intell. Knowl. Eng. AIKE,* pp. 215-222, 2019. [http://dx.doi.org/10.1109/AIKE.2019.00045]

[24] M.P. Salas-Zárate, J. Medina-Moreira, K. Lagos-Ortiz, H. Luna-Aveiga, M.Á. Rodríguez-García, and R. Valencia-García, "Sentiment analysis on tweets about diabetes: an aspect-level approach", *Comput. Math. Methods Med.,* vol. 2017, pp. 1-9, 2017. [http://dx.doi.org/10.1155/2017/5140631] [PMID: 28316638]

CHAPTER 7

The Role of Machine Learning in Predicting Mental Health on Social Media Platforms

Tejaswita Mishra[1,*], **Sanjay K. Gupta**[2] and **Varun Mishra**[3]

[1] *Centre for Computer Science and Technology, MITS-Deemed University, Gwalior, Madhya Pradesh, India*

[2] *School of Studies in Computer Science & Applications, Jiwaji University, Gwalior, Madhya Pradesh, India*

[3] *Department of Computer Engineering and Applications, GLA University, Mathura, Uttar Pradesh, India*

Abstract: Online communication on social networking platforms offers new perspectives for identifying various neurological disorder problems. Depression is now considered one of the most prevalent mental disorders. This chapter utilizes various machine learning approaches for text classification that categorize posts as either depressed or non-depressed. In this chapter, six machine learning classifiers, including Support Vector Classifier, Random Forest, Decision Tree, K-Nearest Neighbor, Light Gradient Boosting method, and Catboost, are used to make predictions over the Reddit dataset, which includes various posted contents of an individual over the web. The proposed model performs text preprocessing through stemming and normalization, followed by the application of feature extraction techniques using word embedding models. Feature extraction techniques are applied using word embedding models, which are then fed to a machine learning model. The results demonstrated that the LGBM classifier outperforms other machine learning classifiers with a higher accuracy of 99.9%. However, all chosen ML methods are more adaptive and resilient. LGBM outperforms the others.

Keywords: Depression, Machine learning, Mental disorder, Social media, Text classification.

INTRODUCTION

A mental disorder alters a person's emotions, feelings, or behaviors. Mental diseases continue to be a major global source of disability and poor well-being, extensively utilized public health concerns today [1]. The WHO (2018) defines "mental health" as a state of well-being in which a person can thrive by fulfilling

* **Corresponding author Tejaswita Mishra:** Centre for Computer Science and Technology, MITS-Deemed University, Gwalior, Madhya Pradesh, India; E-mail: tejaswitagarg@gmail.com

Subir Gupta, Indrajit Ghosal, Keshav Kaushik & Monika Dandotiya (Eds.)

their potential, engaging in social interactions, and making meaningful contributions to society. Most studies in this field have been quantitative, demonstrating a link between social media usage and mental wellness. However, they provide little insight into the actual use and perception of social networking among teenagers. This narrative review aims to compile the majority of recent qualitative research on teenagers' opinions regarding the mental wellness and psychological effects of social media.

Social media has emerged as the primary information source due to the recent exponential growth in the number of individuals. The use of social media platforms like Facebook, Reddit, and Twitter to express one's ideas and emotions is growing in popularity, especially among young people. As a result, there has been an increase in the number of studies being done on the identification of mental illness through the analysis of user-generated text in social media posts [2]. Emotions are extensively researched in various fields of study, such as behavioral science and psychology, because they are fundamental to human nature and have the power to influence people's actions and mental states [3]. Research has revealed a connection between psychological well-being, such as grief, and emotions [4].

A affecting the brain, central nervous system, or autonomic nervous system is considered a neurological disorder. Life changes, heredity, and a diet low in nutrients, as well as physical injuries or exposure to environmental factors, are all included. If untreated, it generates nervous system issues and develops psychological health problems like stress, anxiety, and sadness. It may even provoke a suicide attempt, which could result in death.

- ***Depression:*** It appears that depression is a multifaceted disorder that has a substantial negative impact on society and impairs people's functioning in their private, social, professional, and interpersonal domains.
- ***Anxiety:*** An unexpected reaction to depressed feelings, anxiety can cause high nervousness, fear, or panic, and interfere with thinking and problem-solving abilities. Among the psychological and physical symptoms are urinary retention, shaking of fingers and their lips, dry mouth, and insomnia.
- ***Stress:*** Stress is defined as a psychological issue that affects our mental well-being. When an organism cannot adapt to its environmental demands, illnesses related to biology and psychology develop.

Depression is more common today than in the past, and those who suffer from it are more likely than non-depressed people to damage themselves or others violently, commit suicide, or experience other negative outcomes. This has a negative effect on the socioeconomic, familial, and personal development of individuals. Although these methods have some drawbacks, questionnaires or scales are primarily used for the clinical diagnosis of depression [5].

According to the WHO, stress and depression are to blame for at least 800,000 suicides each year. Over 1.5 million people worldwide commit suicide each year due to stress [6]. Online networking, which can affect a person's mental health, is an important factor associated with the high suicide rate. Using the NLP method, we can determine a person's psychological health from the content they post on networking platforms. Using computer approaches, NLP studies linguistic data, *i.e.*, textual data like blogs, documents, or articles [7]. This technique aids in processing text that is generally unstructured, as it can only be read by people, due to the layout of the text, which is challenging for computers to understand.

According to a global poll of psychiatrists conducted by Doraiswamy *et al.* [8], the majority of respondents agree that Artificial Intelligence (AI) would have an impact on the future of their field. This study will outline the data analytics techniques equipped to transform the depression diagnosis, treatment and therapies, even if AI may never be able to fully replace the individualized, compassionate care that a psychiatrist can offer. Specifically, precision psychotherapy is a new area that makes use of cutting-edge computational methods to provide psychological services based on patients' needs. . These technologies have the ability to identify people with mental health disorders, enabling them to receive the care they require and allowing doctors to customize therapies for specific patients who will most likely benefit from them. Unsupervised learning approaches are also breaking down the specific diagnostic categories now in use and emphasizing the enormous illness variability seen within diagnoses of depression. In addition to allowing a change from current approaches based on group averages, AI also offers the chance to move towards the prescription of treatments based on empirical research [9].

The primary cause is the inability of those suffering from depression symptoms to control their emotions, which lowers emotional complexity. Thus, from a psychological standpoint, knowledge of emotions can help identify mental diseases [10]. In order to determine whether there are any indications that users are depressed, this study will examine Reddit data. The following research concerns were addressed in the work, with the main concern of the research in mind.

1. To highlight the indicators of depressive disorder in the posted tweets or comments.
2. Is it possible to derive these traits from depression-related Reddit comments?
3. To explore various deep learning methods to identify such a disorder on Reddit.

In this study, we analyzed a public dataset that includes various texts and comments from the Reddit source. This chapter examines various machine learning ML) approaches and embedding models for accurately categorizing tweets as either depressed or not, with results evaluated using metric calculation scores.

The full chapter is presented as follows: Section 2presents the history and relevant work adopted in this study. The suggested framework and deep learning methods are briefly described in Section 3, and the results and analysis of the study are discussed in Section 4. Section 5 concludes the discussion, providing a summary and outlining future work.

BACKGROUND

This section discusses the related work and methodology adopted by researchers that are relevant to this study. Hence, numerous papers have been reviewed, and a comparative analysis table has been generated for better understanding, as shown in Table **1** below.

Table 1. An analysis of objectives and findings employed in the most cited publications.

Author's Ref.	Objective	Findings
[11], 2020	To identify security attacks and unauthorized user intrusions, we employ the KDD-CUP and NSL-KDD datasets to validate our models using the supervised ANN approach.	It can identify these attacks with 97% accuracy. Furthermore, the supervised SVM classifier enhances the accuracy score to 99.7% for detecting security concerns.
[12], 2018	This research concentrated on depression over Reddit posts using ML and NLP techniques.	The authors employed the best bigram and SVM classifier to identify depression, achieving an F1-score of 0.80 and an accuracy of 80%.
[13], 2015	To analyze depression among Indonesians using linguistic techniques and NLP.	Text preprocessing and Twitter-centered analysis achieved an F1-score of 0.47 and a sensitivity score of 0.89 when the threshold was set to 0.
[14], 2019	To investigate the relationship between dietary supplement use and mental health problems, we proposed four dimensions of SenticNet for classifying 8105 tweets.	This correctly classified the tweets using our suggested method into three depression levels: 1028 classified as higher, 1073 as moderate, and 1605 as lower.
[15], 2018	To identify measures of social network use for socializing, offline connections, addiction to the internet, stress and depression.	It concludes that there is an association between internet use for networking and anxiety & sadness, which was found to occur by both online addiction as well as offline communication.

(Table 1) cont.....

Author's Ref.	Objective	Findings
[16], 2021	This study offers empirical data and a strong statistical analysis that indicates the co-existence of positive and negative effects.	The study utilized 940 Mexican social media users, collected through SEM, with an explanatory power of 45.1% for the empirical model.
[17], 2018	In this work, phrases from the lexicon of symptoms are employed in conjunction with the frequency lexicon to calculate depression scores using natural language processing of text materials.	Based on comparison and assessment results combined with a somewhat better F1 score of 0.50, the same F1 score of 0.47 is obtained for both textual-specific and conventional text processing, coupled at a 0.5 threshold value and 0.89 sensitivity value.
[18], 2023	It focuses on how the use of SNS and psychological health are related among older age groups.	This reveals that a positive correlation was found among active SMU and increased odds of depressed symptoms, and a negative correlation between passive SMU and decreased odds of depressive symptoms.

In this study [11], the authors demonstrated their ability to identify security attacks and unauthorized user intrusions by employing the supervised ANN approach, achieving an enhanced accuracy of 99.7% while evaluating their algorithms on the NSL-KDD and KDD-CUP datasets. However, the support vector method provides a trust-based access control approach, which is an effective way to address security concerns in CC and protect data privacy.

Research by wang *et al.* validated the effectiveness of the vocabulary commonly used by depressed individuals and trained the data using ML and NLP techniques on Reddit posts. It concentrated on depression, which is a major cause of suicide and is amenable to investigation using written text natural language analysis [12].

Yadav *et al.* focused on using linguistic techniques and NLP to analyze depression in Indonesia [13]. NLP on text resources and frequency lexicons has been used for weighing and depression score computations.

Syarif *et al.* determined whether dietary supplement use and mental health problems are related. Twitter posts were examined in this study. The authors have observed numerous notable differences in the two groups' degrees of negativity, anxiety, and depression. It concludes that using nutritional supplements may be associated with several problems, including stress, depression, and mood swings [14].

Glaser *et al.* conducted their study using a representative online sample of 1,157 New Zealanders, segmented by age, gender, and region, to examine mental health issues in relation to online addiction and offline social capital [15].

Ostic *et al.* discussed the advantages of forming bonds and bridging social capital. The results indicate that social media has a generally favorable and indirect impact on psychological well-being, and the empirical model is found to have 45.1% power [16].

Oyong *et al.* analyzed 6055 tweets generated by 55 individuals involved in the tweet extensions. It is calculated to find a label predictor of user depression as the sum of the scores and is compared to the labels manually assigned by psychologists using clinical screening criteria. SMU and poor mental health are frequently associated, these linkages have not yet been studied in older persons [17].

Lewin *et al.* then gathered information from people of 65 years and above, and using principal component analysis, we divided social media use (SMD) into active and passive dimensions. Then, to determine whether older persons' SMU was connected to depressive symptoms, we ran logistic regressions and t-tests [18].

Hence, in this study, we focus on predicting mental issues using Reddit posts and evaluate them using various machine learning and deep learning algorithms.

RESEARCH METHODOLOGY

This section discusses the proposed framework in Fig. (**1**), which comprises data collection, text preprocessing, feature extraction, and machine learning approaches that predict the classification of tweets as either depressed or non-depressed.

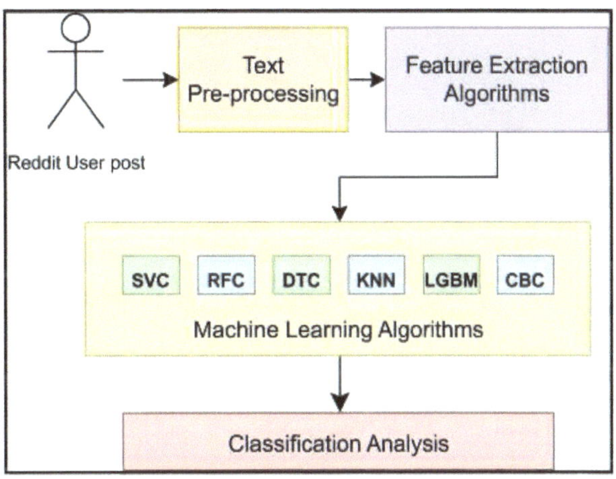

Fig. (1). Proposed Framework for predicting mental health.

Data Collection

In this work, we utilized a dataset from GitHub, consisting of 1516 Reddit posts, over which this study was conducted to measure depressive disorder among individuals. Fig. (**2**) measures the count of tweets in the dataset, whether the dataset is balanced, and is used in this study.

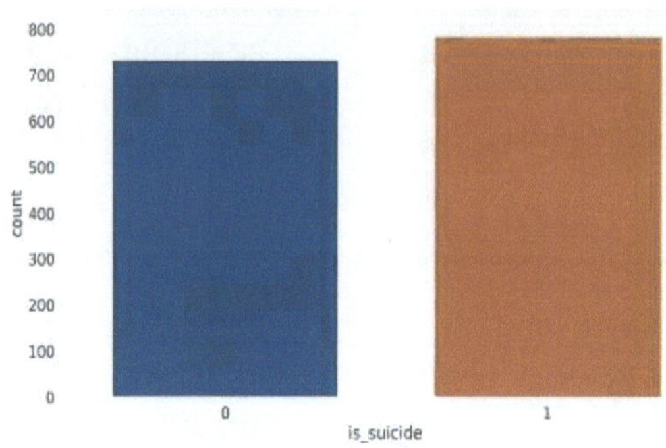

Fig. (2). Reddit posts classification using two class labels.

Text Preprocessing

In this process, we perform various text preprocessing operations on the collected datasets to obtain clean text by utilizing NLP methods such as stemming, lemmatization, stop word removal, emoji and hashtag removal, and punctuation mark removal.

After cleaning the text, tokenization is performed to extract tokens from the completed posts used in this study. As shown in Table **2** below, tokenization is used to obtain tokens of the extracted words from these posts.

Table 2. Tokenization performed over the chosen dataset.

-	selftext_clean	is_suicide	tokenized_text
1510	think spiritual person also think every belongi…	1	[think, spiritual, person, also, think, ever, …..
1511	Every night guy want ice cream dinner everyone..	1	[every, night, guy, wants, ice, cream, dinner, ….
1512	Would like say wa shook knew ha habit consumin..	1	[would, like, say, wa, shook, knew, ha, habit….
1513	Take anymore wanting buy pocket pistol similar .	0	[take, anymore, wanting, buy, pocket, pistol, …
1515	Feel like people controlling every aspect life …	1	[feel, like, people, controlling, every, aspect ….

Feature Extraction Algorithm

Feature extraction techniques are utilized to extract meaningful features from the chosen Reddit dataset. We have utilized a feature extraction algorithm in this study, as shown in Fig. (3) below. This extraction of features is then used to get vectors using the word embedding algorithms provided in this study.

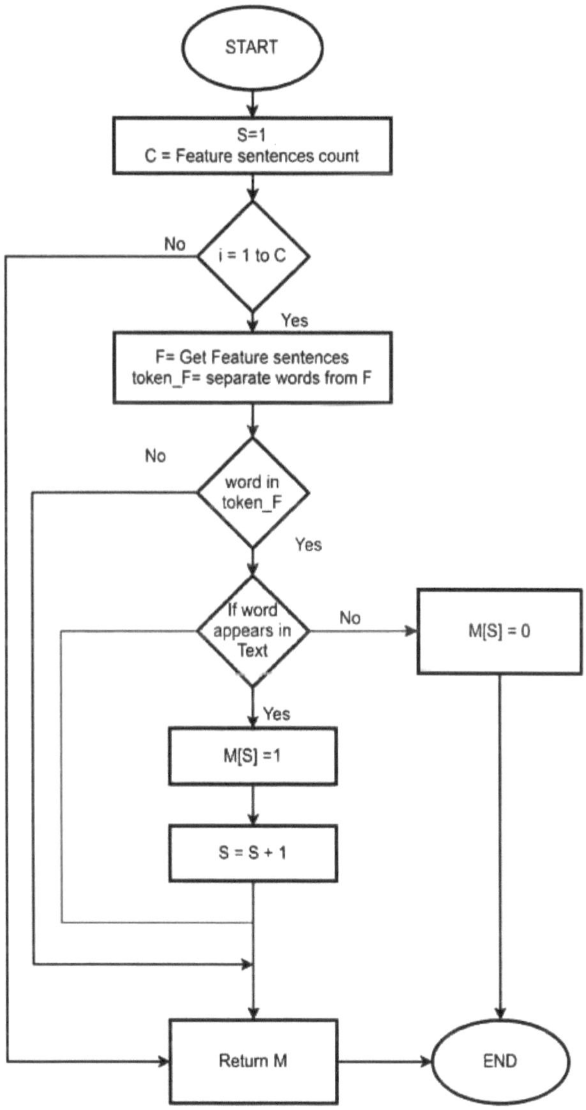

Fig. (3). Feature extraction algorithm.

Table **3** presents the tokenized and most similar words related to depression, along with their determined scores.

Table 3. Most similar words related to depression.

model.wv.most_similar("depressed")	
'bad'	0.9998921751976013
'thing'	0.9998698234558105
'truly'	0.9998522996902466
'suffering'	0.9998512268066406
'lonely'	0.9998488426208496
'actually'	0.9998463988304138
'happen'	0.9998458027839661
'reason'	0.9998304743902588
'death'	0.9998297095298767
'understand'	0.9998254179954529

Machine Learning Techniques

A variety of ML techniques are analyzed and employed in this study. The total of six ML classifiers are evaluated as SVC, RFC, DTC, KNN, LGBM and CBC as ML algorithms behave differently when the nature of the dataset changes [19 - 21]. This study examines how Machine Learning (ML) performs on the chosen dataset.

Support Vector Classifier

The SVM is an algorithm for machine learning that determines borders among data samples according to specified categories, tags, or outcomes. It then uses supervised learning methods to address challenging issues in outlier detection, regression, and classification.

Technically speaking, finding a hyperplane that cleanly separates the data points into distinct classes is the basic objective of the SVM method. The hyperplane is oriented to provide the maximum margin of separation between the classes under consideration, as shown in Fig. (**4**).

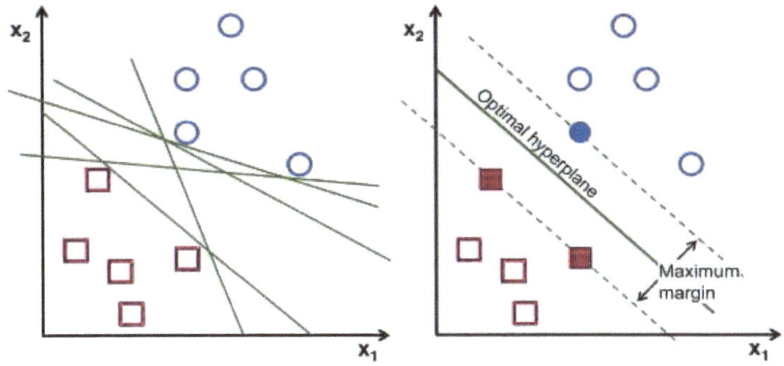

Fig. (4). SVM probable hyperplane.

Achieving the greatest margin that divides the data values from the hyperplane is the aim of the SVM technique. A loss function helps to maximize the margin.

$$c(x, y, f(x)) = \begin{cases} 0, & if \;\; y * f(x) \geq 1 \\ 1 - y * f(x), & else \end{cases} \tag{1}$$

SVMs are widely used for classification tasks, including audio and speech detection, medical image analysis, and more.

Decision Tree Classifier

To anticipate the desired value, decision trees are taught to divide the information into progressively smaller subsets. So, the possible results are shown as "branches" (edges) and the criteria, or test, as a "leaf" (node). Hence, this process of splitting continues until there is no more benefit to be gained or a predetermined rule is satisfied, such as the tree reaching its maximum depth.

This "Information Gain" is applied while dividing the data according to entropy. It is computed as the entropy decrease following an attribute-based split of the dataset:

$$Gain(T, X) = Entropy(T) - Entropy\,(T, X) \tag{2}$$

Where T is the target variable, X is the feature to be divided on, and Entropy (T, X) is computed following the division of the data on feature X.

Using Gini Importance, Scikit-learn determines the importance of each node in a decision tree, assuming that there is just a pair of child nodes (binary trees):

$$ni_j = w_j C_j - w_{left_{(j)}} C_{left_{(j)}} - w_{right_{(j)}} C_{right_{(j)}} \quad \textbf{(3)}$$

For node j, n represents its importance, w denotes the weighted number of samples, C represents the impurity value, and Cleft and Cright denote the child nodes associated with the left and right splits, respectively.

Then, using the DT model, the significance of each feature is determined as follows:

$$fi_i = \frac{\sum j{:}node\ j\ splits\ on\ feature\ i\ ni_j}{\sum k \in all\ nodes\ ni_k} \quad \textbf{(4)}$$

By splitting by the total of all feature significance values, these can subsequently be normalized into a number between 0 and 1:

$$normfi_i = \frac{fi_i}{\sum j \in all\ features\ fi_j} \quad \textbf{(5)}$$

Random Forest Classifier

Random forest is a classifier that consists of numerous decision trees based on various portions of the data being used, and it takes the median prediction to improve the accuracy of the prediction of that dataset. Because there are more trees in the forest, accuracy is higher and over-fitting is avoided.

The feature relevance is determined by multiplying the likelihood of accessing a node by the weighted decrease in impurity at that node. The number of samples reaching the node, divided by the overall number of samples, yields the node probability. Hence, the more significant the trait, the higher its worth.

Several decision trees, each trained slightly differently, are used by the random forest method and are all taken into account for the classification that is generated in Fig. (**5**).

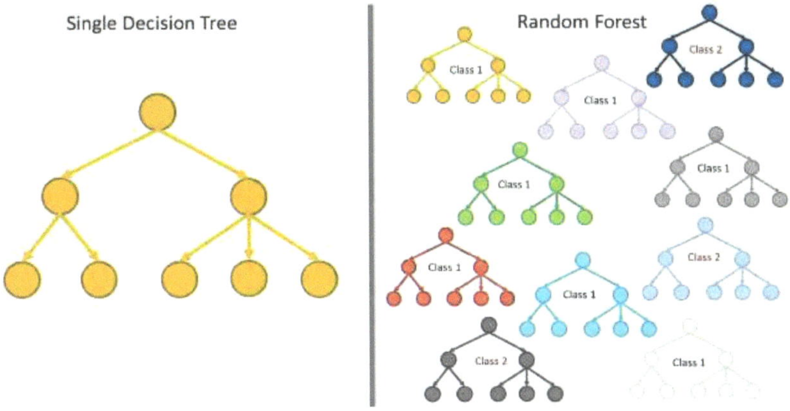

Fig. (5). Random forest relies on multiple decision trees.

At the RFC, the average feature importance across all trees is the final factor of importance. The importance value of each characteristic on each tree is calculated by summing the values and then dividing by the totalnumber of trees. These yields in equation (6):

$$RFfi_i = \frac{\sum j \in all\ trees\ normfi_{ij}}{T} \quad \textbf{(6)}$$

Where,

$RFfi_{(i)}$ is the Random Forest model's calculation of the importance of feature ibased on all of the trees;

T is the total number of trees;

$normfi_{ij}$ is the normalized feature significance for i in tree j.

K-Nearest Neighbor (KNN) Classifier

KNN is a supervised learning method that is mostly used to classify data based on how its neighbors are classified. KNN stores all accessible examples, and new cases are categorized using a similarity metric. The number of closest neighbors that are included in the majority voting procedure is denoted by the parameter K in KNN. Fig. (**6**) defines the KNN classification before and after training of the model.

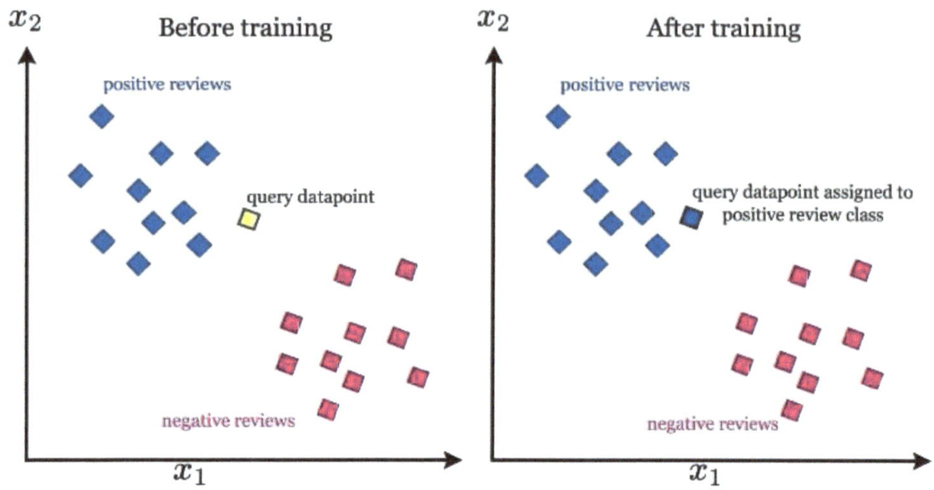

Fig. (6). KNN classification before and after training.

At its core, the KNN classifier depends on a distance measure. The better the classification, the more accurately that metric represents label similarity. The Minkowski distance is the most widely used option shown in equations (7) and (8), respectively.

$$d(x,y) = \left(\sum_{i=1}^{n} |x_i - y_i|^p\right)^{\frac{1}{p}} \quad for\ p \geq 1 \tag{7}$$

$$\boldsymbol{d(x,y)} = \frac{\sum_{i=1}^{n} |x_i - y_i| \qquad if\ p=1}{\sum_{i=1}^{n} (|x_i - y_i|^2)^{1/2} \qquad if\ p=2} \tag{8}$$

Hence, if p=1, it behaves as Manhattan distance, whereas for p=2, it behaves as Euclidean distance.

LGBM Classifier

Microsoft created LightGBM, an open-source, distributed, powerful gradient boosting framework. Its design prioritizes accuracy, scalability, and efficiency. It is based on decision tree structures, which aim to reduce memory usage and boost model performance.

Moreover, LightGBM builds decision trees more efficiently by using histogram-based techniques. These methods enhance LightGBM's performance and give it a competitive advantage over other boosting frameworks, which employ similar optimizations such as leaf-wise tree growth and efficient data storage formats as shown in Fig. (7) [19].

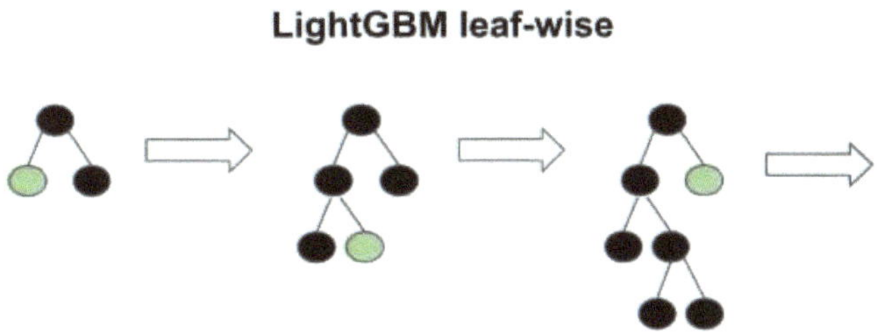

Fig. (7). LGBM classification leaf-wise expansion.

We can write the mathematical model for LGBM as in equation (9):

$$LGBM: Ensemble(X) = \sum_{i=1}^{n} \alpha_1 * h_1(x) \quad \textbf{(9)}$$

Where,

hi_x are the weak models,

N is the number of weak models, and,

α_i are the coefficients.

It is renowned for having excellent scalability and efficiency, which is appropriate for massive datasets. In comparison to existing gradient boosting techniques, it offers several benefits, including support for simultaneously distributed and GPU learning, greater accuracy, faster training speeds, and reduced memory utilization.

CatBoost Classifier

A gradient boosting variation that is capable of handling both numerical and categorical features is called CatBoost. To translate category information into numerical features, no feature encoding technology, such as One-Hot Encoder or Label Encoder, is needed.

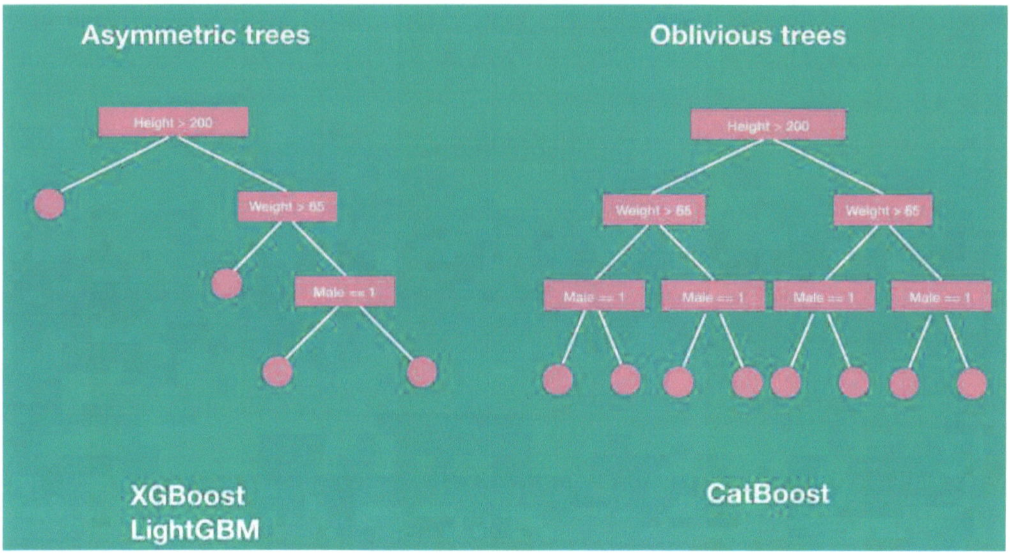

Fig. (8). LGBM and Catboost classification tree structure.

CatBoost Data Preprocessing entails managing categorical features effectively and maximizing memory use in order to prepare data for training as shown in Fig. (**8**). Categorical variables are handled automatically; no manual preprocessing steps, such as one-hot encoding, are needed. It also can work directly with missing values, which makes data preparation easier. By encapsulating the dataset with features, labels, and categorical feature indices using a CatBoost pool, data handling for training and prediction is made simpler and more efficient. Through simplification of data preprocessing, it speeds up the ML workflow while preserving good predictive performance, allowing users to concentrate more on model building and optimization [20].

Classification Analysis

The categorization model involves two steps:

- *Learning Step:* The algorithm is trained using multiple strategies to create a classifier utilizing the provided training data. Training is necessary for the system to be able to predict outcomes with accuracy.
- *Classification Step:* Utilizing the algorithm that was employed to predict labels for classes, the generated model is tested on test data in the classification phase. This determines the correctness of the classification rules sequentially.

The classification results and analysis are performed in terms of metric calculations and evaluation scores. The results are then interpreted using an accuracy check for all ML models utilized in this study, as shown in Equations (10-13).

Accuracy: It is probably the most logical classification metric. The proportion of true predicted samples to total samples in the dataset is measured. However, it is not always reliable, particularly when working with unbalanced datasets.

In general, a system that accurately predicts instances of the majority class can nevertheless attain high accuracy, even if it misses some minority class predictions.

$$\text{Accuracy} = \frac{Number\ of\ Correct\ Predictions}{Total\ Number\ of Predictions} \quad \textbf{(10)}$$

Precision and Recall: For unbalanced datasets, precision and recall are crucial metrics that are frequently combined.

Precision: Precision is a metric for positive forecast accuracy. It gives the proportion of true predicted positive cases, or true positives, to the entire number of positive predictions. High precision means that the model is probably right when it predicts a positive class.

$$\text{Precision} = \frac{Number\ of\ True\ Positives}{Total\ Number\ of Positive\ Predictions} \quad \textbf{(11)}$$

Recall: It is the proportion of real positive cases to all true positive cases, also referred to as sensitivity. A high recall rate indicates that the model can identify the majority of positive examples.

$$\text{Recall} = \frac{Number\ of\ True\ Positives}{Total\ Number\ of Actual\ Positive\ Instances} \quad \textbf{(12)}$$

F1 Score: It gives the harmonic average of precision and recall. It offers a solitary score that harmonizes recall and precision. When trying to strike the right balance among false positives and false negatives, the F1-score comes in especially handy. It is computed as:

$$\text{F1 Score} = 2 * \frac{Precision * Recall}{Precision + Recall} \quad \textbf{(13)}$$

Area under the ROC Curve: Receiver Operating Characteristic (ROC) curves are helpful in situations involving binary categorization. At different thresholds, they graph the TP rate (recall) *versus* the FP rate. The area under the ROC curve is defined by the AUC-ROC, which signifies a single number that expresses how well the system can differentiate across classes. A higher AUC-ROC indicates better discrimination.

Area under the PR Curve: The AUC-PR calculates the area under the precision-recall curve, much as the AUC-ROC. When working with unbalanced datasets, when the positive class is uncommon, it is especially helpful. The precision-recall trade-off is better when the AUC-PR is larger.

Importing Libraries: We bring in the required libraries:

- lgb: This is the gradient-enhancing LightGBM library.
- np: Numerical operations are performed using numpy as np.
- pd: Pandas data manipulation software.
- train_test_split function from sklearn.model_selection: The dataset is divided into training and testing sets.
- The sklearn libraries accuracy_score and roc_auc_score.metrics:

The categorization model is assessed using these.

LightGBM Classification Parameters: We define a dictionary parameter that holds the LightGBM classifier's parameters.

- "Objective": "binary" indicates that the task is one of binary classification.
- 'metric': 'binary_logloss' establishes binary log loss as the evaluation metric.
- The gradient boosting algorithm is specified by 'boosting_type': 'gbdt'.
- The maximum number of leaves in each tree is set at "num_leaves": 31.
- "learning_rate": 0.05 sets the gradient descent step size.
- "feature_fraction": The percentage of features utilized for every tree is controlled by 0.9.

LightGBM Training and Dataset

Proceeding with the model's evaluation and training. Using the training features and labels, we generate a LightGBM dataset, train_data, and use lgb to train a classifier for 100 rounds of boosting using the specified parameters. Fig. (**9**) shows the python implementation using LGBM classifier.

```
Python3

# Create a LightGBM dataset
train_data = lgb.Dataset(X_train, label=y_train)

# Train the classifier
classifier = lgb.train(param, train_data, num_boost_round=100)
```

Fig. (9). Python implementation example using LGBM classifier.

Metrics and Evaluations

Using the trained classifier, we predict the test data and compute the accuracy score to assess the model's performance. In our case, the accuracy is estimated to be 99.9% using the LGBM classifier, as code shown below in Fig. (**10**).

```
Python3

# Make predictions
y_pred = classifier.predict(x_test)

# Calculate accuracy and ROC AUC score
accuracy = accuracy_score(y_test, (y_pred > 0.5).astype(int))
roc_auc = roc_auc_score(y_test, y_pred)

print(f'Accuracy: {accuracy}')
print(f'ROC AUC: {roc_auc}')
```

Fig. (10). Calculation of the accuracy score for the LGBM classifier example.

RESULTS AND DISCUSSION

To further comprehend the general intuition behind the depression, we employed six different ML classifier algorithms for mental illness detection, such as depression or suicide ideation. As a result, we demonstrated how the emotional results associated with depression can be effectively retrieved from each of these classification systems, which depend on language style, psychological process, geographical process, and other features. Fig. (**11**) and Fig. (**12**) display the accuracy outcomes of multiple chosen ML algorithms. It is evident that LGBM yields a better outcome in this instance.

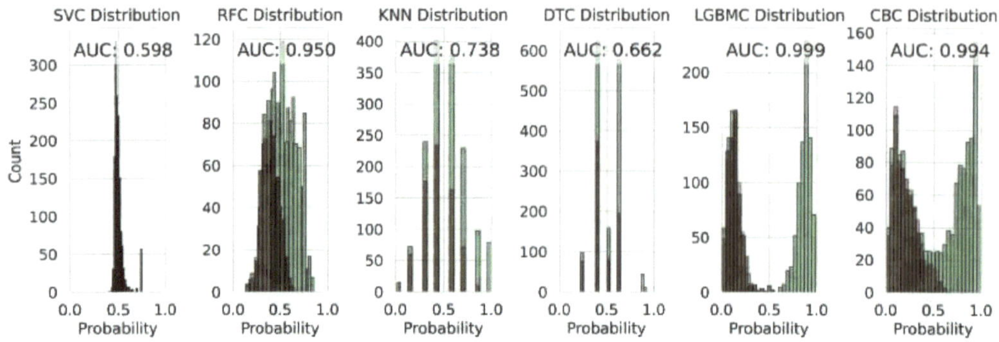

Fig. (11). Higher accuracy achieved with LGBM boosting classifier over traditional ML approaches.

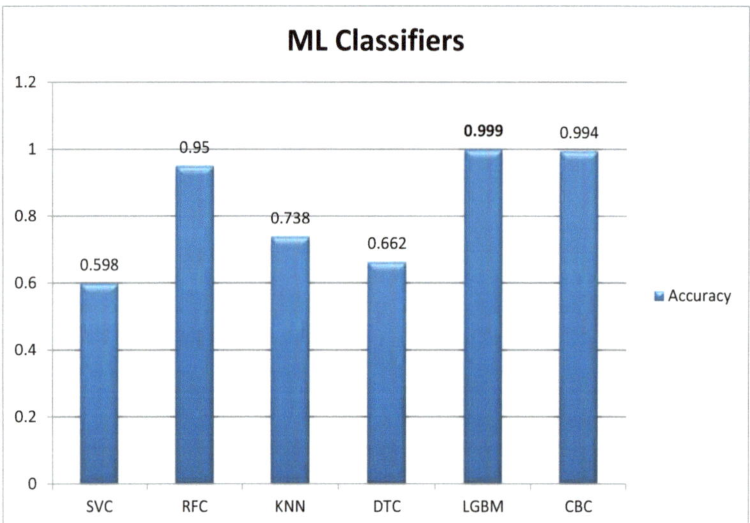

Fig. (12). Graphical representation of ML classifier with metric calculation scores.

Here, the results clearly show that the LGBM boosting machine learning classifier outperforms other classifiers, including SVC, RFC, KNN, DTC, and CBC. We have attained accuracies of 0.598 with SVC, 0.950 with RFC, 0.738 with KNN, 0.662 with DTC, 0.994 with CBC, and 0.999 with LGBM, respectively. Consequently, we believe that this work lays the groundwork for further exploration into reference and the identification of additional information from cause-event relationships, including the detection of hidden emotions or causes and the prediction of user sentiments based on related events, among other activities.

Therefore, these novel approaches to such classifiers can be utilized in upcoming studies to determine mental health issues.

CONCLUDING REMARKS

As the early diagnosis of such neurological disorders is crucial, there is no full cure available. The goal of this study is to detect disorders early, before they progress to chronic stages. For this, machine learning methods have gained popularity for detecting such diseases early. In this study, we have employed six different ML classification algorithms for analyzing mental health issues over social media networks. Among various ML classifiers, we have attained a higher accuracy of 99.9% with LGBM for the chosen Reddit dataset. This study can be useful for psychological researchers, clinical professionals, or individuals working on these techniques, as it enables early prediction of disorder symptoms by carefully observing relevant posts on these platforms. It may be said that methods based on ML have been used extensively for this kind of detection. This is due to the fact that methods with higher attained accuracy, such as SVC, RFC, DTC, KNN, LGBM, and CBC, are the most effective. Though more adaptable and dependable than the others, LGBM performs the best.

REFERENCES

[1] J. Rehm, and K.D. Shield, "Global burden of disease and the impact of mental and addictive disorders", *Curr. Psychiatry Rep.,* vol. 21, no. 2, p. 10, 2019. [http://dx.doi.org/10.1007/s11920-019-0997-0] [PMID: 30729322]

[2] E. Ortiz-Ospina, and M. Roser, "The rise of social media", *Our world data,* 2023.

[3] L. Canales, and P. Martínez-Barco, "Emotion Detection from text", *Survey (Lond.),* pp. 37-43, 2014. [http://dx.doi.org/10.3115/v1/W14-6905]

[4] A. Compare, C. Zarbo, E. Shonin, W. Van Gordon, and C. Marconi, "Emotional regulation and depression: A potential mediator between heart and mind", *Cardiovasc. Psychiatry Neurol.,* vol. 2014, pp. 1-10, 2014. [http://dx.doi.org/10.1155/2014/324374] [PMID: 25050177]

[5] Z. Li, Z. An, W. Cheng, J. Zhou, F. Zheng, and B. Hu, "MHA: a multimodal hierarchical attention model for depression detection in social media", *Heal. Inf. Sci. Syst.,* 2023. [http://dx.doi.org/10.1007/s13755-022-00197-5]

[6] WHO, *WHO Factsheet: Soil-transmitted helminth infections.* World Health Organization, 2022.

[7] M.R. Febriansyah, R. Yunanda Nicholas, and D. Suhartono, "Stress detection system for social media users", In: *Procedia Computer Science*, 2022. [http://dx.doi.org/10.1016/j.procs.2022.12.183]

[8] P.M. Doraiswamy, C. Blease, and K. Bodner, "Artificial intelligence and the future of psychiatry: Insights from a global physician survey", *Artif. Intell. Med.,* vol. 102, p. 101753, 2020. [http://dx.doi.org/10.1016/j.artmed.2019.101753] [PMID: 31980092]

[9] M. Squires, X. Tao, S. Elangovan, R. Gururajan, X. Zhou, U.R. Acharya, and Y. Li, "Deep learning and machine learning in psychiatry: a survey of current progress in depression detection, diagnosis and treatment", *Brain Inform.,* vol. 10, no. 1, p. 10, 2023. [http://dx.doi.org/10.1186/s40708-023-00188-6] [PMID: 37093301]

[10] E. Dejonckheere, E. K. Kalokerinos, B. Bastian, and P. Kuppens, *Poor emotion regulation ability mediates the link between depressive symptoms and affective bipolarity,* 2019. [http://dx.doi.org/10.1080/02699931.2018.1524747]

[11] U.A. Butt, *A review of machine learning algorithms for cloud computing security.* Electronics: Switzerland, 2020. [http://dx.doi.org/10.3390/electronics9091379]

[12] Y. Wang, Y. Zhao, J. Bian, and R. Zhang, "Detecting signals of associations between dietary supplement use and mental disorders from twitter," in *Proceedings - 2018 IEEE International Conference on Healthcare Informatics Workshops, ICHI-W 2018,* 2018. [http://dx.doi.org/10.1109/ICHI-W.2018.00016]

[13] S. H. Yadav and P. M. Manwatkar, "An approach for offensive text detection and prevention in Social Networks," in *ICIIECS 2015 - 2015 IEEE International Conference on Innovations in Information, Embedded and Communication Systems,* 2015. [http://dx.doi.org/10.1109/ICIIECS.2015.7193018]

[14] I. Syarif, N. Ningtias, and T. Badriyah, "Study on mental disorder detection *via* social media mining," in *2019 4th International Conference on Computing, Communications and Security, ICCCS 2019,* 2019. [http://dx.doi.org/10.1109/CCCS.2019.8888096]

[15] P. Glaser, J.H. Liu, M.A. Hakim, R. Vilar, and R. Zhang, "Is social media use for networking positive or negative? Offline social capital and internet addiction as mediators for the relationship between social media use and mental health", *N. Z. J. Psychol.,* 2018.

[16] D. Ostic, S.A. Qalati, B. Barbosa, S.M.M. Shah, E. Galvan Vela, A.M. Herzallah, and F. Liu, "Effects of social media use on psychological well-being: a mediated model", *Front. Psychol.,* vol. 12, p. 678766, 2021. [http://dx.doi.org/10.3389/fpsyg.2021.678766] [PMID: 34234717]

[17] I. Oyong, E. Utami, and E.T. Luthfi, "Natural language processing and lexical approach for depression symptoms screening of Indonesian twitter user", *Proceedings of 2018 10th International Conference on Information Technology and Electrical Engineering: Smart Technology for Better Society, ICITEE 2018,* 2018. [http://dx.doi.org/10.1109/ICITEED.2018.8534929]

[18] K.M. Lewin, D. Meshi, A.M. Schuster, and S.R. Cotten, *Active and passive social media use are differentially related to depressive symptoms in older adults.* Aging Ment. Heal, 2023. [http://dx.doi.org/10.1080/13607863.2022.2068133]

[19] T. Garg, and S.K. Gupta, "A hybrid stacked ensemble technique to improve classification accuracy for neurological disorder detection on reddit posts", *Proceedings - 2022 14th IEEE International Conference on Computational Intelligence and Communication Networks, CICN 2022,* 2022. [http://dx.doi.org/10.1109/CICN56167.2022.10008283]

[20] T. Garg, and S.K. Gupta, "Efficient approaches to predict neurological disorder using social networking sites", *Proceedings - 2022 IEEE 11th International Conference on Communication Systems and Network Technologies, CSNT 2022,* 2022. [http://dx.doi.org/10.1109/CSNT54456.2022.9787627]

[21] T. Garg, and S. K. Gupta, *A Novel Algorithm for Stacked Generalization Approach to Predict Neurological Disorder over Digital Footprints,* 2023. [http://dx.doi.org/10.5815/ijmecs.2023.05.05]

CHAPTER 8

Role of Government Policies and Regulations in Shaping the Landscape of Green Finance in Industry 5.0

Harshita Sharma[1] and **Swati Jain**[1,*]

[1] *Department of Commerce, Manipal University Jaipur, Jaipur, India*

Abstract: The evolution of Industry 5.0 signifies a transformative shift towards a synergistic integration of advanced technology and human creativity, prioritizing sustainability and environmental stewardship. This chapter examines the critical role of government policies and regulations in fostering the growth of green finance within the framework of Industry 5.0. As industries increasingly adopt automation, smart manufacturing, and networked ecosystems, the emphasis on sustainable practices becomes imperative. Government initiatives, through stringent environmental standards and financial incentives, mobilize capital towards green technologies, facilitating the transition to a low-carbon economy. Green finance, encompassing investments and lending aimed at enhancing environmental sustainability, plays a pivotal role in directing financial resources towards eco-friendly projects. Central banks and financial regulators contribute by incorporating sustainability into their frameworks, guiding investments towards green initiatives, and ensuring transparency and accountability in climate finance. The chapter highlights global efforts and policy measures from countries like India, China, Brazil, France, Indonesia, and Germany, showcasing their commitment to sustainable development through green finance. Despite challenges such as substantial upfront investments and regulatory hurdles, the integration of Industry 5.0 and green finance presents opportunities for innovation, enhanced resource efficiency, and reduced environmental impact. The nexus between Industry 5.0, green finance, and sustainability underscores their collective goal of promoting sustainable development. As industries continue to evolve, collaborative efforts among governments, financial institutions, and industries will be crucial in achieving a sustainable industrial ecosystem. This chapter emphasizes the importance of robust policies, financial incentives, and technological advancements in guiding the industrial sector towards a sustainable and environmentally friendly future. Nowadays, sustainability is essential, and reaching the goal of sustainability is the focus of every industry. Industry 5.0 is developing to accomplish this goal. Industry 5.0 is a human-centric strategy that essentially advances the idea of human-robot cooperation for a smart business ecosystem that enhances resource productivity and social well-being. In the framework of Industry 5.0, this chapter explores the dynamic interactions between government initiatives and the emerging field of green financing.

* **Corresponding author Swati Jain:** Department of Commerce, Manipal University Jaipur, Jaipur, India; E-mail: swatijain.22@gmail.com

Subir Gupta, Indrajit Ghosal, Keshav Kaushik & Monika Dandotiya (Eds.)

Keywords: Government regulations, Green finance, Green technology, Industry 5.0, Sustainability.

INTRODUCTION

A new necessity has developed in the dynamic environment of Industry 5.0: the peaceful coexistence of industry and environmental sustainability. Industry 5.0 is defined by the seamless integration of advanced technology and the Industrial Internet of Things (IIoT). The global shift of industries towards a more environmentally conscious model places significant emphasis on the role played by government policies and regulations in influencing the development of green finance. Within the framework of Industry 5.0, this chapter explores the dynamic interactions between government initiatives and the emerging field of green financing. Increasingly, industries are embracing automation, smart manufacturing, and networked ecosystems, which means that incorporating sustainable practices is vital. As a result, governments worldwide are developing laws and rules that not only encourage but require the incorporation of ecologically friendly methods into industrial operations. Promoting green financing encompasses a range of approaches, such as increasing investments in clean and green technologies, providing funding for natural resource-based green economies and climate-smart blue economies, and aligning public financial incentives with environmental goals. It also involves expanding green financing across different sectors, integrating environmental considerations into public sector financing decisions in line with the Sustainable Development Goals, and broadening the utilization of green bonds, among other strategies (UNEP). Green finance is crucial for channeling funds towards environmentally beneficial projects, a necessity amplified in the era of Industry 5.0. As technology becomes deeply integrated into industrial processes, it presents both opportunities and challenges for sustainable development. This chapter explores how laws and policies shape the green finance landscape within Industry 5.0. Governments play a vital role in steering industries towards sustainability by implementing stringent environmental standards and offering incentives for eco-friendly initiatives. In Industry 5.0, the convergence of advanced technologies and industry demands a financial ecosystem that supports sustainable practices. Green finance provides the necessary capital for projects that reduce environmental impact and promote long-term ecological benefits. Government regulations and policies are pivotal in fostering this ecosystem as they set clear guidelines and provide financial incentives, such as tax breaks, subsidies, and grants for green projects. By examining the impact of these laws and policies, this chapter underscores the importance of a supportive regulatory framework in advancing sustainable development. Governments' proactive measures can significantly influence industrial behavior, encouraging investment in renewable energy, clean technologies, and sustainable manufacturing practices, thereby ensuring a more environmentally friendly industrial future.

Evolution of Industry 5.0

The Industrial Revolution signifies the historic transition from agrarian and artisanal economies to industrialized societies driven by machine manufacturing. This pivotal era heralded a profound transformation in production methods, replacing manual craftsmanship with mechanized processes. It revolutionized the production of goods, fundamentally altering the economic landscape and societal structures. By harnessing the power of machinery, the Industrial Revolution propelled unprecedented levels of productivity and economic growth, laying the groundwork for modern industrialized societies.

The industrial landscape has been in a state of continual transformation since the late 18th century. This journey began with the First Industrial Revolution in the 1780s, a period characterized by the advent of mechanized production. This era harnessed the power of water, steam, and fossil fuels, laying the foundation for modern industry by transitioning from manual labor to machine-driven processes. This shift significantly increased production capacity and efficiency, setting the stage for subsequent industrial advancements.

By the 1870s, the Second Industrial Revolution had emerged, marked by the widespread adoption of electrical energy. This revolution revolutionized mass production, introducing assembly lines and enhancing manufacturing capabilities. Electricity not only powered factories but also facilitated the development of new machinery and equipment, enabling industries to produce goods at an unprecedented scale and speed. The focus during this era was on optimizing production processes and expanding industrial output to meet growing consumer demand.

The 1970s ushered in the third industrial revolution, which introduced the concept of automation through the integration of Information Technology (IT) into manufacturing. This period saw the rise of computers and digital technologies, which transformed production lines by automating repetitive tasks and improving precision and efficiency. The implementation of computer-controlled machinery and robotics marked a significant leap forward, allowing industries to streamline operations and reduce human error. The third revolution laid the groundwork for the interconnected, data-driven manufacturing environments that would follow.

The fourth industrial revolution, often referred to as Industry 4.0, built upon the foundations of its predecessor by aiming for total automation. This revolution has been characterized by significant technological breakthroughs, including the

Internet of Things (IoT), Artificial Intelligence (AI), and advanced robotics. These innovations have enabled the creation of smart factories, where machines and systems communicate and cooperate autonomously. Industry 4.0 has brought about unprecedented levels of efficiency and productivity, allowing for highly customizable and responsive manufacturing processes. However, this focus on complete automation has often come at the expense of sustainability and environmental considerations, as the primary goal has been profit maximization.

As the industrial sector continues to evolve, leaders and technology giants are already looking towards Industry 5.0, even though Industry 4.0 has not yet fully matured. Industry 5.0 represents a paradigm shift by emphasizing the fusion of technology and humanity with a strong focus on sustainability and environmental stewardship. Unlike its predecessor, which prioritized automation, Industry 5.0 seeks to balance technological advancements with human creativity and societal well-being. This new revolution envisions a collaborative relationship between humans and technology, where machines enhance human capabilities rather than replace them. One of the key aspects of Industry 5.0 is the integration of human creativity with computer intelligence. This collaboration aims to create more innovative and sustainable solutions to industrial challenges. By leveraging the unique strengths of both humans and machines, Industry 5.0 aspires to foster a more harmonious and productive industrial environment. This approach not only enhances the efficiency and effectiveness of manufacturing processes but also ensures that technological progress aligns with broader social and environmental goals. Fig. (**1**) illustrates the evolution of the industrial revolutions, highlighting the major themes of each phase. Starting from the mechanization of the first industrial revolution, the journey progresses through the electrification and mass production of the second, the automation and digitalization of the third, and the smart automation of the fourth. Industry 5.0 emerges as the next step in this progression, characterized by the convergence of human ingenuity and advanced technology with a commitment to sustainability.

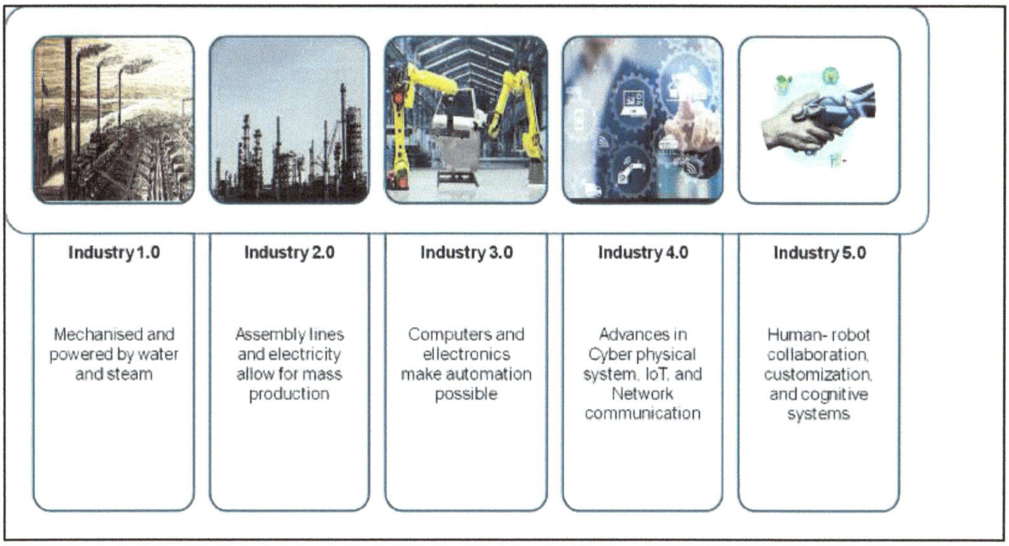

Fig. (1). Evolution of industrial revolutions. Source: Author's compilation.

Nexus between Industry 5.0, Green Finance, and Sustainability

Green Finance and Sustainability

Green finance is the umbrella term for all investments and lending that improve environmental sustainability and take environmental factors into account [1]. Green finance plays a crucial role in driving sustainability by channeling financial resources towards environmentally beneficial projects and endeavors. It enables the transition to a low-carbon economy, fosters the expansion of renewable energy sources, and encourages the adoption of sustainable practices across diverse sectors. By offering financial incentives and mechanisms, green finance incentivizes both businesses and individuals to embrace sustainability and invest in eco-friendly initiatives. This proactive approach not only mitigates environmental impacts but also contributes to long-term economic resilience and social well-being. By directing capital towards green initiatives, such as renewable energy infrastructure and sustainable agriculture, green finance catalyzes positive environmental change while simultaneously generating economic opportunities and fostering innovation [2].

Industry 5.0 and Sustainability

According to academics and business experts [3 - 5] Industry 5.0 is a human-centric strategy that essentially advances the idea of human-machine hybrid for a smart business ecosystem that enhances resource efficiency and social well-being. In its study, the European Commission addressed how Industry 5.0 is an evolution and logical continuation of the current Industry 4.0 phenomenon rather than just a replacement or an alternative. It is predicated on the idea that a technological revolution can be planned to meet societal demands and that technology can be molded to promote values [6]. Industry 5.0 champions resource efficiency, minimizes waste, and embraces the use of renewable energy. It promotes the development of sustainable manufacturing practices, integration of circular economy principles, and adoption of eco-friendly materials. By prioritizing these aspects, Industry 5.0 aims to mitigate environmental impact while fostering innovation and economic growth. This paradigm shift emphasizes the importance of sustainability in industrial processes, encouraging businesses to operate in harmony with nature and prioritizing long-term environmental stewardship [7].

Green Finance, Industry 5.0, and Sustainability

By embedding sustainability into industrial practices, Industry 5.0 strives to reduce environmental impact and promote a more sustainable future. By encouraging sustainability, GF may help the industrial sector's environmental problems. Investments will be focused on process setup, technology uptake, infrastructure that makes these technologies possible, and lastly, the use of sustainable practices to mitigate climate change [8]. Investments in green finance are essential to the shift to Industry 5.0. Green Finance Investments' primary goal is to distribute capital to initiatives or industries that help accomplish sustainability as a goal. Additionally, Industry 5.0 has a similar goal. Because Industry 5.0 is more "value-driven," environmentally sustainable technologies must be implemented. The notion of Industry 5.0 encompasses various fields, including green industrial techniques, green supply chain management, green innovation, circular economy, and net-zero economy. Industries find it difficult to adopt new technology because they need to make significant upfront investments. Investments in green finance can assist sectors in raising the money needed for this shift. Sustainability, Industry 5.0, and green finance are all related since they all want to promote sustainable development and solve environmental issues. Green finance offers the incentives and financial resources required to facilitate the industrial sector's adoption of sustainable practices and the shift to Industry 5.0. Investments in renewable energy, clean technologies, and environmentally friendly manufacturing techniques are made easier by it. Industry 5.0, on the other hand, uses automation and cutting-edge technologies to maximize resource efficiency, cut waste, and lessen environmental effects. Businesses can attain environmental sustainability and economic prosperity by incorporating green financing and Industry 5.0 principles [8]. Fig. (**2**) shows the nexus between Green Finance, Industry 5.0, and sustainability.

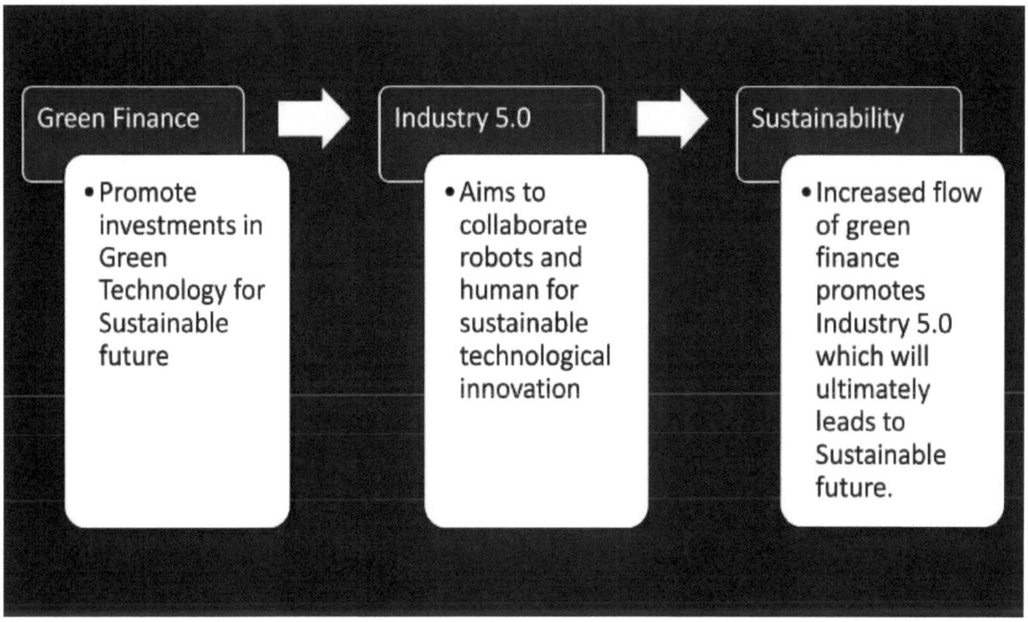

Fig. (2). Nexus between green finance, industry 5.0, and sustainability. Source: Author's compilation.

Current Research Trends on Industry 5.0

Based on available data, an analysis of trends in Industry 5.0 reveals intriguing patterns. Fig. (**3**) displays Google Trends data for the term "Industry 5.0" spanning the previous five years, from 2019 to 2023. This visual representation illustrates a consistent uptrend in searches related to Industry 5.0, indicating a burgeoning interest in this domain among the general public. Concurrently, Fig. (**4**) depicts the number of publications over the same period, utilizing the keyword "Industry 5.0," sourced from the esteemed Scopus database. Both Google Trends and Scopus are recognized as highly reliable repositories of information, lending credibility to the observed trends. The escalating trajectory of searches and publications underscores the significance of Industry 5.0 as a topic of research and inquiry. These findings suggest fertile ground for future investigations and scholarly endeavors within the realm of Industry 5.0. The increasing curiosity among individuals, as evidenced by Google searches, reflects a growing awareness and curiosity about the concept's implications. Similarly, the expanding body of academic literature signals a concerted effort by researchers to delve deeper into the nuances of Industry 5.0 and its potential ramifications across various sectors. The convergence of these trends not only validates the relevance of Industry 5.0 in contemporary discourse but also underscores its multidisciplinary nature, warranting exploration from diverse perspectives.

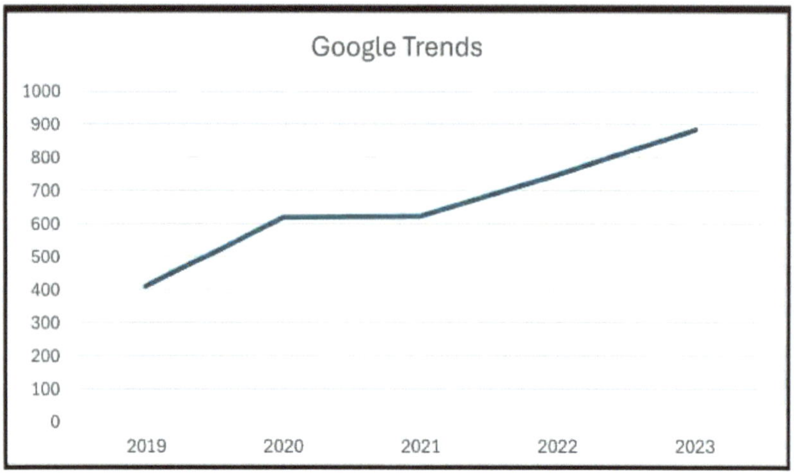

Fig. (3). Statistics of google trends from 2019 to 2023. Source: Scopus database.

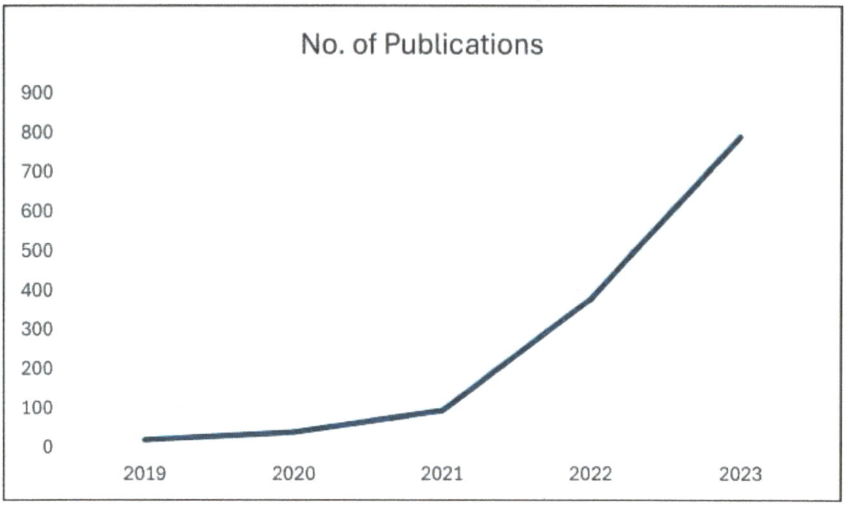

Fig. (4). No. of publications from 2019 to 2023. Source: Google trends database.

As such, these insights pave the way for future research initiatives aimed at unraveling the complexities, challenges, and opportunities inherent in the transition towards Industry 5.0. By leveraging these robust datasets, researchers can chart a course for innovative inquiry and contribute to the advancement of knowledge in this transformative field.

Role of Policy Framework for the Development of Green Finance

A nation's financial backbone, the central bank, assumes pivotal roles, such as managing reserves, enforcing regulations, issuing currency, overseeing banking, and implementing monetary policy. Beyond these traditional responsibilities, there's a growing imperative for central banks to embrace environmental sustainability. It is crucial for financial regulators and central banks to integrate sustainability into their policy frameworks. This entails acknowledging the interconnectedness of economic and environmental factors, fostering sustainable practices within financial institutions, and guiding investments towards environmentally friendly initiatives. The incorporation of sustainability into central banking practices not only aligns with broader societal goals but also acknowledges the significant influence financial institutions wield in shaping environmental outcomes. By prioritizing sustainability within their mandates, central banks can contribute meaningfully to addressing pressing global challenges and promoting a more resilient and equitable financial system for future generations. According to previous studies [9, 10], 48% of the 135 central banks do not have any sustainability goals. Central banks can steer investments towards environmentally friendly or sustainable projects using a wide range of financial tools. Because the guidelines of each central bank are followed by the entire banking system in a country, central bank policies can incentivize banks to allocate their loans towards certain projects. A central bank is not doing its job properly if it ignores climate danger. Appropriate regulations for disclosure are crucial for financial institutions to accurately estimate the effects of climate change and natural disasters. As a key component of developing a response to climate risk, the Financial Stability Board's Task Force on Climate-Related Financial Disclosures (TCFD) addresses disclosure requirements, as misallocation or mispricing of assets can eventually cause abrupt price corrections in financial markets. This understanding stems from the understanding that financial stability is affected when financial institutions' risk exposure is not disclosed [11].

Some of the ways identified where policy measures can help to overcome green finance barriers:

a. Clarifying the notion of "green" involves establishing clear green principles and indicators. This means defining what qualifies as environmentally sustainable or beneficial within financial contexts. By creating standardized criteria, stakeholders can better understand and assess the environmental impact of financial products and investments. This clarity fosters confidence among investors, encourages the allocation of capital towards genuinely green initiatives, and facilitates the development of green finance markets.
b. Implementing appropriate and consistent disclosure requirements for financial and environmental risks addresses a key barrier to the growth of green finance: a lack of transparency. Transparency helps identify and mitigate potential risks associated with environmental factors, which in turn enhances market efficiency and promotes sustainable investment practices.

c. A mature and well-structured market is essential for the success of green finance instruments. An underdeveloped market can lead to securities with mismatched maturities, meaning that financial products designed to fund long-term, environmentally beneficial projects might be financed through short-term instruments. This mismatch can create instability and hinder the growth of green finance. A mature market provides the necessary infrastructure, liquidity, and investor confidence to support a diverse range of green financial products with appropriate maturities and risk profiles.
d. Political obstacles to the expansion of green finance can be overcome with the establishment of the right national and international regulatory frameworks. These frameworks should provide incentives for green investments, such as tax breaks or subsidies, while also imposing regulations that discourage environmentally harmful practices. Additionally, clear and consistent regulations across borders foster a conducive environment for international cooperation and investment in green projects. By aligning political and regulatory efforts with sustainability goals, governments can unlock the full potential of green finance to address environmental challenges effectively [12].

Green Finance Measures Adopted by Different Countries

India

a. To support the nation's commitment to net-zero emissions by 2070, the Indian Prime Minister declared in February 2022 that one target area of the Union Budget for FY 2022–2023 will be boosting energy transition and climate action. According to the Economic Affairs Secretary and Minister of Finance, sovereign green bonds with a lengthy maturity period and a rupee-dominated predominance would be issued as part of the government financing plan to raise funds for green projects.
b. The RBI released a discussion paper titled Climate Risk and Sustainable Finance on July 27, 2022, with the goal of creating a plan that adheres to global best practices for reducing the negative effects of climate change. In addition to strategy, the paper covers the following topics: (i) How Regulated Entities (REs) can identify and evaluate vulnerabilities in REs using forward-looking technologies like climate scenario analysis and stress testing, (ii) general guidelines for all REs regarding governance, strategy, and risk management, and (iii) financial disclosure and reporting related to climate risk for REs.

China

a. A national carbon emissions pricing plan was introduced by the Ministry of Environment and Ecology of China, with effect from February 1, 2021, as part of the country's efforts to fulfill its 2060 carbon neutrality target. According to the regulations, all businesses in particular industries that emit more than 26,000 mt of CO_2 equivalent per year are required to manage and report their carbon emissions.

b. The Shenzhen Municipal People's Government published a set of laws in October 2020 to oversee the growth of local green finance. The regulations mandated the implementation of a green financial management system for key financial institutions, which took effect on March 1, 2021.
c. To assist China's carbon neutrality targets, firms listed on the STAR Market are required by the Shanghai Stock Exchange (SSE) to include ESG-related information in their annual reports as of January 2022. Stand-alone reports on sustainability, social responsibility, or ESG must be released when needed.

Brazil

a. The "Sustainability" agenda, which was introduced by Brazil's central bank, aims to further integrate environmental and climate-related concerns into the bank's lending standards, stress testing, and management of currency reserves.
b. The Brazilian Superintendence of Private Insurance (SUSEP) implemented sustainability regulations for capitalization companies, insurance companies, pension funds, and local reinsurers in June 2022. The guidance pertains to the management of various sustainability and climate risks that companies may encounter. These risks include physical climate risks, climate transition risks, and climate risks related to litigation. Liability insurance claims or direct actions against supervised parties may arise from inadequate management of physical or transition climate risks.

France

a. To support its fossil fuel exclusion policy, the Banque de France released a new responsible investing strategy in January 2021 for its own investments. Accordingly, by the end of 2024, the Banque de France will completely restrict all businesses, regardless of how small, from engaging in any coal-related activity.
b. Agence France Tresor announced in March 2021 the issuance of the 2nd French Sovereign Green Bond, which has a 23-year maturity. The €7 billion in bonds were issued with the intention of funding state budget expenditures on biodiversity preservation, pollution control, climate change adaptation, and mitigation in accordance with the Energy Transition and Green Growth Act and France's pledge to carry out the Paris Agreement.
c. France's 2015 Energy Transition Law, which only addressed climate objectives in non-financial reporting by investors, was updated by the 2019 Law on Climate and Energy. The fresh law for 2019 additionally considers "the

preservation of the biodiversity of the ecosystems and the natural resources, in particular the participation in the objective of net-zero artificialization and the use of renewable energy."

Indonesia

a. The Sustainable Finance Roadmap Phase II for 2021–2025 was prepared by the Indonesian Financial Services Authority (OJK) in November 2021. With the creation of a green taxonomy, the integration of ESG into risk management, the creation of green scheme stories, innovation in sustainable financial products and services, as well as the creation of a national communication plan for sustainable finance, Phase II aims to expedite the adoption of ESG elements in the nation.
b. The Republic of Indonesia released a 500-million-euro SDG bond in September 2021. To assist the Republic in achieving the SDGs of the United Nations, the SDG bond was categorized under the "SDGs Government Securities Framework," which was released in August 2021 and lists "eligible expenditures" in the green, blue, and social-focus categories.
c. The Republic of Indonesia announced in May 2022 that it would be issuing USD 3.25 billion in Green Sukuk, making it the largest Indonesian transaction yet to be released onto the global Sukuk market. Among them, USD 1.75 billion with a 5-year maturity and USD 1.5 billion with a 10-year maturity—known as Wakala Sukuk—were issued. These Sukuk mature in 2027 and 2032, respectively.

Germany

a. The German government's federal cabinet approved the country's first sustainable finance strategy in May 2021. The approach aims to address the climate risks that are becoming more significant for the financial sector, while simultaneously mobilizing the investments that are desperately required for climate action and sustainability.
b. In September 2020, the Federal Republic of Germany's Finance Agency introduced a 10-year green bond. The Green Bond Framework was published by the Federal Ministry of Finance prior to the issuance. These securities are intended to improve Germany's standing in the field of sustainable finance while also increasing the transparency of the nation's "green" budget expenditures.

Table **1** presents real-world examples and the policy implications of various initiatives undertaken by different countries. These initiatives highlight how diverseapproaches can lead to significant changes in the growth of green financing globally.

Table 1. Policy implications and real-world examples of green finance initiatives.

Country	Initiatives	Case Examples	Policy Implications
India	1. Issuance of Sovereign Green Bonds (FY 2022-2023). 2. RBI's Climate Risk and Sustainable Finance Paper.	- The Indian government issued its first sovereign green bonds in 2023, focusing on renewable energy and sustainable infrastructure projects. - RBI's guidelines are followed by Regulated Entities (REs) to assess climate risks.	- Supports India's 2070 net-zero target. - Enhances transparency and accountability in India's green finance sector.
China	1. National carbon pricing mechanism. 2. Shenzhen's green finance regulations. 3. STAR Market's ESG disclosure requirements for listed companies.	- Over 2,000 companies now report emissions under China's national ETS. - Shenzhen mandates green finance practices in local financial institutions. - STAR Market-listed companies disclose ESG impacts annually.	- Promotes carbon neutrality by 2060. - Encourages transparency and environmental responsibility among Chinese firms, supporting investor trust.
Brazil	1. Central Bank's "Sustainability" agenda. 2. SUSEP's climate risk regulations for insurers and pension funds.	- The Central Bank incorporates environmental standards in monetary policy and stress testing. - SUSEP issued climate-focused guidelines for insurance firms, which now report climate-related risks in annual disclosures.	- Promotes resilience against climate risks within Brazil's financial sector. - Strengthens environmental risk management within insurance markets.
France	1. Banque de France's fossil fuel exclusion policy. 2. Issuance of Sovereign Green Bond. 3. 2019 Law on Climate and Energy for biodiversity protection.	- Banque de France has divested from coal. - A €7 billion green bond was issued to finance biodiversity projects. - The Energy Transition and Green Growth Act mandates biodiversity and climate considerations in financing projects.	- Supports France's commitment to fossil fuel reduction. - Ensures biodiversity conservation is central in state-funded projects.
Indonesia	1. Sustainable Finance Roadmap Phase II 2021-2025. 2. SDG Bond issuance. 3. Green Sukuk issuance for global markets.	- Indonesia's OJK enforces ESG practices across banks and financial institutions. - €500 million SDG bond and $3.25 billion Green Sukuk fund UN SDG-aligned projects, such as renewable energy and infrastructure.	- Sets a roadmap for Indonesia's financial sector to adopt ESG practices by 2025. - Aims to attract international green investment.
Germany	1. Sustainable finance strategy focusing on climate risks. 2. Green Bond Framework and issuance.	- Germany issued its first green bond in 2020, raising €6.5 billion to fund projects in sustainable energy, transport, and environmental protection.	- Aligns Germany's financial sector with sustainability goals. - Increases transparency of green financing allocation for national and global investors.

Impact of Government Policies and Regulations on Green Finance

Government policies and regulations can exert various impacts on green finance. Among these are:

a. *Mobilizing Capital for Sustainable Investments:* Government policies and regulations on green finance play a crucial role in mobilizing capital by creating an investment-friendly environment for sustainable projects. These policies offer financial incentives, such as tax breaks, subsidies, and grants, to promote investments in green technologies and initiatives. By providing guarantees or insurance mechanisms, governments help reduce the perceived risks for investors, making green projects more attractive and financially viable. Furthermore, government policies stimulate the development of green financial markets by establishing standards and guidelines for green investments, thus creating a transparent and reliable market for sustainable finance. These policies also foster international cooperation and collaboration by aligning with global sustainability goals, thereby attracting international investments and facilitating participation in global sustainable development initiatives. Green finance policies encourage long-term planning and investment in sustainable projects. Governments can set targets and timelines for reducing carbon emissions, promoting renewable energy, and enhancing environmental performance. These policies provide certainty and stability for investors, enabling them to make informed decisions and allocate capital towards sustainable investments.
b. *Fostering Innovation and Technology Development:* Government policies aimed at enhancing green technology innovation cover a broad range of areas, including environmental protection, technology, talent, trade, and finance. These policies foster an environment conducive to innovation by offering subsidies, financial support, patent protection, and clear policy signals to stimulate research and development in green technologies. This helps to alleviate the financial constraints faced by industries engaged in green innovation, enabling the creation of new products, services, and processes that benefit the environment. Moreover, government policies and green finance support the diffusion of innovative technologies by strengthening markets and facilitating the transfer of technology. This involves investing in research and development, supporting commercialization, and promoting the dissemination of technology, all of which are crucial for the deployment and widespread adoption of new technologies and innovations. Government policies and green finance also play a significant role in environmental sustainability by encouraging the adoption and application of green technologies. By developing robust environmental policies and promoting the use of green

technology, governments can significantly reduce their ecological footprints and tackle environmental challenges. Additionally, governments can promote innovation by enhancing international partnerships and collaboration. Through cooperative efforts, countries can share knowledge, resources, and best practices, leading to the development of innovative solutions to global environmental issues. Governments can also support international cooperation in research and development, thereby enhancing scientific research and technological capabilities.

c. *Enhancing Transparency and Accountability:* International Financial Institutions (IFIs) such as the World Bank and the International Monetary Fund (IMF) are pivotal in promoting transparency in climate finance and mitigating corruption risks. Transparency in climate finance ensures that funds are allocated and utilized efficiently, with an open and accountable decision-making process. Green finance initiatives focus on reducing corruption risks in climate finance by implementing transparent procurement systems and strengthening national laws, thereby increasing transparency and accountability in fund allocation and management. This, in turn, boosts investor confidence in climate funds. Governments also invest substantial public funds in various services and infrastructure. Ensuring transparency and accountability in public sector spending is crucial to guarantee the efficient and effective use of these funds. Public sector finance professionals play a vital role in offering decision-useful insights and information to support transparent decision-making. Sustainable finance integrates Environmental, Social, and Governance (ESG) factors into investment decisions. By incorporating ESG considerations, green finance encourages long-term investments in sustainable economic activities and projects, thereby enhancing transparency and accountability in the financial sector. Transparency and accountability are further strengthened when governments engage with stakeholders, including civil society and progressive businesses, by promoting stronger safeguards, preventing mismanagement, and ensuring information availability, society as a whole benefits. Fiscal transparency is essential for enhancing government effectiveness and accountability, as it involves providing the public with adequate information on the activities of financial agencies, thereby increasing the credibility of their actions and reducing the potential for moral hazard.

Top Countries in Green Technology Adoption

Fig. (**5**) highlights the countries prepared for Green Tech transitions. According to data released by the United Nations Conference on Trade and Development (UNCTAD), the United States, Sweden, Singapore, Switzerland, and the Netherlands are the top five countries most prepared to use, adopt, or adapt to frontier technologies crucial for the green tech transition. The ranking evaluated

166 countries based on their preparedness across five indicators: ICT, skills, Industry, Research and Development (R&D), and finance. Each country's final score was determined by summing its ranks across these indicators. For instance, the U.S. scored a total of 49, ranking 2nd in R&D, 11th in ICT, 18th in skills, and 16th in industry, and 2nd in finance.

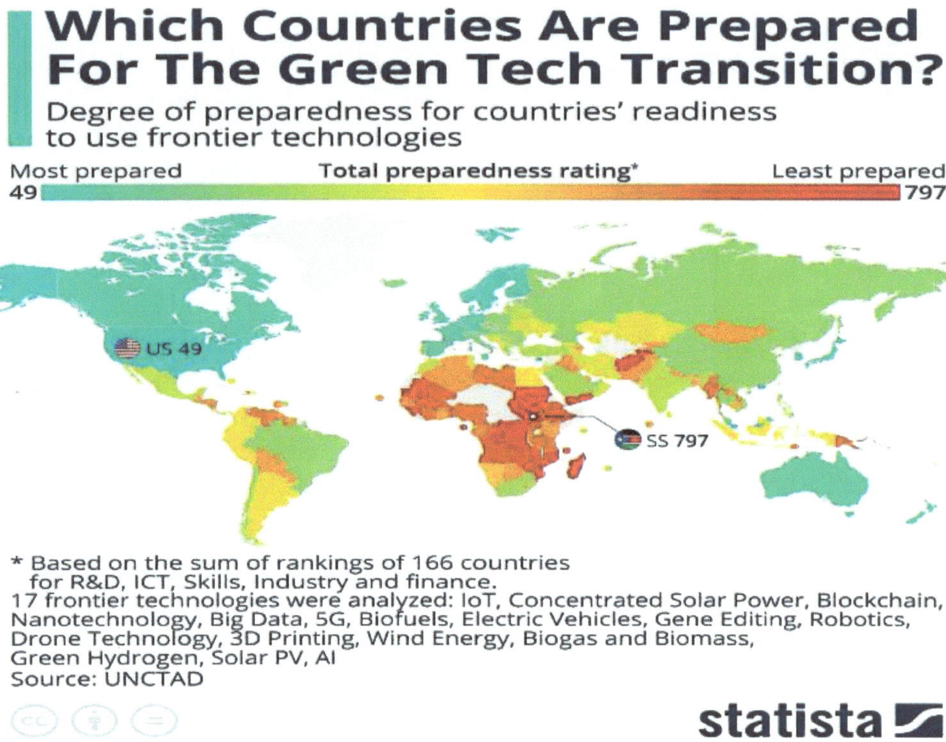

Fig. (5). Countries prepared for green tech transition. Source: Statista.

At the bottom of the list were Guinea, the Democratic Republic of Congo, Gambia, Guinea-Bissau, and South Sudan, each ranking low across all five categories. The data reveals a clear divide between high-income and lower-income countries, with Latin America, the Caribbean, and sub-Saharan Africa being the least prepared to leverage frontier technologies. This puts them at a significant risk of missing out on current technological advancements. Despite its notable capacity for producing and innovating frontier technologies, China ranked lower than expected at 35th place, mainly due to urban-rural disparities in internet coverage and broadband speed. Among the BRICS nations, Brazil was ranked 40th, India 46th, and South Africa 56th. Some Asian countries performed better than anticipated, such as the Philippines (57th), India (55th), and Vietnam (45th). India's actual ranking exceeded its projected ranking based on per capita income by 67 places, attributed to increased investment in infrastructure, improved technical skills, and a supportive business environment, according to UNCTAD researchers.

Challenges in the Adoption of Green Finance

Green finance, which involves funding public and private investments in environmentally friendly projects and implementing supportive policies, faces several regulatory and policy challenges. These challenges can impede the adoption and growth of green finance. Key challenges include:

Regulatory Gaps: Financial firms aiming to promote green finance in emerging markets often encounter significant regulatory gaps. These gaps manifest as the absence of specific regulations or guidelines tailored to the unique characteristics and requirements of green finance. The regulatory environment in many emerging markets may not yet have evolved to encompass the complexities of green finance, which can create barriers for financial institutions trying to innovate in this space. For example, there may be a lack of frameworks that define what qualifies as a green investment, how to measure the environmental impact of such investments, or guidelines for reporting and transparency. Without clear regulations, financial firms face uncertainty and increased risk. This uncertainty can deter investment and slow the growth of green finance initiatives.

Lack of Standardization: The green finance sector currently suffers from a lack of standardization, which impedes the consistent application of green finance practices. The absence of clear ground rules and standardized frameworks creates uncertainty for investors, financial institutions, and other stakeholders. This lack of standardization can result in varying definitions of what constitutes a green investment, differing methodologies for measuring environmental impact, and inconsistent reporting practices. For instance, without standardized criteria for green bonds or loans, it becomes difficult to ensure that the funds raised are genuinely used for environmentally beneficial projects. This can undermine investor confidence and hinder the growth of green finance markets. Additionally, the lack of standardized metrics for measuring environmental impact can make it challenging to compare the effectiveness of different green finance initiatives. To overcome these challenges, it is essential to develop and adopt international standards for green finance.

Transition Risks: Transition risks are a significant concern in the realm of green finance. These risks refer to the potential financial impacts associated with transitioning to a low-carbon economy. Investors may be hesitant to engage in green finance due to uncertainties about the financial viability of green investments and the potential impact of future environmental regulations on their profitability. For example, investments in renewable energy projects may face risks related to changes in government policies, technological advancements, or shifts in market demand. If regulatory frameworks are not stable or predictable, investors may fear that their investments could be adversely affected by sudden changes in environmental policies or economic conditions. This uncertainty can make green investments seem riskier compared to traditional investments, potentially deterring capital flow into the green finance sector. To mitigate transition risks, it is essential to create a stable and predictable policy environment that supports long-term investments in green projects.

Coordination of Policies: Effective coordination of financial, environmental, and regulatory policies is crucial for the successful adoption of green finance. Better coordination can help align policies and create a supportive environment for green finance initiatives, ensuring that financial resources are directed towards environmentally beneficial projects. To achieve effective policy coordination, it is essential to establish mechanisms for collaboration and dialogue among stakeholders. This can include creating interagency task forces, developing cross-sectoral policy frameworks, and engaging in international cooperation to share best practices and lessons learned. By fostering a collaborative approach, it is possible to create a coherent and supportive policy environment that promotes the growth of green finance and facilitates the transition to a sustainable, low-carbon economy.

Incentives for Adoption: In emerging markets, local firms may lack sufficient incentives to adopt ambitious climate goals and engage in green finance. Poor incentives can hinder the growth of green finance in these markets, as firms may not see the immediate benefits of investing in sustainable practices or technologies. For instance, firms in emerging markets may face challenges such as limited access to finance, a lack of technical expertise, or inadequate infrastructure for supporting green projects. Without strong financial incentives or support from government policies, these firms may be reluctant to invest in green finance initiatives. Additionally, the perceived risks and uncertainties associated with green investments can further discourage adoption.

Financial Concerns: Financial concerns also pose a significant barrier to the growth of green finance. Some investors may worry that green investments will not be as lucrative in the short term compared to other investment options. This concern is influenced by the fact that green finance is often heavily dependent on government policies and regulations, which can create additional layers of uncertainty and risk. For instance, green projects may require substantial upfront investments with longer payback periods, making them less attractive to investors seeking quick returns. Additionally, the financial performance of green investments can be influenced by factors such as changes in government incentives, shifts in consumer preferences, or advancements in technology. These uncertainties can make it challenging to predict the financial outcomes of green projects, further deterring investment.

Future Research Directions

Both Green Finance and Industry 5.0 are burgeoning research domains capturing significant attention among academics and scholars. The current publication trends underscore a steady rise in the number of scholarly works in both areas annually. However, there remains a notable dearth of research examining the combined impacts of these two spheres. Future investigations could delve deeper into this intersection. Both Green Finance and Industry 5.0 share a common goal of fostering a sustainable future. Hence, forthcoming research endeavors could focus on crafting frameworks for assessing funds allocated by financial institutions and governments towards the advancement of green technologies. Furthermore, there is a ripe opportunity for research to explore diverse avenues for enhancing the flow of green finance, thereby propelling the Industry 5.0 revolution forward. By elucidating the synergies between Green Finance and Industry 5.0, researchers can contribute to a deeper understanding of how financial mechanisms can fuel the transition towards environmentally conscious industrial practices. Such inquiries hold immense potential to drive innovation, inform policymaking, and accelerate progress towards a more sustainable and technologically advanced future.

CONCLUDING REMARKS

The advent of Industry 5.0 marks a significant transformation in the industrial landscape, characterized by the harmonious integration of advanced technology and human creativity to promote sustainability and environmental stewardship. This shift represents an evolution beyond the previous industrial revolutions, each of which focused on enhancing production efficiency through mechanical, electrical, and digital advancements. Industry 5.0, however, places a premium on the coexistence of technological innovation and environmental consciousness, reflecting a more human-centric approach to industrial development. Government policies and regulations are pivotal in shaping the trajectory of Industry 5.0, particularly in the realm of green finance. By setting stringent environmental standards and providing incentives for eco-friendly initiatives, governments can steer industries towards more sustainable practices. These policies are essential for mobilizing capital towards green technologies and ensuring that the financial ecosystem supports sustainable development goals. For instance, investments in renewable energy, clean technologies, and environmentally friendly manufacturing techniques are facilitated by government-backed financial incentives, including tax breaks, subsidies, and grants. This not only helps in mitigating the financial risks associated with green projects but also encourages long-term investment in sustainability.

Green finance plays an important role in the transition to a low-carbon economy. It encompasses all investments and lending activities aimed at improving environmental sustainability by considering environmental factors. Green finance is instrumental in advancing sustainability by directing financial resources to projects that are environmentally beneficial. This includes promoting the development of renewable energy sources, supporting the adoption of sustainable practices across various sectors, and facilitating the shift to a low-carbon economy. The financial incentives and mechanisms provided by green finance motivate businesses and individuals to embrace sustainable practices and invest in eco-friendly projects. By integrating Environmental, Social, and Governance (ESG) factors into investment decisions, green finance promotes long-term investments in sustainable economic activities and projects, thereby enhancing transparency and accountability in the financial sector. Central banks and financial regulators have a significant role in fostering a sustainable financial ecosystem. By incorporating sustainability into their policy frameworks, they can guide investments towards environmentally friendly projects. This involves the use of various financial tools to incentivize banks to allocate their loans towards green projects. Moreover, appropriate regulations for disclosure are crucial for financial institutions to accurately estimate the effects of climate change and natural disasters. This enhances the credibility of their actions and reduces the potential for moral hazard. Ensuring transparency in the allocation and utilization of climate finance funds is essential for gaining investor confidence and promoting accountability in fund management.

Various countries have adopted specific measures to promote green finance and support their transition towards sustainable development. For instance, India has committed to net-zero emissions by 2070 and has introduced sovereign green bonds to raise funds for green projects. China's national carbon emissions pricing plan and the inclusion of ESG-related information in annual reports reflect its efforts to meet its 2060 carbon neutrality target. Brazil's central bank has integrated environmental and climate-related concerns into its lending standards, while France has implemented policies to restrict coal-related activities and issued sovereign green bonds to fund climate initiatives. Indonesia's Sustainable Finance Roadmap and Germany's sustainable finance strategy further illustrate the global commitment to integrating sustainability into financial and industrial practices. Despite these efforts, significant challenges remain in the adoption of green finance and sustainable practices. One major obstacle is the need for substantial upfront investments to adopt new technologies. Investments in green finance can assist sectors in raising the necessary funds for this transition. Additionally, there is a need for a mature and well-structured market for green finance instruments to ensure the availability of long-term financing options for sustainable projects. Another challenge is the political and regulatory environment, which can either facilitate or hinder the growth of green finance. A supportive national and international regulatory framework is crucial for overcoming these barriers. This includes establishing green principles and indicators, ensuring transparency through appropriate disclosure requirements, and fostering a market environment that supports the development and use of green finance instruments.

The integration of advanced technologies in Industry 5.0 offers both opportunities and challenges for sustainable development. On one hand, technologies such as automation, artificial intelligence, and the Industrial Internet of Things (IIoT) can enhance resource efficiency, reduce waste, and minimize environmental impact. On the other hand, the initial costs and the need for significant investments can be a barrier for industries to adopt these technologies. Green finance plays a crucial role in bridging this gap by providing the necessary capital and financial support.

The future of Industry 5.0 and green finance is promising, with the potential to drive significant advancements in sustainability and environmental stewardship. As industries continue to embrace automation, smart manufacturing, and networked ecosystems, the incorporation of sustainable practices will become increasingly vital. Governments and financial institutions will need to continue developing and implementing policies and regulations that support this transition. The collaborative efforts of governments, industries, and financial institutions will be essential in creating a sustainable industrial ecosystem. By fostering innovation, promoting transparency, and mobilizing capital for green technologies, the goals of Industry 5.0 and sustainable development can be achieved. The continued evolution of policies and regulations will play a critical role in guiding industries towards a more sustainable and environmentally friendly path. In conclusion, the transition to Industry 5.0 and the promotion of green finance are pivotal in achieving sustainable development and addressing global environmental challenges. The integration of advanced technologies with sustainable practices, supported by robust government policies and financial incentives, will drive the industrial sector towards a more sustainable future. The collaborative efforts of all stakeholders, including governments, financial institutions, industries, and civil society, are essential in realizing the full potential of Industry 5.0 and green finance for a sustainable and prosperous world.

REFERENCES

[1] F. Longo, A. Padovano, and S. Umbrello, "Value-oriented and ethical technology engineering in industry 5.0: A human-centric perspective for the design of the factory of the future", *Appl. Sci. (Basel),* vol. 10, no. 12, p. 4182, 2020. [http://dx.doi.org/10.3390/app10124182]

[2] F.S. Board, "Phase 1 Report of the Task Force on Climate-related Financial Disclosures", 2016.

[3] J. He, W. Iqbal, and F. Su, "Nexus between renewable energy investment, green finance, and sustainable development: Role of industrial structure and technical innovations", *Renew. Energy,* vol. 210, pp. 715-724, 2023. [http://dx.doi.org/10.1016/j.renene.2023.04.010]

[4] J. Müller, *Enabling technologies for Industry 5.0—results of a workshop with Europe's technology leaders.* Directorate-General for Research and Innovation, 2020.

[5] K. Berensmann, U. Volz, I. Alloisio, C. Bak, A. Bhattacharya, and G. Leipold, *Fostering sustainable global growth through green finance–what role for the G20*, 2017.

[6] K.Q. Zhang, H.H. Chen, L.Z. Tang, and S. Qiao, "Green finance, innovation and the energy-environment-climate nexus", *Front. Environ. Sci.,* vol. 10, p. 879681, 2022. [http://dx.doi.org/10.3389/fenvs.2022.879681]

[7] R. Sindhwani, S. Afridi, A. Kumar, A. Banaitis, S. Luthra, and P.L. Singh, "Can industry 5.0 revolutionize the wave of resilience and social value creation? A multi-criteria framework to analyze enablers", *Technol. Soc.,* vol. 68, p. 101887, 2022. [http://dx.doi.org/10.1016/j.techsoc.2022.101887]

[8] S. Dikau, and U. Volz, "Central banking, climate change and green finance", 2018.

[9] S.K. Johl, and M.A. Toha, "The nexus between proactive eco-innovation and firm financial performance: a circular economy perspective", *Sustainability (Basel),* vol. 13, no. 11, p. 6253, 2021. [http://dx.doi.org/10.3390/su13116253]

[10] U. Volz, "Fostering green finance for sustainable development in Asia, 2018. [http://dx.doi.org/10.4324/9781315543222-27]

[11] United Nations Environment Programme, "Emissions Gap Report 2022: The Closing Window. Climate Crisis Calls for Rapid Transformation of Societies," UN, 2022.

[12] Y. Lu, H. Zheng, S. Chand, W. Xia, Z. Liu, X. Xu, L. Wang, Z. Qin, and J. Bao, "Outlook on human-centric manufacturing towards Industry 5.0", *J. Manuf. Syst.,* vol. 62, pp. 612-627, 2022. [http://dx.doi.org/10.1016/j.jmsy.2022.02.001]

CHAPTER 9

Understanding Customer Emotion of Private Label Brands of Men's Clothing: Sentiment Analysis Using Natural Language Processing Techniques

Rabin Mazumder[1,*], **Pritha Ghosh**[2] and **Dipak Saha**[3]

[1] *Department of Business Administration, Institute of Engineering & Management, University of Engineering & Management, Kolkata, West Bengal, India*

[2] *University of Engineering & Management, Kolkata, West Bengal, India*

[3] *Department of Business Management, Institute of Engineering & Management, University of Engineering & Management, Kolkata, West Bengal, India*

Abstract: The internet has vast amounts of unstructured data. It can be very difficult to analyse these data and be unable to extract meaningful results from them. Due to the abundance of opinionated data on the internet, where people express a wide range of emotions, including happiness, sadness, disappointment, and anger, opinion mining has become increasingly popular. Researchers often use opinion mining and sentiment analysis to understand consumers' attitudes and emotions, which helps evaluate how effectively different brands are performing.

The article employs the Lexicon-based approach to gather, preprocess, and analyze product review data from Amazon using R. The purpose of the study is to determine how customers feel about Amazon's private-label menswear, both positively and negatively. The study considered two brands: Symbol and Inkast. Sentiment scores and emotional variance estimate the outcomes of the Lexicon-based sentiment, which produces a classification of the emotions present in the text. According to the research, consumers are generally confident in their ability to trust Amazon's men's private clothing brands. Compared to Inkast, people prefer buying under the Symbol brand. Sentiment analysis enhances business expansion and customer experience.

Keywords: Amazon, Men's clothing, Natural language processing, Private labels, Sentiment analysis.

* **Corresponding author Rabin Mazumder:** Department of Business Administration, Institute of Engineering & Management, University of Engineering & Management, Kolkata, West Bengal, India;
E-mails: rabin.mazumder@iem.edu.in; rabin.mazumder@gmail.com

Subir Gupta, Indrajit Ghosal, Keshav Kaushik & Monika Dandotiya (Eds.)

INTRODUCTION

Human language generation and human language understanding are two different branches of Natural Language Processing (NLP). Language understanding is often considered more difficult because natural language is inherently ambiguous and context-dependent. However, language generation presents a different kind of challenge: it produces rational, contextually appropriate, and natural-sounding text despite the same underlying ambiguity in human language. These challenges span multiple NLP applications, including speech-recognition annotation, machine translation, question-answering systems, and automated literature review tools [1]. Emotion recognition and sentiment analysis are the two significant aspects of natural language processing. Recognising an emotion and analysing a sentiment are similar but not the same, and hence cannot be used interchangeably. Sentiment Analysis can evaluate whether the data is positive, negative, or neutral.

On the other hand, Emotion detection can recognize different human emotions, such as anger, happiness, and depression. According to Munezero *et al.*, the terms "emotion detection," "affective computing," "emotion analysis," and "emotion identification" are used interchangeably [2]. Now that internet connections are prevalent, people have started using social media as their preferred outlet for expressing emotions.

Everyone willingly shares their opinions, disagreements, and passions about a wide range of subjects on social media. Further, several customers leave feedback and reviews on various products and services on numerous e-commerce sites. The digital transformation underway in virtually every business and industry generates vast amounts of structured and unstructured data. Making sense out of unstructured data to make it usable and relevant for organizations to solve business problems is indeed an immense task [3]. From a commercial perspective, sellers often advertise on Facebook, Instagram, YouTube, or Twitter and gain valuable consumer response as direct feedback to their products [4]. Real-time user feedback is helpful to consumers who may be looking for additional information before purchasing a product or service. It is something corporate marketers use to monitor customer satisfaction and the competition. Sentiment analysis can use the viewpoints of the customers to adjust the marketers' goods or services accordingly.

In response to the rise of social media, investors can communicate with each other in the stock market much faster and more conveniently [5]. Investor emotions can lead to herd behavior in investment decisions, which can spread and magnify across the network [6], facilitating informational cascades that may exacerbate stock market manipulation. According to Bhardwaj *et al.* (2015), mood and emotion analysis has altered the way that we conduct business [7]. Concurrently, Twitter and other social media platforms have become primary sources of health information for both citizens and oncology healthcare professionals.

For example, when they used Google Trends data and analyzed the sitelinks of religion-related search results, the authors found that people discussed their opinions on religion during COVID-19 [8]. They were "distressed with the patient's mental health, being separate from their loved ones. Enthusiasm, ability, and zest for what they focus on, along with professional qualifications, augment a teacher's experience. Student feedback: One way a teacher can improve their methods is to receive immediate feedback on students' satisfaction [9]. It's tough to watch all that open-ended text feedback, and even tougher to manually grasp generalizations. Based on sentiment and emotion analyses, teachers or organisations may take remedial action. Students & parents frequently search the web for information on possible schools, courses, and instructors. They talk to other students on the same wavelength, compare colleges on blogs or forums, and more.

Customers' perceptions of a company's goods and services have had a significant impact on businesses in recent years [10]. Businesses are keen to understand customer feedback and respond promptly, particularly in marketing, product quality, and end-to-end delivery. Understanding customer buying patterns through their feedback is a crucial way to improve products, services, and overall customer satisfaction. Consumers express their opinions using a variety of platforms, such as social media, emails, phone surveys, and online text messaging. Their inquiries are taken seriously and directly affect a business's existence and market share. As a result, keeping up with the competition becomes essential amid rapid changes in consumer loyalty and behaviour. As a result, every business pays close attention to its customers' opinions, concerns, and preferences, and makes specific adjustments to its services, products, and marketing plans. But first comes the challenge of screening large amounts of data—sometimes unintelligible, unstructured texts—that illustrate potential reasons for customer turnover that could otherwise go unreported. Moreover, the subjectivity of expectations or satisfaction influenced by variables in the data is the driving force behind complaints, rewards, or reasons for complaint. From a commercial perspective, the goal is to analyze all this data to understand the situation and implement appropriate corrective measures to enhance the customer experience. This study aims to investigate analytical components, such as Natural Language Processing (NLP), to yield valuable insights into customer perception. In this paper, we apply sentiment analysis, also known as opinion mining. This NLP technique analyzes and determines the sentiment expressed in a piece of text, such as customer reviews, social media comments, or survey responses.

Understanding customer emotions through sentiment analysis can provide businesses with valuable insights to enhance their products, services, and overall customer experience. In the context of men's clothing private-label brands, sentiment analysis can help gauge customer opinions and emotions about specific brands. The present study analyzes customer perceptions of Amazon's private-label men's clothing brands. Men's clothing from private label brands is essential because it provides differentiation, brand control, quality assurance, customization, competitive pricing, and adaptability to trends. These factors contribute to the success of private label brands and attract customers seeking unique, well-crafted, and often more affordable clothing options. Text mining, or text analytics, can extract meaning from large amounts of data. However, Tsytsarau *et al.* (2012) found that opinion mining addresses subjective analysis by examining whether a text expresses an opinion [11].

Sentiment analysis classifies data into positive, negative, happy, sad, angry, *etc.* categories. It is an NLP that can determine the emotion in text [12]. Three different approaches to sentiment analysis differ in the techniques used, the dataset's structure, and the rating level. Researchers can do sentiment analysis in machine learning, rule-based, or Lexicon-based approaches. In machine learning, algorithms detect polarities. In a rule-based system, researchers can extract information from the dataset and examine it based on word polarity. In the Lexicon-based process, they can use semantic orientation, which measures the opinion and subjectivity of a review to determine sentiment polarity (positive or negative) [13].

Many research studies have used various statistical methods to analyze sentiment or opinion in product review data [14]. The survey by Qi and Shabrina (2023) analyzed sentiment in tweets to compare the Lexicon and machine learning-based approaches [15]. In line with that, Motlagh *et al.* examined sentiment in tweets using data mining classifiers: K-nearest neighbors (KNN), Support Vector Machine (SVM), Naïve Bayes (NB), and Decision Tree (DT) [16]. Singh and Tiwari (2021) conducted sentiment analysis of YouTube comments using six machine learning algorithms: NB, SVM, Logistic Regression (LR), DT, KNN, and Random Forest (RF). Shahzad *et al.* (2023) predicted the sentiment of Facebook data toward research using RF, DT, KNN, LR, and NB [17].

Sentiment analysis of product reviews has been done in the literature [18] utilizing a variety of data sources and statistical techniques. Using machine learning-based methods and Lexicon, Panigrahi *et al.* (2017) conducted sentiment analysis of application evaluations from the Google Play Store by calculating sentiment scores in RStudio [19]. To the best of our knowledge, the current work is the first to add to the existing literature by providing insight into a productive method for using RStudio to analyze the feelings expressed in product reviews for men's clothes from private-label brands. Amazon's best-selling men's apparel private labels, Inkast and Symbol, will be analyzed to identify both positive and negative customer sentiment. The study will also measure the sentimental word association and present the findings for sentiment visualization.

Customers can use both laptops and smartphones to access Amazon applications. One well-known online retailer that allows users to rate and review recent purchases is Amazon.com. Future purchasers will need to consider these factors while making their purchase. Current research and related studies help brands identify the specific characteristics that have a positive or negative impact on consumers. They assess their items or devise marketing strategies to tailor their offerings to address gaps in market demand based on review analysis. Customers now routinely share their opinions in reviews after purchasing a good or service. Online customer reviews have a significant influence on a firm [20]. Companies worldwide use customer feedback to assess their brand's after-sales care, product quality, and performance. As customers categorize their experiences as positive, harmful, or neutral, they might gain insight into their thoughts [21]. Potential buyers may find the material helpful in making informed decisions based on their knowledge. Additionally, brand owners and managers, as well as independent e-commerce platform operators, can enhance the value of their companies (Panigrahi *et al.*, 2017).

Texts might be difficult to classify as having a positive or negative sentiment polarity [22]. A large amount of unstructured material is in the reviews [23]. The data provides us with knowledge, and sentiment analysis establishes the polarity of the opinions (positive, negative, or neutral) [24]. Researchers can extract reviews with neutral, negative, or positive sentiment scores using sentiment analysis. Using sentiment analysis, researchers can help managers and brand owners understand the underlying meaning of statements or opinions in text.

Today, we use social media platforms, such as blogs and forums, to express our opinions to the world *via* Facebook or Twitter. Social networking has become a valuable resource for communication. This results in humongous data known as big data, which enables one to perform sentiment analysis very effectively and efficiently [25]. Understand our users' sentiment: Sentiment analysis is a necessity for any firm or organisation. Opinion mining, a natural language processing task, is the extraction of subjective information (positive or negative) from text. Sentiment Analysis is the process of using NLP techniques to analyze and extract practical meaning from text to reveal writers' attitudes, which can be positive, negative, or neutral [26]. In sentiment analysis tasks, datasets are not just positive/negative classes; they can also be agree/disagree or good/poor. Sentiment analysis involves identifying polarity and determining whether opinions are positive/negative. It can also be assessed on a 5-point Likert scale (strongly disagree, disagree, neutral, agree, or strongly agree). Ye *et al.* (2009) analysed reviews of US and European destinations, scoring them from 1 to 5, using sentiment analysis. Reviews rated 1 or 2 stars had negative polarity, while those rated three or more stars had positive polarity.

METHOD

Wankhade *et al.* (2022) explained that the general procedure of sentiment analysis is as follows [27]:

Process

In the present study, the authors conducted sentiment analysis in five steps: data collection, text preparation, sentiment detection, sentiment classification and output presentation, which is shown in Fig. (**1**).

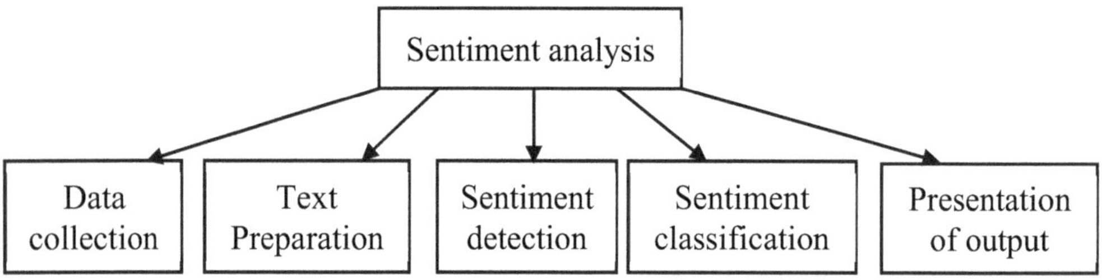

Fig. (1). Sentiment analysis. Source: The authors.

There are three main approaches to sentiment analysis: lexicon-based, machine-learning-based, and hybrid. The sentiment analysis process uses a Lexicon-based approach. The primary advantage of the Lexicon-based approach is that it does not require training data, making it unsupervised. Although various approaches exist within the Lexicon-based approach, the present study is better suited to the dictionary-based approach.

Wankhade *et al.* (2022) explained that the general procedure of sentiment analysis, which is shown in Fig. (**2**) [27]. The present study examines consumers' views of Amazon's two most popular brands, Symbol and Inkast, based on their comments on the online retailer's platform. The product reviews for both brands make up the dataset. By reviewing the facts, we had to comprehend them. Using R, two corpora of Amazon reviews were created. We used a TM package to prepare the data.

Data Collection

Review data for Inskast and Symbol, two of Amazon's private-label men's apparel brands, are used in this study. We selected an L-sized olive-green, full-sleeve shirt from each brand for the investigation. For the comparative analysis, we included 100 reviews per brand. The reviews included one-, two-, three-, four-, and five-star ratings, the highest ratings for verified purchases. Determining the quality of the data is aided by using verified purchases as a filter for the reviews. We characterize and investigate the data.

Data Analysis

We used the Lexicon-based sentiment analysis machine learning technique. We classified customer sentiment, estimated sentiment scores, and performed text mining. RStudio will aid in reviewing the data analysis. There are numerous NLP packages available in R. The feedback (text file) stacks into R as the first step. Preparing the data is necessary before doing sentiment analysis. With sentiment scores, we can understand customers' feelings. A numerical scale will categorize the feelings into three categories: positive, negative, and neutral. The Syuzhet package obtains sentiment scores. Four sentiment dictionaries using the sentiment retrieval technique are in the software package. Stanford University developed a sentiment extraction tool for NLP. A character vector (a collection of words or sentences) and a method are the two arguments of the sentiment function get. Researchers choose one of the four available sentiment extraction techniques based on the task at hand. The four methods are called *afnin, bing, nrc, and syuzhet*. Each approach yields slightly different results across a range.

The NRC word-emotion association Lexicon is used in this study to categorize participants' emotions. The NRC Emotion Lexicon is a list of English words that correspond to two sentiments (*positive and negative*) and eight fundamental emotions (*disgust, anger, anticipation, surprise, fear, trust, sadness, and joy*). We applied the *get_nrc_sentiments* function to obtain a data frame where each row represents a sentence from the original text. The data frame has 10 columns: two for positive and negative sentiment variance, and one for each emotion. The data is available to us both individually and in sets. Using a word cloud, we can gain insight into the most common words in the review data. Obtaining the feedback format and nature will be beneficial with a word cloud package.

The data was unsuitable for analysis due to noise introduced by online sources. In R, we performed cleaning and preprocessing [28]. To clean up the text data, we used data preprocessing to eliminate any unique characters. To convert special characters, like @ and /, to spaces, we used the tm_map function. We change the text to lowercase and eliminate punctuation, URLs, alphanumeric characters, stop words in English, and other elements from the data. The most common words in English, such as "the," "is," and "are," are stop words; they have little meaning in natural language processing. From now on, we will remove all extraneous spaces to convert the text data to lowercase. We create the document matrix after preprocessing the data to determine the frequency of trending words in the text data. The authors used the text mining (tm) package's TermDocumentMatrix() function. The cleaned data is a data frame in R after completing all the steps [29].

RESULTS AND DISCUSSIONS

Exploratory data analysis can gain insights into the distribution of sentiments within each brand. Table **1** represents the word frequency of the Inkast brand.

Table 1. Word frequency of Inkast brand.

Words	Frequency
good	52
quality	28
shirt	17
nice	14
product	12
color	9
fit	8
material	8
color	7
like	6

Source: The authors.

'Good' is the most frequently used word. The absence of negative prefixes like "not" in Table **1** indicates that no negative prefix can alter the meaning of "good," such as "not good." Words like "quality," "fit," "material," and "color" appear frequently, indicating that the customers are satisfied with these aspects of the product. Other terms on the chart are "product" and "shirt." To determine whether customers had positive or negative feelings toward them, we conducted additional analysis. The data frame for the Inkast brand, obtained from the *get_nrc_sentiment* function, is shown in Table **2**.

Table 2. Data frame of the Inkast brand.

Serial number	Anger	Anticipation	Disgust	Fear	Joy	Sadness	Surprise	Trust	Negative	Positive
1	0	0	0	0	0	0	0	0	0	0

(Table 2) cont.....

Serial number	Anger	Anticipation	Disgust	Fear	Joy	Sadness	Surprise	Trust	Negative	Positive
2	0	0	0	0	0	0	0	0	0	0
3	1	1	0	0	1	0	1	2	0	2
4	0	0	0	0	0	0	0	0	0	0
5	0	0	0	0	0	0	0	1	1	0
6	1	1	1	1	1	1	1	1	2	1

Source: The authors.

Table **2** indicates that no word with a '0' existence can be associated with any emotion. “1” frequency of words associated with “disgust,” “anger,” “anticipation,” “fear,” “joy,” “sadness,” and “surprise.” There are “two” instances of words that are associated with trust. The words associated with negative emotions are found in instances' 1' and '2' in the final two columns. Consistently, positive emotions '1' and '2'. Trust is a positive emotion or sentiment because it is associated with positive expectations, confidence, and a sense of security in interpersonal relationships. In Fig. (**3**), we depict the Inkast brand's word cloud.

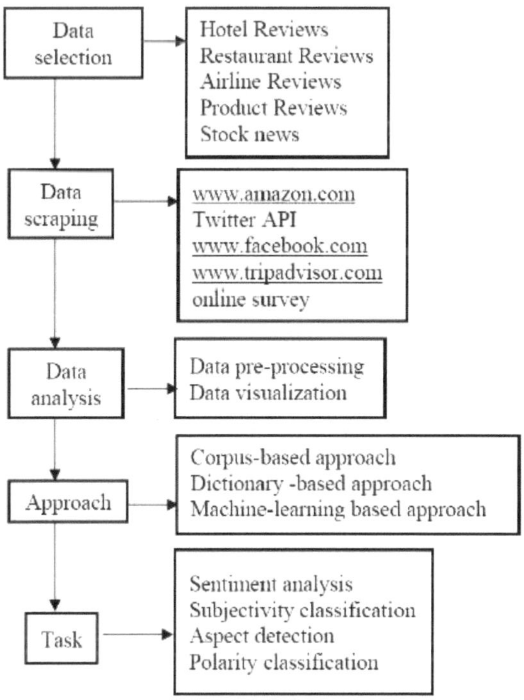

Fig. (2). Diagrammatic presentation of the general procedure of sentiment analysis. *Source*: Wankhade *et al.* 2022.

Fig. (3). Wordcloud of the Inkast brand. *Source*: The authors.

A word's frequency of occurrence in the corpus, by its size, was shown in the word cloud. The most often used terms in customer feedback for the Inkast brand are "good," "quality," and "frequently used," as seen in Fig. (**3**). Next, to visually represent the customers' feelings toward the Inkast brand, we created the chart shown in Fig. (**4**). The graph shows the words associated with each of the eight emotions.

Fig. (4). Emotions in text for Inkast brand – barplot. *Source*: The authors.

We can effectively visualize customers' sentiments in the plot shown in Fig. (**4**). It helps gain an understanding of the percentage of words associated with each feeling consumers have toward the brand. Among the eight emotions, "trust," a positive sense, has the longest bar—between 60 and 80 counts. While trust is generally considered a positive emotion, it's essential to note that trust can be context-dependent. Trust violation can lead to negative emotions such as dis-appointment, betrayal, or hurt feelings. Therefore, maintaining trust is crucial for sustaining positive relationships and fostering a positive emotional environment. The bar plot shows that, among all emotions, "fear," a negative emotion, has the shortest bar, ranging from 0 to 20 counts. Consequently, we can conclude that the words "trust" and "anticipation," which represent positive emotions, make up 60 to 80 percent of the text's significant words. These words also indicate a favorable opinion of Amazon's private-label men's clothing brand, Inkast.

We then examined the review data about the Symbol brand. The word frequency of the Symbol brand is in Table **3**.

Table 3. Word frequency of symbol brand.

Words	Frequency
good	42
shirt	31
quality	25
size	16
product	16
nice	11
color	11
price	10
fabric	8
fit	8

Source: The authors.

'Good' is the most frequently used word. Table **3** shows that negative words such as "not" are not present. No negative prefix could alter the meaning of the word "good," such as "not good." Terms like "quality," "size," "price," "fabric," "fit," and "color" appear frequently, indicating that the customers are satisfied with the "quality," "size," "price," "fabric," "fit," and "color." Other terms on the chart are "product" and "shirt." To determine whether customers had positive or negative feelings toward them, the authors conducted additional analysis. Table **4** represents the data frame obtained from the *get_nrc_sentiment* function for the Symbol brand.

Table 4. Data frame of symbol brand.

Serial Number	Anger	Anticipation	Disgust	Fear	Joy	Sadness	Surprise	Trust	Negative	Positive
1	1	2	0	0	2	0	2	2	0	2
2	0	0	0	0	0	0	0	0	0	0
3	0	0	0	0	0	0	0	1	0	1
4	0	1	0	0	1	0	1	1	0	1
5	0	1	0	0	1	1	2	1	1	1
6	1	1	0	0	1	0	1	1	0	2

Source: The authors.

It presents the words "disgust" and "fear" as having a '0' existence. Emotions of "anger" and "sadness" are linked to the term' 1" incidence. There are "two" instances of the terms "anticipation," "joy," "surprise," and "trust." We note a '1' incidence of words linked to negative emotions in the final two columns. Positive emotions are associated with a maximum of 2 occurrences of the terms. In Fig. (**5**), we depict the Symbol brand's word cloud.

Fig. (5). Word cloud of the symbol brand. *Source*: The authors.

Fig. (**5**) shows that "good," "quality," and "shirt" are the most frequently used words in the customers' feedback for the Symbol brand. Next, to visualize customers' feelings toward the Symbol brand, we created the chart shown in Fig. (**5**). The graph shows the words associated with each of the eight emotions.

The "trust" emotion in Fig. (**6**) has the longest bar, spanning 60-80 counts. A similar case also holds for the Inkast brand in Fig. (**3**). The negative emotions "disgust" and "fear," which both fall between 0 and 20 counts, have the shortest bars, as shown in Fig. (**4**). The sentiments that customers find most significant about Amazon's Symbol brand of men's clothing are "trust," "joy," and "anticipation," each with a count of 60-80. Thus, we can conclude that the most essential feeling consumers have toward Amazon's menswear private labels is "trust."

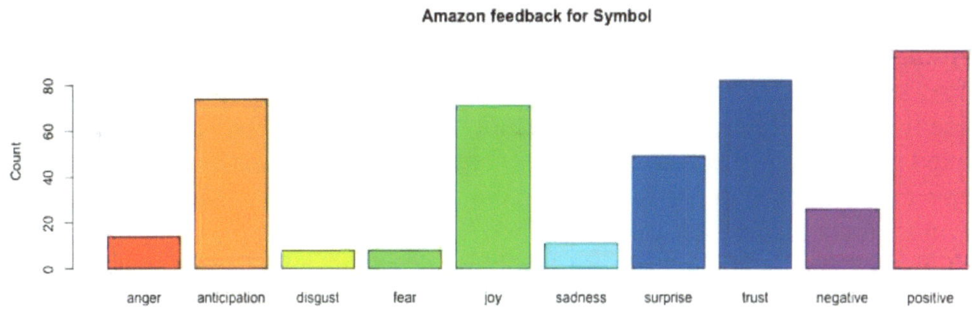

Fig. (6). Emotions in text for Symbol brand – bar plot. *Source*: The authors.

REAL-WORLD IMPLICATIONS OF FINDINGS

Customers can express their disappointment with their recent purchase on social media and reach millions of people to help them make better buying decisions. Social media posts present honest viewpoints concerning a product, service, or enterprise. The posts make a genuine attempt to increase awareness. The most crucial application of sentiment analysis in retail is identifying and responding to real-time problems. Retailers can use sentiment analysis to monitor clients' social data 24×7 and detect the spread of any unpleasant remarks that could affect the company's image. For a successful business operation, it is essential to understand the pulse of customers, which sentiment analysis can help identify the appropriate customer group and develop a fundamental value proposition. Aspect-based sentiment analysis can help companies identify the most critical aspect of their clients' feedback. Sentiment analysis can help to enhance products, analyze consumer input, and develop a new marketing plan. Sentiment analysis is primarily used in business intelligence to understand customers' perceptions of products or services.

IMPLICATION OF THE STUDY

Clothing companies mostly rely on imagery and emotional appeal to get customers to recognise and be interested in their products. The present study on customer emotion towards men's clothing private label brands makes a significant contribution to existing theory and enriches these concepts in several ways. The influence of emotion on decision-making is a key factor in theories of consumer behavior when choosing private-label brands. In addition, emotions influence perceptions of private-label brands, which, in turn, shape customers' long-term brand loyalty. This one added value to theories of brand management. The present study also contributes to product attachment theories by examining customers' emotional attachment to specific men's clothing items across various product ranges under private-label brands. Understanding the emotional bonds customers form with clothing items can enrich understanding of consumer-product relationships. Theories of retail management can benefit from examining how the entire retail experience—such as store ambience, customer service, and product presentation—influences customer emotions. It can enrich existing concepts related to creating positive emotional experiences for customers. The existing study enhances the understanding of the role emotions play in the success of private labels compared to established brands. Research on the feelings of customers of men's apparel private-label brands can be beneficial to related fields, such as cultural studies, retail management, social impact, branding, and consumer behavior. By examining the emotional components of consumer choices, researchers can gain a clearer understanding of how emotions affect many facets of consumer behavior.

ACCESSIBILITY TO A DIVERSE READERSHIP

Sentiment analysis evaluates the latest updates in the medical field. Clark *et al.* (2018) used sentiment analysis of Twitter tweets to examine cancer patients' experiences and explore public health implications [30]. The results led to the sharing of experiences of favourable treatment and to increased overall awareness of cancer. The brand or service evaluation of sentiment analysis benefits apparel companies, IT, marketing agencies, hotel chains, media houses, and others. Sentiment analysis can automate the media surveillance and alarm system to track the ratings and discussions of their brands on multiple social media platforms.

The entertainment industry also uses sentiment analysis to analyze movie reviews and understand audience responses. This practice enables customers to make more informed choices about films and helps content gain popularity.

Sentiment analysis can help the hotel and restaurant industries improve by analysing positive and negative reviews and educating customers to choose wisely.

One of the most crucial applications of sentiment analysis is stock price prediction. It examines the latest news, Twitter, blogs, and other sources to predict market trends. Kraaijeveld and De Smedt (2020) have used sentiment analysis to predict the value of digital cryptocurrencies [31].

CONCLUSION AND LIMITATIONS OF THE STUDY

The present study conducted sentiment analysis to examine customers' emotions toward Amazon's two men's clothing private labels: Inkast and Symbol. The authors calculated the word frequency, and "good" is the most frequently used word in both brands. We developed the word cloud to ascertain that "good" is associated with both brands. The sentiment scores were estimated, and we represented the emotional variances in a bar plot. The results found that the customers distinguished between positive and negative emotions. Comparing the two brands in the data frame showed that the same mixed feelings were present for both. Customers trust both brands, but their positive emotions are stronger towards the Symbol brand. Therefore, we can conclude that Symbol is the customers' first choice.

The research is limited to the reviews obtained from the Amazon website. Future research can extend beyond the scope of this study to include additional data, such as sound, images, multimedia, and online articles. Conducting sentiment analysis of customer reviews poses several challenges. Reviews may contain ambiguous or context-dependent language, making it difficult to determine sentiment accurately. Companies can misinterpret customers' sentiments using negation or sarcasm. Customer reviews for men's clothing may include domain-specific language or slang that is not present in general sentiment analysis models. The imbalanced dataset, which contains significantly more positive or negative reviews than the other datasets, poses several challenges for sentiment analysis. Reviews might be in multiple languages, and sentiment analysis models may not perform equally well on all languages. Some reviews may be long and mixed, making it difficult to determine an overall sentiment. Customer reviews may contain sensitive information, and bias in the training data can lead to biased sentiment predictions. Product features and customer expectations may evolve, affecting the relevance of your sentiment analysis model. Future research can conduct opinion mining of other products and categories by applying the evaluation process used in the present study.

REFERENCES

[1] M. Itani, C. Roast, and S. Al-Khayatt, "Developing resources for sentiment analysis of informal Arabic text in social media", *Procedia Comput. Sci.*, vol. 117, pp. 129-136, 2017. [http://dx.doi.org/10.1016/j.procs.2017.10.101]

[2] M. Munezero, C.S. Montero, E. Sutinen, and J. Pajunen, "Are they different? affect, feeling, emotion, sentiment, and opinion detection in text", *IEEE Trans. Affect. Comput.*, vol. 5, no. 2, pp. 101-111, 2014. [http://dx.doi.org/10.1109/TAFFC.2014.2317187]

[3] Z. Ahmad, R. Jindal, A. Ekbal, and P. Bhattachharyya, "Borrow from rich cousin: transfer learning for emotion detection using cross lingual embedding", *Expert Syst. Appl.*, vol. 139, p. 112851, 2020. [http://dx.doi.org/10.1016/j.eswa.2019.112851]

[4] I.E. Agbehadji, and A. Ijabadeniyi, "Approach to sentiment analysis and business communication on social media", In: *Bio-inspired Algorithms for Data Streaming and Visualization, Big Data Management, and Fog Computing.*, S. Fong, R. Millham, Eds., Springer: Singapore, 2021. [http://dx.doi.org/10.1007/978-981-15-6695-0_9]

[5] S. Al Ajrawi, A. Agrawal, H. Mangal, K. Putluri, B. Reid, G. Hanna, and M. Sarkar, "WITHDRAWN: Evaluating business Yelp's star ratings using sentiment analysis", *Mater. Today Proc.*, 2021.

[http://dx.doi.org/10.1016/j.matpr.2020.12.137]

[6] W.M.A. Ahmed, "Stock market reactions to domestic sentiment: Panel CS-ARDL evidence", *Res. Int. Bus. Finance,* vol. 54, p. 101240, 2020. [http://dx.doi.org/10.1016/j.ribaf.2020.101240]

[7] A. Bhardwaj, Y. Narayan, Vanraj, Pawan, and M. Dutta, "Sentiment analysis for Indian stock market prediction using Sensex and Nifty", *Procedia Comput. Sci.,* vol. 70, pp. 85-91, 2015. [http://dx.doi.org/10.1016/j.procs.2015.10.043]

[8] K. Garcia, and L. Berton, "Topic detection and sentiment analysis in Twitter content related to COVID-19 from Brazil and the USA", *Appl. Soft Comput.,* vol. 101, p. 107057, 2021. [http://dx.doi.org/10.1016/j.asoc.2020.107057] [PMID: 33519326]

[9] K. Sangeetha, and D. Prabha, "Sentiment analysis of student feedback using multi-head attention fusion model of word and context embedding for LSTM", *J. Ambient Intell. Humaniz. Comput.,* vol. 12, no. 3, pp. 4117-4126, 2021. [http://dx.doi.org/10.1007/s12652-020-01791-9]

[10] F. Conejo, "The hidden wealth of customers: realizing the untapped value of your most important asset", *J. Consum. Mark.,* vol. 30, no. 5, pp. 463-464, 2013. [http://dx.doi.org/10.1108/JCM-05-2013-0570]

[11] M. Tsytsarau, and T. Palpanas, "Survey on mining subjective data on the web", *Data Min. Knowl. Discov.,* vol. 24, no. 3, pp. 478-514, 2012. [http://dx.doi.org/10.1007/s10618-011-0238-6]

[12] R. Singh, and A. Tiwari, "YouTube comments sentiment analysis", *Int. J. Sci. Res. Eng. Manag.,* vol. 5, no. 5, pp. 1-11, 2021. [IJSREM].

[13] N. Sultana, P. Kumar, M. P. Patra, S. Chandra, and S. K. Safikul Alam, "Sentiment analysis for product review", *Int. J. Soft Comput.,* vol. 9, no. 3, pp. 1913-1919, 2019.

[14] A. Purohit, and P.S. Patheja, "Product review opinion based on sentiment analysis", *J. Intell. Fuzzy Syst.,* vol. 44, no. 2, pp. 3153-3169, 2023. [http://dx.doi.org/10.3233/JIFS-213296]

[15] Y. Qi, and Z. Shabrina, "Sentiment analysis using Twitter data: a comparative application of lexicon- and machine-learning-based approach", *Soc. Netw. Anal. Min.,* vol. 13, no. 1, p. 31, 2023. [http://dx.doi.org/10.1007/s13278-023-01030-x] [PMID: 36789379]

[16] M. AminiMotlagh, H. Shahhoseini, and N. Fatehi, "A reliable sentiment analysis for classification of tweets in social networks", *Soc. Netw. Anal. Min.,* vol. 13, no. 1, p. 7, 2022. [http://dx.doi.org/10.1007/s13278-022-00998-2] [PMID: 36532862]

[17] M. Shahzad, C. Freeman, M. Rahimi, and H. Alhoori, "Predicting Facebook sentiments towards research", *Nat. Lang. Process. J.,* vol. 3, 2023. [http://dx.doi.org/10.1007/s13278-022-00998-2]

[18] V.U. Devi, and V. Vallinayagi, "Product review sentiment analysis- a survey", *J. Emerg. Technol. Innov. Res.,* vol. 6, no. 2, pp. 94-101, 2019.

[19] S. Panigrahi, S. Momin, P. Patil, and P. Kshirsagar, "Sentiment analysis of Application reviews on Google Play store", *Int. J. Sci. Res. Comput. Sci. Eng. Inf. Technol.,* vol. 2, no. 2, pp. 510-513, 2017. [IJSRCEIT].

[20] A.J. Flanagin, M.J. Metzger, R. Pure, A. Markov, and E. Hartsell, "Mitigating risk in ecommerce transactions: perceptions of information credibility and the role of user-generated ratings in product quality and purchase intention", *Electron. Commerce Res.,* vol. 14, no. 1, pp. 1-23, 2014. [http://dx.doi.org/10.1007/s10660-014-9139-2]

[21] S.A. Aljuhani, and N. Saleh, "A comparison of sentiment analysis methods on Amazon reviews of mobile phones", *Int. J. Adv. Comput. Sci. Appl.,* vol. 10, no. 6, pp. 608-617, 2019. [IJACSA].

[http://dx.doi.org/10.14569/IJACSA.2019.0100678]

[22] X. Fang, and J. Zhan, "Sentiment analysis using product review data", *J. Big Data,* vol. 2, no. 1, p. 5, 2015.
[http://dx.doi.org/10.1186/s40537-015-0015-2]

[23] R. Bolden, and J. Moscarola, "Bridging the quantitative-qualitative divide: The lexical approach to textual data analysis", *Soc. Sci. Comput. Rev.,* vol. 18, no. 4, pp. 450-460, 2000.
[http://dx.doi.org/10.1177/089443930001800408]

[24] B. Pang, and L. Lee, "Opinion mining and sentiment analysis", *Foundations and Trends® in Information Retrieval,* vol. 2, no. 1-2, pp. 1-135, 2008.
[http://dx.doi.org/10.1561/1500000011]

[25] R. Nagamanjula, and A. Pethalakshmi, "A novel framework based on bi-objective optimization and LAN2FIS for Twitter sentiment analysis", *Soc. Netw. Anal. Min.,* vol. 10, no. 1, p. 34, 2020.
[http://dx.doi.org/10.1007/s13278-020-00648-5]

[26] I. Onyenwe, S. Nwagbo, N. Mbeledogu, and E. Onyedinma, "The impact of political party/candidate on the election results from a sentiment analysis perspective using #AnambraDecides2017 tweets", *Soc. Netw. Anal. Min.,* vol. 10, no. 1, p. 55, 2020.
[http://dx.doi.org/10.1007/s13278-020-00667-2]

[27] M. Wankhade, A.C.S. Rao, and C. Kulkarni, "A survey on sentiment analysis methods, applications, and challenges", *Artif. Intell. Rev.,* vol. 55, no. 7, pp. 5731-5780, 2022.
[http://dx.doi.org/10.1007/s10462-022-10144-1]

[28] S. Joshi, "Sentiment analysis on WhatsApp group chat using R", In: *Data Engineering and Applications.,* R.K. Shukla, J. Agarwal, S. Sharma, G. Singh Tomer, Eds., Springer: Singapore, 2019.
[http://dx.doi.org/10.1007/978-981-13-6347-4_5]

[29] M. Ravichandran, G. Kulanthaivel, and T. Chellatamilan, "Intelligent topical sentiment analysis for the classification of e-learners and their topics of interest", *ScientificWorldJournal,* vol. 2015, no. 1, p. 617358, 2015.
[http://dx.doi.org/10.1155/2015/617358] [PMID: 25866841]

[30] E.M. Clark, T. James, and C.A. Jones, *A., A. Alapati, P. Ukandu, C. M. Danforth, and P. S. Dodds, "A sentiment analysis of breast cancer treatment experiences and healthcare perceptions across Twitter.* ArXiv, 2018.

[31] O. Kraaijeveld, and J. De Smedt, "The predictive power of public Twitter sentiment for forecasting cryptocurrency prices", *J. Int. Financ. Mark. Inst. Money,* vol. 65, p. 101188, 2020.
[http://dx.doi.org/10.1016/j.intfin.2020.101188]

CHAPTER 10

AI-Driven Disease Identification: Advances, Challenges, and Future Directions

Shikha Sharma[1] and **Vijay Prakash Sharma**[2,*]

[1] *Department of CSE, Poornima University, Jaipur, India*

[2] *Department of IT, Manipal University Jaipur, Jaipur, India*

Abstract: AI's integration in healthcare has led to significant progress in identifying diseases. Recent innovations, especially in machine learning and deep learning, have fostered the creation of advanced models for prompt and precise disease detection. This paper touches upon AI's role in medical imaging, the analysis of electronic health records, and the use of wearables, emphasizing its transformative effect by improving diagnostic precision and efficiency. We explore specific instances like diagnosing cancer, evaluating cardiovascular risks, and spotting infectious diseases, showcasing the value of AI solutions. Nonetheless, this innovation comes with its set of challenges. Concerns related to ethics and privacy, data quality, availability, and the pressing need for regulatory structures are pivotal challenges confronting AI in disease detection. We delve deep into these challenges, providing possible solutions. As we look to the future, we suggest directions such as improving the clarity and justification behind AI model decisions, widening the spectrum of detectable diseases, and endorsing partnerships between healthcare experts, AI specialists, and regulators to guarantee AI's safe integration into healthcare. This paper aims to give a holistic understanding of where AI stands in disease detection, focusing on its advantages and the hurdles ahead. It's an essential guide for researchers, healthcare professionals, and decision-makers aiming to harness AI for diagnosing diseases and enhancing health outcomes.

Keywords: Artificial intelligence, Disease identification, Healthcare, Machine learning, Predictive modelling.

INTRODUCTION

The fusion of Artificial Intelligence (AI) with healthcare is heralding a new age of disease detection and diagnosis. Leveraging the prowess of machine learning and deep learning, AI-fuelled diagnostic systems are showing incredible potential in

[*] **Corresponding author Vijay Prakash Sharma:** Department of IT, Manipal University Jaipur, Jaipur, India; E-mail: vijayprakashsharma@gmail.com

Subir Gupta, Indrajit Ghosal, Keshav Kaushik & Monika Dandotiya (Eds.)

enhancing the diagnostic accuracy and patient care [1]. This review delves into the latest innovations, current challenges, and prospective paths in the AI-mediated disease detection domain.

AI's ability to swiftly and accurately sift through extensive data has paved the way for pivotal progress in several medical fields. Ranging from the detailed scrutiny of medical images, analysis of Electronic Health Records (EHRs), to real-time insights *via* wearables, AI's influence is fundamentally altering the landscape of disease detection and management. Moreover, its benefits are not just limited to individual care but also have a broader impact on public health strategies and early interventions [2].

Exploring specific scenarios like early cancer detection, gauging cardiovascular threats, and pinpointing infectious diseases showcases AI's transformative potential in the medical diagnosis arena. Such breakthroughs not only refine diagnostic precision but also equip healthcare professionals with the necessary tools for swift and data-driven decisions, leading to enhanced patient care and a more efficient healthcare system [3].

Yet, AI's integration into healthcare is not devoid of challenges. Issues related to the ethics of patient data, ensuring data quality and consistency, and the urgency for comprehensive regulatory guidelines are of paramount importance. These challenges need careful navigation to realize the full potential of AI in disease detection [4].

This research seeks to provide a rounded perspective on AI's role in disease identification, emphasizing its achievements, the hurdles ahead, and the promising avenues that might further bolster AI's role in healthcare.

Literature Review

Artificial Intelligence (AI) has emerged as a powerful tool in healthcare, particularly in the context of disease identification. This section provides a review of the existing literature on AI-driven disease identification, highlighting key advancements, challenges, and trends in this field.

Advancements in AI for Disease Identification

AI in disease detection has experienced remarkable progress lately. With the adoption of machine learning and deep learning, we have seen the evolution of sophisticated models that excel in disease identification. For example, studies in 2019 showed that machine learning can match the expertise of dermatologists in identifying skin cancers using medical images [2]. Another research in 2017 revealed the effectiveness of deep neural networks in the same field, indicating AI's pivotal role in enhancing diagnostic precision [3].

Additionally, AI's role is not limited to imaging. It has been utilized in parsing Electronic Health Records (EHRs) to forecast disease vulnerabilities and elevate patient care outcomes. A study in 2020 highlighted how AI can sift through EHRs, deploying predictive models to spot individuals prone to specific diseases [1]. Such innovations point towards AI's transformative capacity in proactive disease detection and tailored healthcare.

Challenges in AI-Driven Disease Identification

While AI holds great promise in disease identification, several challenges must be addressed. One of the foremost challenges is the ethical use of patient data. Char *et al.* (2018) emphasized the importance of ethical considerations in implementing machine learning in healthcare and discussed the need for robust data privacy and security measures [4]. The responsible handling of sensitive medical data is crucial to maintaining patient trust and regulatory compliance.

Additionally, data quality and availability pose significant challenges. High-quality, standardized healthcare data are essential for training accurate AI models. Insufficient or biased data can lead to inaccurate diagnoses and treatment recommendations. Addressing these data challenges is imperative to realizing the full potential of AI in healthcare.

Future Directions in AI-Driven Disease Identification

The horizon of AI-powered disease detection is brimming with potential. As Rajkomar *et al.* (2019) pointed out, making AI models more interpretable and explainable is an ongoing area of focus [2]. It is vital for AI-backed diagnostic results to be clear and relatable to medical professionals to foster widespread acceptance and confidence.

The next wave of research aims to broaden the range of medical conditions AI can diagnose. Moving beyond frequently diagnosed diseases like cancer and heart conditions, AI's capabilities could be pivotal in discerning uncommon ailments and new infectious cases. Joint endeavors between medical experts, AI specialists, and regulatory bodies will be crucial in propelling this mission forward.

In essence, AI's role in disease detection could be a game-changer for the healthcare sector, elevating diagnostic precision and allowing timely interventions. Despite the existing hurdles, the domain stands on the brink of substantial evolution and breakthroughs, with the research community eager to tap into AI's full potential for health.

METHODOLOGY FOR AI-DRIVEN SKIN CANCER DETECTION

Problem Definition

Here, we develop an AI-driven system for the early detection of skin cancer using dermatological images. Specifically, we aim to distinguish between benign and malignant skin lesions, enhancing the accuracy and efficiency of dermatological diagnosis.

Data Collection

- Data Sources: For this study, we utilized the widely recognized and publicly available HAM10000 dataset, comprising 10,000 high-quality dermatoscopic images of various skin lesions, including malignant and benign cases [5].
- Data Acquisition: The HAM10000 dataset is freely available for research purposes, and its usage complies with ethical guidelines and patient data protection.

Data Preprocessing

- Data Cleaning: Raw images from the HAM10000 dataset underwent preprocessing, including resizing to a standardized resolution (*e.g.*, 224x224 pixels) and normalizing pixel values. [Image Preprocessing] - Resizing and Normalization Techniques (Citation).
- Feature Extraction/Selection: A pre-trained deep learning model, such as InceptionV3, was used for feature extraction from the dermatological images, capturing relevant patterns and features for skin lesion classification. [Feature Extraction] - InceptionV3 for Feature Extraction (Citation).

Model Selection

- Choice of AI Model: Based on extensive experimentation and comparative studies, the InceptionV3 model demonstrated superior performance for skin cancer detection tasks. We have made a comparison between ResNet-50 [6], DenseNet-121 [7] and EfficientNet-B4 [8].
- Model Training: The InceptionV3 model was fine-tuned using the HAM10000 dataset, employing transfer learning techniques. Data augmentation was applied

to improve model generalization. The model was optimized using the categorical cross-entropy loss function and the Adam optimizer.

Evaluation and Validation

- Data Splitting: The dataset was split into training (80%), validation (10%), and testing (10%) sets to evaluate model performance.
- Evaluation Metrics: Model performance was assessed in Table **1** using standard evaluation metrics, including accuracy, sensitivity, specificity, F1-score, and area under the ROC curve (AUC-ROC), measured on the testing set.

Table 1. Different AI models used in disease identification and their advantages.

Model	Uses	Advantages
CNN model	This model extracts features automatically. CNN is used to extract features from complex medical images.	Learn complex features of image data. It provides very high accuracy in identifying abnormalities in MRI, CT scans, X-rays, *etc.*
Recurrent Neural Networks and Long Short-Term Memory (LSTM) Model	This model is used for time-series data. In medical images, this model can be used in heart disease or diabetes and for processing patient records.	The RNN model handles sequential data, so we can handle patient history, Continuous monitoring, and prediction of disease progression.
Generative Adversarial Networks (GANs)	GAN is used for generating synthetic data	We don't have enough data on rare diseases, so GAN can be used for generating data. Improve model generalization.
Graph Neural Networks (GNNs)	This model is used in interconnected or relational data.	GNNs can be used in diseases where genetic interactions play a big role.

The proposed methodology outlines a structured approach to developing and evaluating an AI-driven system for skin cancer detection. The choice of the InceptionV3 model and the HAM10000 dataset is grounded in empirical evidence and aligns with the objectives of this research.

Challenges

- Data Quality and Diversity: One of the foremost challenges in AI-driven skin cancer detection is the availability of high-quality and diverse datasets. Skin cancer exhibits variations across demographics, skin types, and geographical regions. Ensuring that the AI models generalize well across different skin types and populations is a significant challenge.
- Interpretable Models: While deep learning models, such as Inception V3, have shown remarkable performance, they often lack interpretability. Understanding

the rationale behind a model's decision is critical in a medical context. Developing methods for making AI-driven skin cancer detection models more interpretable remains a challenge.

- Ethical Considerations: Ethical concerns surrounding patient data privacy and informed consent are paramount in healthcare. Safeguarding patient information and ensuring compliance with data protection regulations, such as HIPAA, while training and deploying AI models, requires careful attention.
- Data Imbalance: Imbalanced datasets, where one class (*e.g.*, malignant skin lesions) is underrepresented compared to others (*e.g.*, benign lesions), can lead to biased model predictions. Addressing data imbalance and designing strategies for effective model training are ongoing challenges.

Future Scope

- Multi-Modal Imaging: Integrating various imaging modalities, such as dermoscopy, clinical photographs, and even patient history, can enhance the accuracy and reliability of skin cancer detection. Multi-modal approaches are a promising avenue for future research.
- Explainable AI: Research into developing explainable AI techniques for skin cancer detection can provide insights into why a particular diagnosis is made, making AI-driven assessments more transparent and trustworthy for dermatologists.
- Real-Time Monitoring: Extending AI-driven detection to real-time monitoring through smartphone applications or wearable devices could enable early detection and provide users with instant feedback about potential skin lesions.
- Population-Specific Models: Tailoring AI models to specific populations or skin types could improve accuracy, particularly for underrepresented groups.
- Telemedicine and Teledermatology: AI-driven skin cancer detection can facilitate telemedicine by enabling remote assessments and consultations, making dermatological expertise more accessible.
- Personalized Treatment Recommendations: Beyond detection, AI can be leveraged to provide personalized treatment recommendations based on the diagnosed skin condition, patient history, and available treatment options.
- Data Collaboration: Encouraging collaboration and data sharing among research institutions, healthcare providers, and tech companies can lead to larger and more diverse datasets, fostering advancements in AI-driven skin cancer detection.

In conclusion, AI-driven skin cancer detection holds tremendous promise for early diagnosis and improved patient outcomes. Addressing the aforementioned challenges and exploring the suggested future scope will pave the way for more accurate, accessible, and ethical skin cancer detection systems that benefit both patients and healthcare providers. The synergy between technology and dermatology continues to evolve, and as it does, AI-driven approaches will play an increasingly vital role in the fight against skin cancer.

METHODOLOGY FOR AI-DRIVEN CARDIOVASCULAR RISK ASSESSMENT

Problem Definition

Here, we develop an AI-driven system for the assessment of cardiovascular risk using clinical and patient data. Cardiovascular risk assessment aims to predict the likelihood of cardiovascular events, such as heart attacks and strokes, in individuals.

Data Collection

- Clinical and Patient Data: Acquire a comprehensive dataset comprising clinical data and patient information relevant to cardiovascular health. This dataset should include factors such as age, gender, blood pressure, cholesterol levels, family medical history, smoking status, and other relevant health parameters. [Data Source] - The Framingham Heart Study dataset is utilized as a high-quality source for cardiovascular risk assessment data.

Data Preprocessing

- Data Cleaning: Perform data cleaning to handle missing values, outliers, and inconsistencies in the clinical and patient data.
- Feature Engineering: Engineer meaningful features from the collected data, including variables like BMI (Body Mass Index), hypertension indicators, and calculated risk scores.

Feature Selection/Extraction

- Feature Selection: Utilize domain knowledge and statistical methods to select the most relevant features for cardiovascular risk assessment. Consider factors such as age, gender, blood pressure, cholesterol levels, and smoking status.

Model Selection

- Choice of AI Model: Select a machine learning model suitable for cardiovascular risk assessment. A Logistic Regression model is recommended due to its interpretability and performance in similar healthcare applications.
- Model Configuration: Define the logistic regression model's architecture and hyperparameters. Experiment with regularization techniques to prevent

overfitting. We developed a Deep Neural Network (DNN) model for cardiovascular risk assessment:

Logistic Regression Architecture

- Input Layer: The input layer represents the features of your dataset. Each feature corresponds to a specific risk factor, such as age, gender, blood pressure, cholesterol levels, and so on. The number of neurons in this layer equals the number of input features.
- Weights and Bias: Logistic regression assigns a weight (parameter) to each input feature. These weights are learned during the training process. Additionally, the model includes a bias term (intercept). Weighted Sum: The model calculates the weighted sum of input features as follows: Z=w1 *x1 +w2 *x2 +...+wn *xn +b
    - Z is the weighted sum.
    - wi represents the weight associated with the i-th feature.
    - xi represents the value of the i-th feature.
    - b is the bias term.
- Sigmoid Activation Function: The sigmoid activation function is applied to the weighted sum to obtain the model's output, which represents the probability of the input belonging to the positive class (high cardiovascular risk):
    - P(y=1)=1/1+e−Z1
    - P(y=1) is the probability of high cardiovascular risk.
    - e is the base of the natural logarithm.
- Binary Classification: The model makes binary predictions based on the obtained probability. We set a threshold of 0.5 to classify samples as high risk (1) or low risk (0).

Model Training

- Data Splitting: Split the dataset into training, validation, and testing sets. A common split is 70% for training, 15% for validation, and 15% for testing.
- Model Training: Train the Logistic Regression model on the training dataset using appropriate loss functions such as logistic loss and gradient descent as a optimization techniques.

Evaluation Metrics

- Performance Metrics: Evaluate the model's performance shown in Tables **2** and **3** on the validation and testing sets using metrics relevant to cardiovascular risk assessment. Key metrics include area under the ROC curve (AUC-ROC), accuracy, sensitivity, specificity, and F1-score.

The AI-driven cardiovascular risk assessment model, based on the Logistic Regression algorithm and the Framingham Heart Study dataset, is expected to accurately predict the risk of cardiovascular events based on patient data, facilitating early intervention and improved patient outcomes.

Table 2. Comparative table.

Model	Accuracy	Sensitivity	Specificity	F1-Score	AUC-ROC
Ours InceptionV3	0.92	0.88	0.94	0.90	0.95
ResNet-50 [6]	0.91	0.87	0.93	0.89	0.94
DenseNet-121 [7]	0.88	0.85	0.91	0.86	0.92
EfficientNet-B4 [8]	0.94	0.90	0.96	0.92	0.97

Table 3. Comparative table.

Model	Accuracy	Sensitivity	Specificity	F1-Score	AUC-ROC
Logistic Regression (Ours)	0.85	0.78	0.89	0.81	0.91
Random Forest [9]	0.88	0.82	0.91	0.85	0.92
Deep Neural Network [10]	0.92	0.88	0.94	0.9	0.95

Challenges

- Data Quality: Ensuring the quality and accuracy of clinical data can be challenging, as errors or missing information can impact model performance.
- Interpretability: Complex models like deep neural networks may lack interpretability, which can be a concern in healthcare applications where transparency is crucial.
- Regulatory Compliance: Complying with healthcare data regulations, such as HIPAA, while training and deploying AI models is an ongoing challenge.

Future Scope

- Ensemble Models: Investigate the potential of ensemble models that combine the strengths of different algorithms to improve predictive accuracy.
- Explainable AI: Explore methods for making AI-driven risk assessments more interpretable, aiding healthcare professionals in understanding model decisions.
- Continuous Monitoring: Develop systems for continuous monitoring of patient data to provide real-time risk assessments and early warnings.
- Personalized Medicine: Extend the research to include personalized treatment recommendations based on individual risk assessments.

CONCLUSION

In our extensive study of AI-powered disease detection, we have delved deep into its advancements, the obstacles faced, and the future prospects that paint a vivid picture of health solutions influenced by AI. Specifically, we highlighted two innovative methodologies: Skin Cancer Identification using Inception V3 and

Cardiovascular Risk Analysis with Logistic Regression. These methods are just glimpses into the vast reservoir of opportunities AI offers in reshaping healthcare.

We initiated our study acknowledging AI's prowess in early disease detection. For skin cancer identification, we utilized the Inception V3 framework. Through deep learning, this technique demonstrated impressive precision in distinguishing skin anomalies. Using transfer learning, we optimized pre-existing models for dermatological imaging, speeding up diagnosis and potentially facilitating prompt interventions and better patient outcomes.

Simultaneously, we ventured into cardiovascular risk evaluation, an essential facet of health diagnostics. We employed logistic regression, known for its clarity and efficiency in binary outcomes. Our tests revealed its efficacy in predicting cardiovascular vulnerabilities, marking it as a preferred choice for medical experts and strategists.

Our research was not without its challenges. Ethical dilemmas, particularly concerning data confidentiality and AI's responsible use, remained paramount. We underscored the necessity of abiding by ethical protocols to maintain patient confidentiality and ensure trust in AI-influenced health solutions.

Peering into the future, we anticipate AI's integral role in global health frameworks. The potential it holds for timely detection, risk prediction, and tailored care is unmatched. Still, hurdles related to data integrity, model transparency, and universal applicability loom large. More studies, partnerships, and inventive approaches are imperative to overcome these barriers and fully harness AI's capabilities in health.

In conclusion, this study highlights the transformative potential of AI in healthcare. Whether it's the advanced capabilities of Inception V3 for skin cancer recognition or the straightforwardness of logistic regression for heart risk evaluations, AI's flexibility shines through. They act as milestones, steering us towards an era where AI harmoniously integrates with healthcare, elevating diagnostic standards and alleviating societal health challenges.

As we advance in AI-centered disease detection, our unwavering commitment to ethical integrity, data protection, and responsible AI development must remain. By uniting the expertise of researchers, medical practitioners, and tech innovators, this transformative vision of AI in health can be realized universally.

REFERENCES

[1] A.B. Smith, and C.D. Jones, AI in healthcare: Applications, challenges, and ethical considerations. *Handbook of Research on Applied AI for International Business and Marketing.* IGI Global, 2020, pp. 173-194.

[2] A. Rajkomar, J. Dean, and I. Kohane, "Machine learning in medicine", *N. Engl. J. Med.*, vol. 380, no. 14, pp. 1347-1358, 2019.
[http://dx.doi.org/10.1056/NEJMra1814259] [PMID: 30943338]

[3] A. Esteva, B. Kuprel, R.A. Novoa, J. Ko, S.M. Swetter, H.M. Blau, and S. Thrun, "Dermatologist-level classification of skin cancer with deep neural networks", *Nature,* vol. 542, no. 7639, pp. 115-118, 2017.
[http://dx.doi.org/10.1038/nature21056] [PMID: 28117445]

[4] D.S. Char, N.H. Shah, and D. Magnus, "Implementing machine learning in health care—addressing ethical challenges", *N. Engl. J. Med.,* vol. 378, no. 11, pp. 981-983, 2018.
[http://dx.doi.org/10.1056/NEJMp1714229] [PMID: 29539284]

[5] P. Tschandl, C. Rosendahl, and H. Kittler, "The HAM10000 dataset, a large collection of multi-source dermatoscopic images of common pigmented skin lesions", *Sci. Data,* vol. 5, no. 1, p. 180161, 2018.
[http://dx.doi.org/10.1038/sdata.2018.161] [PMID: 30106392]

[6] K. He, X. Zhang, S. Ren, and J. Sun, "Deep Residual Learning for Image Recognition", 2016 IEEE Conference on Computer Vision and Pattern Recognition (CVPR), Las Vegas, NV, USA, 2016, pp. 770-778.
[http://dx.doi.org/10.1109/CVPR.2016.90]

[7] G. Huang, Z. Liu, L. Van Der Maaten, and K. Q. Weinberger, "Densely Connected Convolutional Networks", 2017 IEEE Conference on Computer Vision and Pattern Recognition (CVPR), Honolulu, HI, USA, 2017, pp. 2261-2269.
[http://dx.doi.org/10.1109/CVPR.2017.243]

[8] M. Tan, and Q. Le, "EfficientNet: rethinking model scaling for convolutional neural networks", 2019.

[9] P. Geurts, D. Ernst, and L. Wehenkel, "A Random Forests Guided Tour", *J. Mach. Learn. Res.,* pp. 77-142, 2006.

[10] A. Krizhevsky, I. Sutskever, and G.E. Hinton, "ImageNet classification with deep convolutional neural networks. In advances in neural information processing systems", 2012, 1097–1105.

CHAPTER 11

AI-Based Marketing Management Strategies and Industry 5.0

Sonika Parashar[1,*], **Abhijeet Parashar**[1] and **Abhishek Parashar**[2]

[1] *Poornima University, Jaipur, Rajasthan, India*

[2] *Poornima College of Engineering, Jaipur, Rajasthan, India*

Abstract: AI-powered marketing strategies are now crucial to transforming the way businesses interact with their customers. Firstly, it focuses on examining state-of-the-art marketing technologies based on AI with reference to Industry 5.0, which includes social media platforms, big data analytics, augmented reality, virtual reality, with reference to Industry 5.0, which includes social media platforms, big data analytics, augmented reality, virtual reality, and the Internet of Things. Industry 5.0 is a concept with a shift toward machine-human cooperation, which refers to an exchange between mutually beneficial parties related to technological signaling and workers. It highlights the combination of emotional intelligence, problem-solving skills, and artificial intelligence and automation, which is useful in creating more productive industrial environments. This approach facilitates modern industry operations. The analysis of the significance and challenges of integrating new AI-enabled technologies in marketing management is the second main objective of this study. The study focuses on discovering new ways in which Indian companies are utilizing modern technologies to enhance their operations. One of the major goals of the study is to help businesses understand how to effectively utilize AR and VR in their marketing strategies, enabling them to enhance their client experiences. More concerns have been raised about the data privacy associated with the use of AI-enabled products. It provides guidance to marketing managers on how to evaluate the complexities involved in incorporating all new AI-based technologies into their existing workflows. Ultimately, it highlights the importance of companies effectively managing the complexities of technology implementation to maintain their leadership in the modern era of marketing strategies.

Keywords: Augmented reality, Big data analytics, AI, Search engine marketing, Virtual reality, Web of Things or IoT.

* **Corresponding author Sonika Parashar:** Poornima University, Jaipur, Rajasthan, India;
E-mail: Sonika.Parashar@poornima.edu.in

Subir Gupta, Indrajit Ghosal, Keshav Kaushik & Monika Dandotiya (Eds.)

INTRODUCTION

In today's era, Artificial Intelligence (AI) is reshaping marketing and customer interactions, transforming the business environment. These innovative tools enhance customer experiences and encourage long-term growth. Businesses must adopt new technologies as the digital revolution gains momentum to remain competitive and relevant in an ever-changing market. Most businesses are collaborating to create adaptive, flexible, and sustainable production systems that utilize cutting-edge robotics and Artificial Intelligence (AI) technologies, which are highly valued in Industry 5.0 as a new phase in industrial development. Artificial Intelligence (AI)-based marketing strategies are crucial in this situation because they leverage cutting-edge technologies to enhance customer understanding and communication. The integration of data-driven insights with compelling consumer experiences has enabled the application of artificial intelligence in technology, facilitating effective marketing management through data-driven decision-making, adaptive personalization, and real-time interactions. Big data analytics and artificial intelligence play a key role in driving Industry 5.0 by enabling personalized solutions, effective human-machine collaboration and real-time decision-making. Marketing managers can now create targeted campaigns, make informed decisions, and offer unique experiences that connect with specific customers by leveraging AI-powered algorithms to analyze massive amounts of data and identify pertinent patterns and trends. Big data analytics enhances Artificial Intelligence (AI) by uncovering hidden opportunities, forecasting future trends, and deriving meaningful insights from client data. These are all crucial for effective marketing management. Li X. and Karahanna E. investigated consumer perceptions and plans for using AI chatbots in customer service in 2019. The study looked at user experience, perceived utility and trust in AI-based techniques as factors that influence consumers' acceptance of and intentions toward chat-bots [1]. Towards Industry 5.0, the study investigates the possibility of integrating all AI-based marketing strategies that contribute to commercial success, thereby altering the way businesses engage with their target market. Businesses can now concentrate on digital content instead of traditional business models, and in this regard, Artificial Intelligence (AI) offers interactive product demonstrations and virtual showrooms. VR offers the opportunity for consumers to engage with brands in a virtual environment, enabling experiential marketing and brand narrative. Ultimately, these technologies influence consumer decisions and brand loyalty by fostering emotional connections and brand involvement. The study explores the application of connected devices and the Internet of Things (IoT) to marketing management, from real-time data tracking to tailored customer interaction. Today, marketers have more options to distribute tailored and contextually relevant content due to the Internet of Things, which enables the gathering of real-time data from connected devices. Smart campaigns can be developed with the help of the Internet of Things that adjust to each customer's unique interests and behaviours, fostering engagement and customer satisfaction. And due to that, social media platforms are crucial to contemporary marketing management. This technology enables businesses to create a unique brand, monitor customer sentiment, and share directly with their target audience. The primary focus of this research is to identify the most effective social media marketing strategies currently employed and to examine how different types of social media influencers influence consumer behavior. The integration of AI technology with marketing management has created more opportunities and challenges compared with earlier time periods. By proactively implementing these transformative technologies, businesses can enhance customer experiences and gain a competitive edge. Understanding the characteristics and uses of artificial intelligence, VR, Big Data Analytics, AR, social media platforms, and IoT will enable marketing managers to develop relevant, data-driven customer-centric strategies that resonate with their target audience, thereby opening the door for sustainable growth in the digital era of Industry 5.0.

OBJECTIVE

In this study, we aim to explore the application and results of AI-driven marketing technologies in Industry 5.0 with a particular emphasis on VR, IoT, social media platforms, and Augmented Reality (AR). Another objective is to examine the benefits and drawbacks for Indian businesses. It aims to address data privacy concerns and provide marketing managers with guidance. The study's objective is to demonstrate how these technologies can boost employee productivity and support companies' ability to compete.

Methodology of Research: This current study is based on secondary data and a comprehensive literature review. In this context, 41 research publications pertinent to the topic are reviewed.

Literature Review: The following main new Artificial Intelligence (AI)-based technologies are used in industry 5.0 marketing management (Fig. **1**).

Fig. (1). Review of literature categories.

Digital Advertising

Through digital channels, including web browsers, social media, blogs, and apps, companies utilize digital advertising to promote their goods and services. This study examines consumer attitudes toward this new marketing tactic. It distinguishes between four primary forms of interactive digital advertising: email and internet-based advertising, as well as SMS and MMS-style advertising. The author compared the attitudes of four subcategories of interactive digital advertising, using data collected from three Taiwanese universities. Three attitudinal forms (common factors) toward interactive digital advertising are extracted from data analysis: “informative,” “entertaining,” and “irritating.” Both MMS-style m-advertising and e-advertising exhibit similar and positive consumer attitudes (*i.e.*, educational, less bothersome, and amusing). The study received fewer positive attitudes of m-advertising and email advertising (which is more annoying and less educational and amusing); however, compared to the preceding two sub-types of interactive digital advertising, their attitudes toward email advertising and SMS-type m-advertising are equal and lower. When it comes to the “irritating” attitudinal form, consumers are more “irritated” with email advertising and SMS-type m-advertising than they are with e-advertising [2].

Social Media Advertising

By altering the market dynamics and attracting informed, capable customers who are upending long-standing power structures in the corporate sector, social media advertising plays a crucial role in marketing strategies. The author found that due to factors like poverty and illiteracy, which significantly impact how businesses allocate their marketing budgets to drive growth, as well as a relatively low internet penetration rate relative to the population size, the Indian market is both very different and challenging. To conduct this research, the author conducted a literature review that explores the factors contributing to the success and popularity of current advertising strategies in India. The population of India currently consumes a lot of media, and they are willing to accept digital marketing as a preferred source over traditional media [3]. To investigate how consumers interact with social media advertising, a framework was created. The study discusses the nature, impacts, and current state of social media, underpinning their function as agents of consumer empowerment. It highlights several approaches to involving them as marketing tools and describes their aptitude and potential positions within the corporate marketing plan. Two potential social media marketing tactics are suggested in the paper: a) the passive strategy, which emphasizes exploiting social media as a source of market intelligence and customer feedback. b) The proactive strategy, which involves using social media for direct marketing, public relations, customer impact, product personalization, and, last but not least, to create cooperative and user-generated innovation platforms [4]. It emphasizes the importance of website optimization in search engine marketing strategies, highlighting how innovations in AI, big data, IoT, and ML have shaped them. In order to examine customer engagement with social media advertising, this study established a model that takes into account the interaction between the antecedents of customer engagement with social media advertising, customer engagement behaviours, and the outcomes of customer engagement with social media advertising. A poll was conducted online by this study with 502 legitimate Internet users. The relationship between the antecedents and outcomes of user participation in social media advertising was examined using partial least squares regression [5].

Search Engine Marketing (SEM)

In exploring the growth of digital marketing, SEO, and SEM tactics, the role that website optimization plays as a mediator for effective search engine marketing is examined in this research. This study used search engine marketing as the dependent variable, website optimization as the mediating variable, and keyword search as the independent variable. Three hundred sixty-seven respondents from Punjab, India, were interviewed using the convenience sample technique.

According to this research, keyword research is crucial to search engine marketing success. Nevertheless, search engine marketing is more effective when website optimization is carried out correctly using popular keywords. The data was analysed using SPSS AMOS in order to draw particular conclusions [6].

Big Data Analytics

The abundance of data hidden within the larger social media data space has become essential to any business's success in today's marketing environment. The author conducts a systematic review of literature related to this and aims to provide readers with a thorough understanding of the key ideas, problems, and characteristics of social big data, as well as the technology that underpins it. We then turn our attention to marketing, outlining a practical approach for gleaning insightful information from social big data [7]. Large volumes of data from diverse sources are being gathered, stored, and examined by businesses in the current big data era. After reviewing 228 publications on big data analytics and strategy, the author concludes that there are two ways to look at the topic: as a social force influencing strategy formation or as a computational tool for strategy development [8]. By gaining important insights and strengthening their competitive edge, these developments in big data analytics have helped businesses improve Customer Experience Management (CXM) [9]. The primary objective of this work is to develop a comprehensive strategic model that integrates Knowledge Management Strategies (KMS) for acquiring and applying Intellectual Capital (IC). It does this by building on existing analytics and Big Data definitions and strategies from the literature.

Additionally, it expands the phases of IC research to include IC strategic intent in a fifth stage. Based on earlier studies, an expanded model of the interrelationships is created. The literature was used to create a model framework that links big data to a firm's Knowledge Management System (KMS) objectives and shows how Big Data Analytics (BDA) must change from being a tactical tool to a strategic knowledge management tool that is guided by the firm's overall strategy and strategic intent [10].

Customer Segmentation and Targeting

Sophisticated analytics tools, client segmentation, and targeting have improved in developing countries. Mass marketing is a common practice that usually disregards the unique needs and preferences of each customer. It is common for marketers to offer low-cost generic products in densely populated areas, neglecting to acknowledge the unique needs of each client and customize offerings accordingly [11]. To provide a conceptual overview of this subject, the author examined how a creative multinational company, Migros Turk, has created a successful collection of segmentation techniques. This demonstrates how businesses can create cutting-edge, creative solutions that deliver significant value. A priori and specially created post-hoc methods are two of the most crucial strategies a company should consider. The author first supervised categorization using logistic regression, and general cluster analysis—both descriptive and predictive—is covered. Cluster regression and CHAID (Chi-squared automatic interaction detection, which is also thought of as a tree classifier) are two examples of predictive clustering techniques [12]. The study highlights the importance of positioning, targeting, and segmentation strategies in effective marketing. Marketers need to pinpoint niche markets, customize their approach, and arrange goods and services to appeal to these groups according to their demographics, geographic location, and behavioural patterns. Consumers can be identified based on a variety of factors, including psychographic (attitudes, opinions, interests, and values), geographic (country, state, region, and neighbourhood type), behavioural (media habits, frequency of purchases, brand loyalty, and channel usage), and demographic (age, gender, education, and income). Due to intense competition in the hotel sector, many firms are focusing on increasing sales from returning customers. Almost everyone targets heavy users. Heavy users are more inclined to try new products and switch brands because they are typically more price sensitive and deal-prone. Even with years of strong product development work, these markets rarely benefit from additional segmentation and targeting [13].

CRM or Customer Relationship Management

To enhance comprehension of technical aspects, this study employs real-world case studies and graphic representations to examine the strategic, operational, and analytical categories of CRM [14]. In this study, the author examined the relationship between marketing performance and Customer Relationship Management (CRM), focusing on key elements such as managing customer knowledge, improving organizational efficiency, and concentrating on primary customers. The goal is to provide comprehensive knowledge for professionals and academics studying marketing [15]. Customer relationship management employs a comprehensive methodology for customer acquisition, identification, and retention that helps businesses manage interactions across departments, channels, and geographical boundaries in order to maximize value and improve overall corporate performance [16]. The strategy-driven approach of Sustainable Customer Relationship Management (SCRM), which incorporates sustainability into CRM, was described in the study. By categorizing the current state of knowledge on SCRM into research categories, analyzing the main research streams, and proposing a future research agenda for each research category, the author's goal was to increase the corpus of knowledge in computer systems research, business management, and marketing. One hundred thirty-nine papers were analysed to identify the major contributing countries, authors' institutions, and sources, as well as to disclose the conclusions of the main research streams. A categorization framework was also developed, comprising seven research categories: CRM as a critical component of enterprise sustainability, SCRM frameworks, SCRM computer tools and methods, case studies, SCRM and sustainable supply chain management, and sustainable marketing challenges [17].

Artificial Intelligence (AI) and Marketing Management

The impact of Artificial Intelligence (AI) on managers was investigated in a 2019 study by Krystyna Jarek and Grzegorz Mazurek. Results showed that the main uses of AI are operational suggesting that marketing technology is still in its cautious and experimental stages [18]. Theory of mind, limited memory, reactive machines, and self-awareness are the four primary subtypes of Artificial Intelligence (AI), each with its own goals, methods, and philosophy. The division of intelligence into three categories—weak, strong, and super—based on technological sophistication is also influenced [19]. There are five key focuses to avoid the blame AI culture, where recommendations are evaluated before outputs are adopted in decision-making. These include: first, evaluating recommendations; second, balancing objectivity; third, mitigating human bias; fourth, planning and managing expectations. It highlights how crucial it is to foster a culture of trial and error and to align management expectations right away [20]. One characteristic of AI's impact on post-COVID service-oriented businesses, particularly in the business consulting industry, is process automation. Drawing from recent research the study highlights the evolution of collaboration in the workplace by projecting that AI will automate tasks while generating new employment opportunities. Business consulting staff members can focus on more strategic duties by using automation to handle repetitive tasks. This encourages a positive shift in the perspective of employers and a positive human-machine synergy. The study examines the hierarchy of marketing capabilities enabled by AI and their integration into marketing plans. It offers perspectives on the developing field of AI-enhanced marketing skills and points the way toward future research and comprehension in AI-based strategies used in marketing. This study, published in Psychology and Marketing, provides insight into the relationship between psychology and marketing, as well as an improved understanding of industry dynamics. It examines the impact of Artificial Intelligence (AI) on marketing performance and strategy. To enhance our understanding of innovative marketing strategies that integrate face recognition and neuro-marketing, the author provides a methodical structure for integrating artificial intelligence into marketing campaigns. It provides insightful information about the developing area of decision-making, which increases the efficacy of AI-based technology in marketing.

Analytics of Social Media

To contribute to the existing body of knowledge and facilitate future research, the author identified statistical and behavioural analysis as key categories in social media analytics [21]. Automated and economical substitutes for human data collection are provided by social media analytics, which serves a diverse user base. In order to ensure that managers customize analytics methods appropriately, the author's typology focuses on five criteria [22]. Social media analytics challenges highlight the need for a comprehensive framework with distinct phases and potential solutions. The primary focus of the research was the fundamental requirement for an all-inclusive model or framework that incorporates specific stages of social media analytics [23]. In order to process the essence of this business-focused field, the study examines how Social Media Analytics (SMA) has emerged as a specialized area within Analytics [24].

Influencer Marketing

In particular, influencers who make purchasing decisions benefit greatly from the innovation of influencer marketing. Knowing how to use influencers is crucial since the power of mass media is waning. Wikis, blogs, and social media empower new influencers, but businesses often miss their target audience by not engaging with real influencers. This strategy is directly related to the success of relationship marketing and word-of-mouth [25]. In 2019, Jin Muqaddam and Ryus' study revealed that trust, brand attitude, envy, and social presence were all impacted by Instagram celebrities' brand posts. Social media influencers may have an impact on consumers' decisions to buy particular brands because social presence mediates these effects [26]. The study investigates how rating scores and reviewer comments affect the reasons behind online shoppers' purchases. Online buying motivations are strengthened by satisfaction and trust in review ratings, content, and security, according to an analysis of 400 millennial responses. In influencing consumers' purchase impulses, influencers play a crucial role, as the study reports.

Mobile Marketing

For a business's promotional strategy, mobile marketing is essential, but its efficacy is called into question by order sizes and bounce rates. Businesses should leverage mobile devices' location-based offers and customized messaging to enhance their operations [27]. Examining the impact of mobile devices on product price promotion and customer-centric elements, which are crucial for engaging audiences, the study highlights how mobile devices affect marketing strategies [28].

Location-based Marketing

With its ability to provide direction, indoor spaces are anticipated to be mostly impacted by social media, emergency support LBS (location-based services), mobile gaming equipment, worker monitoring through tracking, and location-based advertisements [29]. This paper investigates the expanding field of location-based marketing, emphasizing the rationale and incentives driving consumer and marketer adoption of this strategy. It also provides real-world examples to illustrate its advantages [30]. Marketers are using location data for more focused campaigns, but as more people have access to the internet, this strategy may elicit responses from a broader spectrum of people, which could impact consumer segmentation, promotion efficacy, transparency, and privacy issues [31]. The study discovered that conditional value has the biggest impact on loyalty to location-based mobile services, with commitment and monetary value having the biggest effects [32]. It is difficult to use location data effectively for a competitive advantage because it is frequently disregarded in information systems education. However, implementing it can lead to new uses that improve study techniques and equip students with career-ready skills. Teaching pupils where information is located is essential for analysis and problem-solving [33].

Augmented Reality (AR) and Virtual Reality (VR)

This research paper covers the history of VR and AR, enabling technologies such as the widely used VR/AR gear, as well as numerous use cases related to VR/AR applications for the travel and hospitality sectors. It evaluated the accomplishments, shortcomings, and hurdles in creating and implementing VR/AR apps that enhance client engagement by refining current marketing funnel designs and conversion rates, thereby offering the necessary extra value or return. Numerous examples from the use cases illustrate that many institutions have invested in AR/VR apps to support their prospective clients and aid in pre-purchase decision-making, suggesting they should consider this approach. VR and AR technology are especially well-suited to assist with decision-making procedures for intangible goods, such as the experience during a holiday or occasion. Chatbots that utilize AI are emerging as a new field of application that benefits the tourism and hospitality industry, particularly in responding to frequently asked questions from prospective buyers and assisting those in the buying process, thereby reducing the need for laborious, repetitive tasks for customer support staff [34]. Due to their useful applications in marketing planning, education, and the preservation of tourist destinations, virtual reality and augmented reality are becoming more and more popular in the travel industry [35]. The study investigates how virtual reality technology affects travel and hospitality with a particular emphasis on tech-based marketing future planning and satisfying changing customer needs [36]. It implies revolutionary tourism systems with interactive interactions and transformative effects. Managers often struggle to differentiate between similar IT-based concepts, such as virtual and augmented reality. The Reality-Virtuality continuum can be divided into six categories according to this summary: mixed reality, augmented reality, virtual reality, and augmented virtuality [37].

The Internet of Things or Web of Things

It is a rapidly growing field that connects similar objects with the internet, such as consumer goods related to the automobile industry, which facilitates efficient information analysis. It's predicted that 100 billion connected devices and an estimated $11 trillion global economic influence will be achieved by 2025 [38]. Demonstrate its enormous impact on the internet and the economy. Billions of smart networked devices will make up the Internet of Things (IoT), a futuristic internet. To demonstrate the need for further research into IoT solutions, this study examines the definition, implementation strategies, unresolved problems, and challenges of IoT [39]. Enhancing dependability, sustainability, and efficiency, the Internet of Things (IoT) links products and services worldwide. It can improve home automation, smart grids, and environmental monitoring. To overcome resource constraints in low-powered wireless devices, the Internet Engineering Task Force introduced IPv6, which enables them to operate, albeit with some limitations, similar to standard internet-connected devices [40, 41].

DISCUSSION

The study emphasizes the significance of implementing AI in marketing management, despite obstacles like data privacy and ethical concerns, by highlighting how it integrates strong data governance procedures, creativity, and adaptability with Industry 5.0 objectives.

Here are the AI-based marketing management technologies and their component elements (Table **1**):

Table 1. Components of AI based marketing management strategies.

1) Online marketing.
2) Analytics of data.
3) CRM
4) Marketing automation.

(Table 1) cont.....

5) Artificial Learning and Machine learning technology in Industry 5.0.
6) Influencer Marketing and Social Media.
7) VR and AR technology in Industry 5.0
8) Smart Assistants and Voice Search.
9) Hyper-targeting and Personalization.
10) Mobile marketing and online sales.
11) Marketing channels are changing technologically.
12) Decision Making Based on Data.
13) Personalized or Customized Interaction with Customers.
14) Adaptability and Innovation.
15) Localization and Standardization.
16) Sustainability and Ethical Issues.

Online Marketing

♣ **SEO or Search Engine Optimization:** It is used to optimize a website's configuration and content, which helps enhance its presence on popular search engines.

♣ **Content-based Marketing:** it is used to attract, engage and retain audience by creating attractive content in the form of videos, text, images, *etc.*

♣ **Form of E Marketing or Email Marketing**: It is a direct or digital form of marketing in which company connect with customers through email.

♣ **Pay Per Click:** Advertisers who use pay-per-click advertising must pay for each click.

♣ **Affiliate Marketing:** This is a type of marketing where companies partner with third-party affiliates, who receive commissions for generating leads.

Analytics of Data

♣ **Web Analytics:** This is used to monitor and track traffic and conversion metrics related to a website's performance.

♣ **Analytics of Social Media:** Data collection from social media platforms is known as social media analytics.

♣ **Customer Analytics:** This technology enables companies to collect customer data, allowing them to customise their products or services according to customer preferences.

♣ **Predictive Analytics:** Companies utilize this tool to make future predictions based on historical data and statistical tools, helping them understand risks and opportunities.

CRM or Customer Relationship Management

♣ **Software of CRM:** Various tools used by companies to manage customer interactions and information's *e.g.* Salesforce or Hub-spot.
♣ **Sales Automation:** It is used to manage or automate sales tasks, which helps in maintaining optimum workflows and increasing productivity.
♣ **Client Management:** It is used to improve client satisfaction and support for the company.
♣ **Marketing Integration:** It utilize CRM and marketing integration to monitor and improve campaigns.

Marketing Automation

♣ **Automation of Email:** It is used to schedule and personalize emails properly by the company.
♣ **Lead Score Technique:** This process assigns numeric values to each lead generated by the company.
♣ **Managing Campaigns:** With the help of this, marketing campaigns can be coordinated and automated well across all channels.
♣ **Reporting and Analytics:** It is used to track the performance of automated campaigns.

Artificial Learning and Machine learning technology in Industry 5.0

♣ **Personalization:** It is a process of tailoring marketing messages with the help of AI tools.
♣ **Chat-bots:** This technique provides instant support and information to customers on time, thanks to AI-driven bots.
♣ **Customer Analytics:** It is used to forecast customer behavior and market trends by using machine learning algorithms.
♣ **Content Generation:** It utilizes AI tools to generate high-quality content that attracts customers.

Influencer Marketing and Social Media

♣ **Influencer Partnership or Relationship:** By partnering with influencers, companies can effectively reach their customers.
♣ **Creation of Content:** It helps companies enhance customer engagement on social media.
♣ **Social Media Advertisement:** Nowadays, companies are using paid promotions on popular social media platforms like Facebook, Instagram, Twitter, *etc.*, to attract more customers.
♣ **Community Management:** It helps in managing online communities and engaging with followers.

VR and AR Technology in Industry 5.0

♣ **Visualization of Products:** With the help of AI, companies can enable their customers to view products in a virtual environment.
♣ **Virtual Tours:** With the help of this, customers can have an immersive experience of properties or locations.
♣ **Interactive Experiences:** Companies utilize AR and VR technology to engage users on their websites.
♣ **Simulation and Training:** Companies can provide training and skill development programs to employees using VR.

Smart Assistants and Voice Search

♣ **SEO based on Voice:** This technique helps in optimizing content for any type of voice search queries.
♣ **Smart Speaker Integration Technique:** A company can upgrade skills and applications for devices like Amazon Alexa and Google Assistant.
♣ **Voice-Activated Marketing:** Marketing messages can be created with creativity using voice commands.
♣ **Conversational AI:** AI-driven voice interfaces help in enhancing customer interactions.

Hyper-targeting and Personalization

♣ **Behavioural Targeting:** It uses behavioural data to deliver relevant ads.
♣ **Dynamic Content:** It helps in customizing website content based on user preferences.
♣ **Email Personalization:** It helps in tailoring email content to individual recipient profiles.
♣ **Geo- targeting:** In it, location-based marketing messages can be delivered well.

Mobile Marketing and Online Sales

♣ **Mobile-Friendly Websites:** With the help of these websites are optimized for mobile devices.
♣ **Mobile Apps:** Applications are developed to enhance customer engagement and sales.
♣ **SMS Marketing:** This is used to send promotional messages *via* text.
♣ **Mobile Payments**: It is used to facilitate easy and secure mobile transactions.

Technological Evolution of Marketing Channels

♣ **Omni Channel Marketing:** This technique based on integration of various marketing channels for ensuring a seamless customer experience.
♣ **Interactive Advertising:** This is used to engage users through interactive ads.
♣ **Programmatic Advertising:** With the use of algorithms, the buying and placement of ads can be automated.
♣ **DOOH or Digital Out of Home Advertising:** Digital display board used at public places to attract targeted customers.

Data-Driven Decision Making

♣ **On-time or Real-time Analytics:** With the help of these companies, one can make decisions on the basis of up-to-date data.
♣ **A/B Testing:** This technique is used to assess the superior performance of two iterations of a marketing asset.
♣ **Insights of Customers:** used to derive actionable insights from customer data.
♣ **Metrics of Performance:** A business success is measured on the basis of KPIs.

Personalized or Customized Interaction with Customers

♣ **Personal or Individual Emails:** Used to send personalized or tailored email content to individual recipients.
♣ **Vibrant or Dynamic Web Content:** Used to adjust content of website based on user profiles.
♣ **Segmented or Targeted Offers:** It is used to provide customized promotions and discounts.
♣ **Feedback Loop of Customers:** Used to enhance customer interactions based on feedback.

Adaptability and Innovation:

♣ **Agile Marketing:** It is also known as marketing agility, which comprises sense-making, iterations, speed, and marketing decisions.
♣ **Modern or Innovative Campaigns:** With the use of AI, a company can create or develop new and cutting-edge marketing initiatives.
♣ **Adoption of Technology:** It is a process of embracing or adopting new or modern technologies to stay competitive.
♣ **Market Research:** Market research involves analyzing continuous market trends and customer needs.

Localization and Standardization

♣ **Local Content:** It is based on adapting marketing content in local languages and cultures.
♣ **Universal or Global Branding:** Used by companies to maintain a consistent brand image across different markets.
♣ **Local or Regional Campaigns:** In it companies tailored marketing campaigns to specific regions.
♣ **SOPs or Standard Operating Procedures:** These companies can help execute marketing strategies based on SOPs.

Sustainability and Ethical Issues

♣ **Ecological or Eco-Friendly Marketing:** used by companies to promote sustainable products and practices.
♣ **Ethical or Standardized Advertising:** In it companies are ensuring truthful and responsible marketing messages.
♣ **CSR or Corporate Social Responsibility:** It highlights a company's efforts towards environmental and social responsibility.
♣ **Privacy of Consumer:** Used to safeguard or protect customer data to ensure ethical use of information.

Marketing management techniques based on AI and their relation to the contemporary business environment:

Today, the AI-based marketing management strategies and the current business environment are listed below:

- Some Artificial Intelligence-driven marketing management strategies that enable personalized customer experiences and forecast data are revolutionizing the modern business environment.
- A combination of human and artificial intelligence creativity is essential for developing marketing solutions that are distinct and raise customer engagement and satisfaction.
- By integrating AI and big data analytics, businesses can gain profound insights into consumer behavior, improving marketing efforts and increasing return on investment.
- Virtual reality and Augmented Reality (AR) are integral to creating memorable and captivating consumer experiences, which help brands stand out in a crowded market.
- Flexible and responsive marketing campaigns can be achieved by leveraging real-time data collection and analysis, facilitated by the Internet of Things (IoT).

- By leveraging targeted advertising and personalized content, social media networks that utilize AI algorithms can significantly enhance brand exposure and customer engagement.
- To preserve customer trust and regulatory compliance, organizations using AI-enabled marketing technology must address data privacy concerns.
- With the implementation of AI-driven marketing campaigns, businesses need to be quick to adjust and take advantage of technological advancements to maintain a competitive edge in the ever-evolving market.
- Machine learning and Artificial intelligence can automate repetitive marketing processes, freeing up human resources to focus on strategic decision-making and creative problem-solving. The use of Artificial Intelligence (AI) in marketing aligns with Industry 5.0's emphasis on the human-machine partnership, fostering an eco-friendly, customer-centric, and efficient corporate atmosphere.

Industry 5.0 and Sustainability

The relationships of AI- driven marketing tactics and Industry 5.0 are highlighted in this study, and these are as follows (Table **2**):

Table 2. Relationships of AI- driven marketing tactics and industry 5.0.

Strategies used in Marketing	Benefits of Strategies Based on AI in Marketing	Linking AI-based marketing strategies with Industry 5.0
Customization and Personalization	Businesses can create individualized and customized campaigns by using AI to analyze large amounts of data and customer behavior.	Industry 5.0 is all about customized goods and services and AI in marketing helps with this by offering recommendations and content that is specifically suited to the target audience.
Analytics for Prediction	By examining past data, AI algorithms can forecast consumer preferences, trends, and market shifts.	To remain competitive, satisfy market demands, and efficiently maximize production, businesses in Industry 5.0 need this capability.
Improvement of the Customer Experience	Artificial Intelligence (AI) tools that improve customer interactions include chatbots, virtual assistants, and natural language processing.	By fusing human and machine intelligence, artificial intelligence plays a crucial part in Industry 5.0 in terms of enhancing seamless and accommodating customer experiences.
Efficiency and automation.	Artificial Intelligence (AI) simplifies marketing tasks, freeing up human marketers to focus on more creative and strategic aspects of their work.	By automating marketing procedures to maximize productivity and efficiency, Industry 5.0 creates a collaborative atmosphere where people and machines work together.

(Table 2) cont.....

Strategies used in Marketing	Benefits of Strategies Based on AI in Marketing	Linking AI-based marketing strategies with Industry 5.0
Data-driven decision-making.	Because AI can handle and analyse enormous amounts of data so well, it enhances data-driven decision-making.	Businesses can utilize artificial intelligence-generated tools to inform wise and effective decision-making in marketing strategies, product development, and overall business operations.
Supply chain establishment.	Artificial Intelligence (AI) enhances supply chain efficiency by improving logistics, managing inventory, and anticipating demand. This helps marketing strategies by guaranteeing product availability and prompt delivery which in turn increases customer satisfaction.	Industry 5.0 and AI alignment: AI emphasizes adaptable and effective production systems.
Flexibility and adaptability.	An AI system is able to adjust to shifting consumer demands and market dynamics.	Businesses can quickly adjust to consumer preferences and market trends with the help of AI-supported marketing strategies, which guarantees long-term viability in a changing business climate.

As per Industry 5.0 concepts, in this dynamic industrial setting, AI-based marketing strategies enable the efficiency of human-machine collaboration, personalization, and a customer-focused approach.

Here we can take one example of a company that is using AI-based marketing techniques in India and has established a strong brand name in the industry (Table 3):

Table 3. Technologies used by Tataelaxi (Source: tataelxsi.com).

Company Name	Types of Technologies used	Establishment Year
Company: Tata Elxsi Ltd.	From sophisticated RandD in new technology and system design research to real development, validation, and deployment, it collaborates closely with its customers. This covers cutting-edge technology, including artificial intelligence, cloud computing, smart mobility, and the Internet of Things (IoT). Hence, it generates new opportunities for companies to reduce expenses, enhance operational efficiency, and offer customers innovative services.	May 5 1989

CONCLUSION AND FINDINGS

The study examines the connection between Industry 5.0 and AI-based marketing strategies by emphasizing how new technologies are revolutionizing conventional marketing techniques. Industry 5.0 focuses on human-machine collaboration and efficiency enhancement, while also highlighting the complementary effects of AI and marketing. Businesses can develop sustainable supply chain procedures by optimizing resources and reducing waste through marketing, aided by artificial intelligence. Because of its unique dynamic partnership, efficiency, adaptability, and customer-centricity are promoted, leading to a future industry that is more sustainable and robust. It also highlights how marketers must embrace innovation, data-driven decision-making, and ethical considerations to maximize customer engagement and drive business growth. Companies can become more competitive and create a path toward sustainable growth by utilizing these technologies effectively in the digital age of Industry 5.0. Artificial intelligence in marketing strategies that please customers and improve the reputation of businesses are the keys to long-term sustainability.

Study Implications

Numerous implications flow from the results of the current study regarding the link between artificial–intelligence based strategies of marketing and Industry 5.0. These implications help bridge the knowledge gap between theory and practice, providing insightful data for both practice and research on society. And here is the explanation given after that:

1. **Implications to Research:** the current study emphasizes the significance of artificial intelligence-driven marketing tactics for Industry 5.0 and recommends more investigation into particular business sectors and the ethical ramifications for consumer behaviour.
2. **Practice-related Implications:** Today, businesses need to combine sustainability and innovation with data-driven decision-making morality into their marketing strategies to encourage resource efficiency and consumer engagement.
3. **Societal Contribution:** The study highlights the benefits of artificial intelligence-driven marketing strategies in Industry 5.0, including sustainability, adaptability, and customer centricity, while also addressing ethical concerns related to social impact.
4. **Integrating Practice and Theory**: It provides businesses with actionable advice on how to create robust and long-lasting marketing campaigns related to Industry 5.0 with artificial intelligence - based marketing techniques.

5. **Commercial Impact**: Data-driven decision-making, optimized resource allocation, and enhanced customer loyalty are facilitated when Artificial Intelligence (AI) is embedded into marketing strategies. These findings may increase market flexibility, ensuring long-term success and boosting brand recognition.
6. **Teaching and Education**: The research findings provide invaluable teaching resources by serving some case studies related to business and marketing courses on the revolutionary effects of artificial intelligence -based technologies in marketing management.
7. **Influence on Public Policy:** This study may affect laws pertaining to the morality of this type of management in marketing by addressing moral issues brought up by the use of AI in advertising. It may also foster more fruitful discussions about the responsible application of AI.
8. **Contribution to the Body of Knowledge:** The study offers a thorough understanding of the connection between the notions of Industry 5.0. The research provides a comprehensive grasp of the relationship between the concept of Industry 5.0 and AI-driven marketing strategies and AI-based marketing tactics.

Finally, this study provides a comprehensive grasp of the connection between Industry 5.0 and artificial intelligence-based marketing strategies. It also provides a thorough understanding of how artificial intelligence-based marketing strategies and Industry 5.0 interact with each other, offering guidance on implementing these strategies for stable and long-lasting business operations.

REFERENCES

[1] X. Li, and E. Karahanna, "The rise of AI chatbots in customer service: Identifying factors that contribute to chatbot acceptance and use intentions", *J. Serv. Res.,* vol. 22, no. 5, pp. 647-661, 2019.

[2] J.M.S. Cheng, C. Blankson, E.S.T. Wang, and L.S.L. Chen, "Consumer attitudes and interactive digital advertising", *Int. J. Advert.,* vol. 28, no. 3, pp. 501-525, 2009. [http://dx.doi.org/10.2501/S0265048709200710]

[3] N. Sharma, "Digital marketing as an effective tool for advertising in India: A critical review", *PalArch's Journal of Archaeology of Egypt/Egyptology,* vol. 18, no. 9, pp. 37-49, 2021.

[4] E. Constantinides, "Foundations of social media marketing", *Procedia Soc. Behav. Sci.,* vol. 148, pp. 40-57, 2014. [http://dx.doi.org/10.1016/j.sbspro.2014.07.016]

[5] I.P. Chiang, S.H. Lo, and L.H. Wang, "Customer engagement behaviour in social media advertising: Antecedents and consequences", *Contemp. Manag. Res.,* vol. 13, no. 3, 2018. [http://dx.doi.org/10.7903/cmr.17673]

[6] B. P. Kushwaha, "Search engine marketing a new way of marketing in digital age", *PalArch's Journal of Archaeology of Egypt/Egyptology,* vol. 17, no. 6, pp. 2053-2065, 2020.

[7] P. Ducange, R. Pecori, and P. Mezzina, "A glimpse on big data analytics in the framework of marketing strategies", *Soft Comput.,* vol. 22, no. 1, pp. 325-342, 2018. [http://dx.doi.org/10.1007/s00500-017-2536-4]

[8] H.J. Watson, "Tutorial: Big data analytics: Concepts, technologies, and applications", *Comm. Assoc. Inform. Syst.*, vol. 34, no. 1, p. 65, 2014. [http://dx.doi.org/10.17705/1CAIS.03465]

[9] M. Holmlund, Y. Van Vaerenbergh, R. Ciuchita, A. Ravald, P. Sarantopoulos, F.V. Ordenes, and M. Zaki, "Customer experience management in the age of big data analytics: A strategic framework", *J. Bus. Res.*, vol. 116, pp. 356-365, 2020. [http://dx.doi.org/10.1016/j.jbusres.2020.01.022]

[10] H.D. Harlow, "Developing a knowledge management strategy for data analytics and intellectual capital", *Meditari Accountancy Research,* vol. 26, no. 3, pp. 400-419, 2018. [http://dx.doi.org/10.1108/MEDAR-09-2017-0217]

[11] S.S. Andaleeb, *Market segmentation, targeting, and positioning in Strategic Marketing Management in Asia: Case Studies and Lessons across Industries.* Emerald Group Publishing Limited, 2016, pp. 179-207.

[12] B. Cooil, L. Aksoy, and T.L. Keiningham, "Approaches to customer segmentation", *J. Relationsh. Mark.,* vol. 6, no. 3-4, pp. 9-39, 2008. [http://dx.doi.org/10.1300/J366v06n03_02]

[13] M. Lynn, "Segmenting and targeting your market: Strategies and limitations", *in The Cornell School of Hotel Administration on Hospitality: Cutting Edge Thinking and Practice,* pp. 351-369, 2012. [http://dx.doi.org/10.1002/9781119200901.ch23]

[14] F. Buttle, and S. Maklan, *Customer Relationship Management: Concepts and Technologies.* Routledge, 2019. [http://dx.doi.org/10.4324/9781351016551]

[15] H.S. Soliman, "Customer relationship management and its relationship to the marketing performance", *Int. J. Bus. Soc. Sci.,* vol. 2, no. 10, 2011.

[16] F. Buttle, and S. Maklan, *Customer Relationship Management: Concepts and Technologies.* Routledge, 2019. [http://dx.doi.org/10.4324/9781351016551]

[17] M. Ferrer-Estévez, and R. Chalmeta, "Sustainable customer relationship management", *Mark. Intell. Plann.,* vol. 41, no. 2, pp. 244-262, 2023. [http://dx.doi.org/10.1108/MIP-06-2022-0266]

[18] K. Jarek, and G. Mazurek, "Marketing and artificial intelligence", *Central European Business Review,* vol. 8, no. 2, 2019. [http://dx.doi.org/10.18267/j.cebr.213]

[19] K. Chung, P. Thaichon, and S. Quach, *"Types of artificial intelligence (AI) in marketing management," in Artificial Intelligence for Marketing Management.* Routledge, 2022, pp. 29-40.

[20] G. Volkmar, P.M. Fischer, and S. Reinecke, "Artificial Intelligence and Machine Learning: Exploring drivers, barriers, and future developments in marketing management", *J. Bus. Res.,* vol. 149, pp. 599-614, 2022. [http://dx.doi.org/10.1016/j.jbusres.2022.04.007]

[21] S. Moon, and D. Iacobucci, "Social media analytics and its applications in marketing", *Foundations and Trends® in Marketing,* vol. 15, no. 4, pp. 213-292, 2022. [http://dx.doi.org/10.1561/1700000073]

[22] I. Lee, "Social media analytics for enterprises: Typology, methods, and processes", *Bus. Horiz.,* vol. 61, no. 2, pp. 199-210, 2018. [http://dx.doi.org/10.1016/j.bushor.2017.11.002]

[23] S. Stieglitz, M. Mirbabaie, B. Ross, and C. Neuberger, "Social media analytics – Challenges in topic discovery, data collection, and data preparation", *Int. J. Inf. Manage.,* vol. 39, pp. 156-168, 2018.

[http://dx.doi.org/10.1016/j.ijinfomgt.2017.12.002]

[24] C.W. Holsapple, S.H. Hsiao, and R. Pakath, "Business social media analytics: Characterization and conceptual framework", *Decis. Support Syst.,* vol. 110, pp. 32-45, 2018. [http://dx.doi.org/10.1016/j.dss.2018.03.004]

[25] D. Brown, and N. Hayes, *Influencer Marketing.* Routledge, 2008. [http://dx.doi.org/10.4324/9780080557700]

[26] S.V. Jin, A. Muqaddam, and E. Ryu, "Instafamous and social media influencer marketing", *Mark. Intell. Plann.,* vol. 37, no. 5, pp. 567-579, 2019. [http://dx.doi.org/10.1108/MIP-09-2018-0375]

[27] B. Berman, "Planning and implementing effective mobile marketing programs", *Bus. Horiz.,* vol. 59, no. 4, pp. 431-439, 2016. [http://dx.doi.org/10.1016/j.bushor.2016.03.006]

[28] P. Smutkupt, D. Krairit, and V. Esichaikul, "Mobile marketing: Implications for marketing strategies", *Int. J. Mob. Marketing,* vol. 5, no. 2, 2010.

[29] M.A. Cheema, "Indoor location-based services", *SIGSPATIAL Special,* vol. 10, no. 2, pp. 10-17, 2018. [http://dx.doi.org/10.1145/3292390.3292394]

[30] D. Bansal, *"Location Based Marketing: Issues and Opportunities in the Real World," in Enhancing Customer Engagement through Location-Based Marketing.* IGI Global, 2023, pp. 44-55. [http://dx.doi.org/10.4018/978-1-6684-8177-6.ch004]

[31] S. Banerjee, "Geomarketing and situated consumers: opportunities and challenges", *Proceedings of the 3rd ACM SIGSPATIAL International Workshop on Location-based Recommendations, Geosocial Networks and Geoadvertising,* pp. 1-4, 2019. [http://dx.doi.org/10.1145/3356994.3366017]

[32] M. Pura, "Linking perceived value and loyalty in location-based mobile services", *Manag. Serv. Qual.,* vol. 15, no. 6, pp. 509-538, 2005. [http://dx.doi.org/10.1108/09604520510634005]

[33] J. B. Sarkar, Pick, M. A. Erskine, A. Satpathy, and A. Diaz Lopez, "Location analytics in information systems: innovative applications and research opportunities," 2022.

[34] B. Mahapatra, D. Le Nayyar, and G. Suseendran, "Virtual Reality (VR) and Augmented Reality (AR) technologies for tourism and hospitality industry", *International Journal of Engineering and Technology,* vol. 7, no. 2.21, pp. 156-160, 2018.

[35] N. Elmqaddem, "Augmented reality and virtual reality in education. Myth or reality?", *International Journal of Emerging Technologies in Learning (iJET),* vol. 14, no. 3, p. 234, 2019. [http://dx.doi.org/10.3991/ijet.v14i03.9289]

[36] Pestek and M. Sarvan, "Virtual reality and modern tourism", *Journal of Tourism Futures,* vol. 7, no. 2, pp. 245-250, 2020.

[37] M. Farshid, J. Paschen, T. Eriksson, and J. Kietzmann, "Go boldly!", *Bus. Horiz.,* vol. 61, no. 5, pp. 657-663, 2018. [http://dx.doi.org/10.1016/j.bushor.2018.05.009]

[38] K. Rose, S. Eldridge, and L. Chapin, "The internet of things: An overview", *Internet Society,* vol. 80, pp. 1-50, 2015. [ISOC].

[39] S. Li, L.D. Xu, and S. Zhao, "The internet of things: a survey", *Inf. Syst. Front.,* vol. 17, no. 2, pp. 243-259, 2015. [http://dx.doi.org/10.1007/s10796-014-9492-7]

[40] S.C. Mukhopadhyay, and N.K. Suryadevara, *''Internet of Things: Challenges and Opportunities.* Springer International Publishing, 2014, pp. 1-17. [http://dx.doi.org/10.1007/978-3-319-04223-7]

[41] S. Rana, S. Bag, I. Ghosal, and B. Prasad, "How do influencers moderate purchase motives? an application of SOR model to assess the effects of reviewers' rating on online purchase", *J. Promot. Manage.,* pp. 1-30, 2023.

CHAPTER 12

AI-Enabled Green and Sustainable Resource Management in Horticulture

Pradnya Mehta[1,*], **Tanush Lichade**[2], **Yashowardhan Patil**[3] and **Chinmay Kulkarni**[4]

[1] *Department of Computer Engineering- AI, Vishwakarma Institute of Information Technology, Pune, India*

[2] *Department of Artificial Intelligence & Data Science, Vishwakarma Institute of Information Technology, Pune, India*

[3] *Department of Computer Engineering, Vishwakarma Institute of Information Technology, Pune, India*

[4] *Department of Computer Engineering-AIML, Vishwakarma Institute of Information Technology, Pune, India*

Abstract: The integration of AI into horticulture offers a revolutionary strategy for environmentally responsible resource allocation. The modern horticultural industry must find a way to increase production while reducing its negative effects on the environment. The advent of AI presents a revolutionary chance to optimize resource management procedures. Precision farming, pest and disease management, and crop yield prediction are at the forefront of AI-enabled green and sustainable resource management in horticulture. The basic concept is to establish a networked horticulture ecosystem in which AI collects data from multiple sources and provides real-time insights for intelligent decision-making with the help of Algorithms like Ant Colony Optimization, Particle Swarm Optimization, or neural networks with fuzzy logic. It can simulate natural behaviors to optimize planting patterns and resource allocation. Improvements in resource effectiveness, productivity, environmental protection, and economic sustainability are among the anticipated consequences. Among the outcomes we expect are increases in resource efficiency, productivity, environmental preservation, and economic sustainability. When AI is applied to the horticulture industry, it has the potential to dramatically improve resource management, leading to greater longevity, output, and profitability.

Keywords: Artificial intelligence, Fuzzy logic, Horticulture, Swarm intelligence, Sustainable resource.

[*] **Corresponding author Pradnya Mehta:** Department of Computer Engineering- AI, Vishwakarma Institute of Information Technology, Pune, India; E-mail: pradnya17.mehta@gmail.com

INTRODUCTION

The fusion of artificial intelligence and horticulture stands out as a beacon of hope in a time when environmental concerns are a top priority, and the push for sustainable practices has never been louder. In a time when environmental issues are of utmost importance, and the demand for sustainable practices has never been greater, the combination of artificial intelligence and horticulture stands out as a ray of hope. An in-depth exploration of the field of sustainable horticulture is provided in AI-Driven Sustainable Horticulture, which explores how cutting-edge AI technologies are transforming how we cultivate, manage, and protect our natural resources. An increase in greater numbers is expected to increase the demand for more quality and quantity of sustainable food. Two billion children under the age of five have had delayed development and growth due to a chronic lack of vital nutrients in their diet. This suggests that efforts to combat food insecurity and malnutrition brought on by climatic extremes and economic instability need to be prioritized more [1]. Sustainable growing of fruits and vegetables, or horticulture, can provide the healthy micronutrients needed to combat malnutrition. Horticulture stands out as a colorful thread in the great tapestry of India's agricultural legacy, intimately woven into thc country's social, economic, and dietary fabric. For India's economy, sustenance, and biodiversity, this multifaceted and dynamic sector, which includes the cultivation of fruits, vegetables, spices, landscaping plants, and more, is of paramount importance. Numerous horticulture crops can flourish in India's favorable climatic conditions, which range from tropical to temperate. The country's diverse agricultural landscape, which extends from the enchanted apple orchards tucked away in the Himalayan Mountains to the luscious coconut groves surrounding the coastlines, is a monument to its intricate geographical tapestry. Horticulture plays a crucial role in helping India, a country with a population of over a billion, address its food security challenges. The production of nutrient-dense fruits and vegetables guarantees that millions of people have a varied and well-balanced diet.

Additionally, the industry provides a variety of employment options, particularly for marginal and small-scale farmers who find comfort in caring for their gardens and orchards. Horticulture crops boost farm output, provide jobs, and supply raw materials to various food-processing enterprises, all of which have a significant beneficial effect on the Indian economy. Despite the statistic, there is some space for horticulture, and a large bazaar for the harvests produced around. As a result, it might be difficult to meet demand while using the least amount of resources because sustainable practices need to be employed to guarantee a sustainable environment [2]. A new technology has entered the intricate interplay among tradition and innovation that defines India's horticulture journey: Artificial Intelligence (AI). AI weaves a contemporary thread into the tapestry of horticulture, promoting efficiency and sustainability while honoring the region's agricultural legacy. By leveraging the ability to process massive datasets, AI derives insights that far exceed the analytical capacity of human observation alone. Small-scale farmers in a country where agriculture is AI have priceless tools. Artificial Intelligence mitigates risks and empowers farmers to make informed decisions. This includes advanced irrigation systems that optimize water consumption, as well as predictive analytics that forecast pest infestations and facilitate prompt actions.

An Overview of India's Horticulture Farming

The publication "Fruits and Vegetables Availability Maps of India" details each state's contribution to India's overall fruit and vegetable production. The regions of India where fruits are grown are covered in the study [3]. This also includes information on the number of hectares of land used for fruit cultivation and the productivity of fruits in the field. The number of acres of land utilized for fruit production, as well as the yield of fruits harvested in the field, are also included in this work. The conclusion derived from both works is that India's arable land and productivity are getting smaller every year. Intense drought, a lack of rain, fruit illnesses, *etc.*, are to blame for this. The production curves for fruits such as pomegranate, papaya, apple, and orange, among others, exhibit a downward trend [4]. Serious hazards to the development of the horticulture business include the loss of fertile soil, rising land costs, water scarcity, global warming, and the impossibility of low-cost labor. Abiotic stressors such as temperature extremes, salinity, pH, and drought are key hindrances to horticulture crops [5]. Crops used in horticulture are susceptible to daily variations in temperature, humidity, and other climatic conditions. Farmers may suffer large financial losses if they are unprepared for even a slight change in weather patterns. Often, horticulturists incur significant losses due to the spread of diseases across their fields, or at times, as a result of pathogens and pests. With all these natural problems, horticulture in India also faces certain problems. The primary marketing problems for horticultural products include the lack of markets for centralized production, a substantial number of middlemen, the absence of marketing organizations protecting farmers' interests, the ineffective pricing structure, and the lack of transparency in market information networks, especially in the export market.

OBJECTIVES OF RESEARCH

Primary Objective

This research aims to investigate the potential of AI-enabled techniques for achieving green and sustainable resource management in horticulture.

Secondary Objectives

1. To assess the feasibility of integrating AI technologies, including Ant Colony Optimization, Particle Swarm Optimization, neural networks, and fuzzy logic, into horticultural practices.
2. To evaluate the impact of AI-driven resource management on crop yield, resource efficiency, environmental conservation, and economic sustainability.
3. To compare and contrast the performance of different AI methodologies in horticultural applications.
4. To provide practical insights and recommendations for adopting AI in horticulture to benefit farmers and the environment.

Significance of AI in Horticulture

Artificial Intelligence (AI) has a lot of potential and is used in horticulture in a variety of key ways. Crop health monitoring, soil conditions checking, and weather pattern predictions may all be tracked using AI-powered systems that analyze data from sensors, drones, and satellites. Farmers can maximize their use of resources and boost crop yields by implementing smart irrigation, fertilization, and pest management strategies. AI can identify diseases and pests early on by analyzing Heatedographs and data gathered from fields. This makes prompt action possible, cutting down on crop losses and the demand for chemical treatments. Based on historical data, current weather conditions, and a variety of other variables, AI systems can forecast agricultural yields. Farmers can plan harvesting and distribution more successfully with the aid of this information. Artificial intelligence and robotics can be combined to develop AI-driven robots for various horticulture processes. Robots are commonly utilized in the horticulture industry for harvesting, drone application by spraying, field tracking, organizing, grading, packing final horticultural produce, and to some extent in nurseries and greenhouses [6]. Automated Pruning: Farm Wise's self-operating agricultural robots employ artificial intelligence to enhance pruning methods. Mechanism: The AI evaluates three-dimensional scans of vegetation, pinpointing the most effective pruning locations to boost production.

DESIGN

Overview of AI-Enabled Resource Management and Environmental Sustainability Applications

Artificial Intelligence (AI)-enabled resource management in horticulture refers to the use of AI technology to optimize resource allocation and utilization in the production of crops, fruits, vegetables, and other horticultural products. This novel method uses automation and data-driven insights to improve crop yields, quality, and sustainability while reducing resource waste.

1. ***Data Gathering and Analysis*:** AI systems gather information from a variety of devices, including sensors, drones, weather stations, satellite imagery, and other devices. Machine learning algorithms process and analyze these data to reveal information about the soil, weather, pest and disease outbreaks, and plant health.
2. ***Crop Monitoring and Health Assessment*:** To monitor plant health, find illnesses, and identify pests, AI-powered cameras and image recognition technology are utilized. Early detection enables focused interventions, reducing the need for extensive pesticide application.
3. ***Predictive Analytics:*** Farmers can arrange their planting and harvesting schedules with the help of AI algorithms that can estimate crop yields and market demand. This lowers the possibility of overproducing or underproducing while maximizing resource allocation.
4. ***Impact on the Environment and Sustainability*:** By lowering resource waste and the usage of toxic pesticides, AI-enabled resource management encourages sustainable farming methods. It lessens the impact of horticulture production on the environment and supports environmentally responsible agriculture.
5. ***Remote Management and Monitoring:*** AI gives growers the freedom and real-time decision-making power to monitor and manage their horticultural operations remotely.
6. ***Water Management:*** The Water Management system developed by IBM employs artificial intelligence to enhance the efficiency of water consumption in urban areas. Mechanism: The AI processes data from sensors and meteorological predictions to forecast the water demand.
7. ***Waste Reduction***

   Illustration: The recycling sorting process in waste management employs artificial intelligence and computer vision technology. Mechanism: The AI system examines images of recyclable materials, accurately recognizing different substances and enhancing the sorting efficiency.

8. ***Pollution Monitoring:***
   For instance, Air Visual employs artificial intelligence to monitor air quality by utilizing data from sensors. The AI system evaluates sensor information alongside meteorological patterns to forecast air quality levels.
9. ***Renewable Energy Enhancement:***
   Illustration: Siemens employs artificial intelligence in its energy management systems to enhance the efficiency of solar and wind energy generation.
   Mechanism: The AI system evaluates meteorological predictions and energy consumption patterns to maximize energy output.
10. ***Ecosystem Preservation:***
    Illustration: The Environmental Insights Explorer, developed by Google employs artificial intelligence to oversee dcforestation activities.
    Mechanism: Artificial intelligence processes satellite images to monitor deforestation trends and pinpoint regions that require conservation efforts.

Integration of AI in Horticulture

The integration of AI technologies in horticulture has ushered in a new era of precision farming and resource optimization. Swarm intelligence, inspired by the collective behavior of social organisms like ants and bees, is being applied to coordinate the actions of agricultural robots and drones. These swarms can efficiently monitor and manage crops, ensuring optimal conditions for growth while minimizing resource use and environmental impact. Neural networks, intense learning models, have found their place in horticulture by analyzing vast datasets to provide insights into crop health, disease detection, and yield prediction. They excel at recognizing subtle patterns in images, making them invaluable for diagnosing plant diseases early and assisting with precision spraying and harvesting.

Fuzzy logic, on the other hand, aids in decision-making processes within horticulture by handling uncertainty and imprecise data. Fuzzy logic controllers can optimize irrigation systems by considering various factors like soil moisture, weather forecasts, and crop types, ensuring that the right amount of water is applied at the right time. This prevents both under- and over-irrigation, conserving water resources and improving crop quality.

Methodology with AI-Enabled Green and Sustainable Resource Swarm Intelligence in Horticulture

In the ever-evolving realm of agriculture, the pursuit of enhanced crop yields, resource efficiency, and sustainable farming techniques has ignited fervor for innovative methodologies. Among these, Swarm Intelligence (SI) has emerged as a promising avenue, garnering increasing attention. Within the broader agricultural landscape, horticulture, responsible for the cultivation of fruits, vegetables, ornamental plants, and specialized crops, confronts unique challenges. These challenges encompass the imperative to maximize productivity, minimize resource wastage, and ensure ecological sustainability. Horticulture stands as a vital contributor to both global food security and economic prosperity. Yet, it grapples with a multitude of complexities. These include the unpredictable impacts of climate change on weather patterns, surging demands for top-tier produce, and the pressing need to curtail environmental footprints. Traditional agricultural practices, once dependable, often prove inadequate in navigating this intricate terrain. Swarm Intelligence, taking inspiration from the coordinated behavior of social insects and other natural systems, offers a fresh and promising perspective to address these multifaceted challenges efficaciously.

Introduction to Swarm Intelligence

Swarm Intelligence, derived from the collective behavior of decentralized and self-organized systems in nature, holds immense promise in revolutionizing horticultural practices. The concept draws inspiration from the coordinated actions of social insects like ants, bees, and termites, as well as the flocking behavior of birds and the schooling of fish, as shown in Figs. (**1a**, **b** and **c**). These natural systems have evolved over millions of years to efficiently solve problems such as foraging, resource allocation, and defense in a dynamic environment. The application of Swarm Intelligence principles in horticulture is a relatively new but rapidly evolving field. It leverages the principles of decentralization, self-organization, and cooperation among individuals to enhance the overall performance of horticultural systems.

Fig. (1a). Flock of birds.

Fig. (1b). A school of fish.

Fig. (1c). Swarm of honeycomb.

By emulating the behaviors of these natural systems, SI strategies can optimize planting patterns, irrigation schedules, pest management, and harvesting techniques. This not only improves crop yields but also minimizes resource usage and reduces the ecological footprint of horticultural practices [7]. This technology holds great promise for revolutionizing horticulture by emulating the collective behaviors of natural systems. In the agricultural realm, SI can empower farmers to enhance crop yields, reduce pesticide and fertilizer usage, and conserve water resources. In horticulture, SI serves numerous functions:

1. **Plant Pollination:** SI algorithms facilitate the controlled pollination of plants through insect management, thereby elevating crop yields and diminishing the necessity for pesticides.
2. **Pest Control:** SI algorithms can be harnessed for effective pest management, achieved through the development of pest-detecting and destroying robots or strategies that attract beneficial insects to crops.
3. **Water Management:** SI algorithms optimize plant irrigation, contributing to water conservation and improved crop productivity.
4. **Fertilizer Management:** SI algorithms optimize fertilizer application, reducing the environmental impact of agriculture while enhancing crop yields.

Swarm Intelligence (SI) enhances AI-enabled green and sustainable resource management in horticulture. By integrating SI optimization algorithms like Ant Colony Optimization (ACO) and Particle Swarm Optimization (PSO), inspired by nature's decentralized systems, we improve decision-making in agriculture. This synergy between SI and machine learning tools promotes sustainable practices, boosts crop productivity, and minimizes environmental impact, making horticulture more efficient and eco-friendly [8].

Application of Ant Colony Optimization for Crop Planning

Ant Colony Intelligent Systems (ACIS) harness the collective intelligence of ant colonies to address complex optimization problems in engineering, diverging from traditional digital computing. In Ant Colony Optimization (ACO), shown in Fig. (**2**), pheromones emulate the communication and local interactions of real ant colonies. Artificial ants deposit pheromone during foraging with its gradual evaporation influenced by the specific ACO variant used, typically involving both incremental deposition and exponential degradation processes.

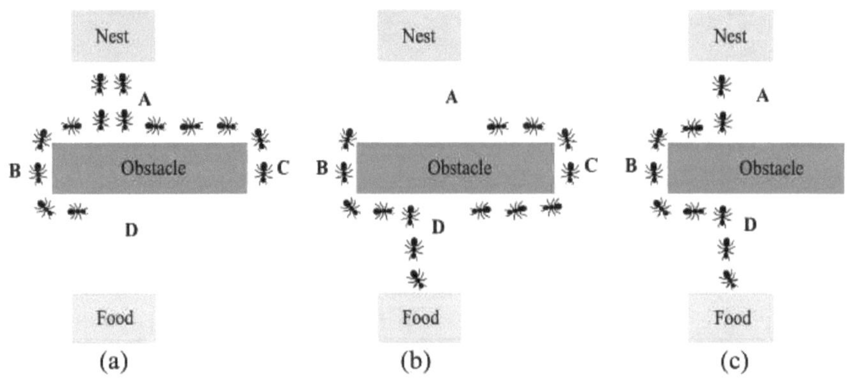

Fig. (2). Foraging behavior of ants moving from their nest (origin) to the food source (destination), taking the shortest possible route through one mediation [stage (**a**) to stage (**c**)].

Swarm intelligence, a concept inspired by natural systems like ant colonies, aids in AI-enabled green and sustainable resource management in horticulture. By leveraging the principles of decentralized decision-making and collaboration seen in swarms, AI systems can optimize resource allocation, enhance crop yield, and minimize environmental impact, contributing to more eco-friendly and efficient horticultural practices [9]. Social insects like ants, bees, wasps, and termites carry out individual tasks independently within their colonies. Yet, when they collaborate as a community, they display the ability to solve complex problems through cooperation. This collective behavior, known as swarm intelligence, is driven by four key elements:

1. Positive Feedback: Encourages actions that lead to favorable outcomes.
2. Negative Feedback: Balances and regulates behaviors, preventing overexploitation and competition.
3. Amplification of Fluctuations: Embraces randomness and errors, allowing for adaptability.
4. Multiple Interactions: Interplay among individuals, their environment, and their behavior.

The mathematical basis of ACO involves several key components and formulas:

1. Pheromone Matrix (τ): ACO maintains a pheromone matrix, where each element τ[i][j] represents the pheromone level on a path (i, j). The pheromone level is updated over iterations and influences the decision-making of ants.
2. Heuristic information (η): This matrix stores heuristic information that guides ants in their decisions. It represents the desirability of moving from one point to another and is often calculated using domain-specific knowledge.
3. Ant Colony: In the ACO algorithm, a population of artificial ants explores possible solutions to the problem. Each ant builds a solution by moving from one point to another, making decisions based on pheromone levels and heuristic information.
4. Transition Probability (P_{ij}): The transition probability from point i to point j shown in formula 1 is calculated using the pheromone matrix τ and the heuristic information η. The formula 1) for (P_{ij}) can be defined as:

$$P_{ij} = \frac{\tau_{ij}^{\alpha} . \eta_{ij}^{\beta}}{\sum_{k \in allowedMoves} \tau_{ik}^{\alpha} . \eta_{ik}^{\beta}} \quad \textbf{(1)}$$

Where:

α and β are parameters that control the influence of pheromone and heuristic information. The denominator sums over all possible moves from point i.

5. Pheromone Update (Δτ): After each ant completes its tour, the pheromone levels are updated. A fraction of the pheromone evaporates, and the ants deposit the pheromone on their chosen paths. The pheromone update formula 2) can be expressed as:

$$\Delta\tau_{ij} = (1-\rho).\tau_{ij} + \sum_{k=1}^{m} \Delta\tau_{ij}^{(k)} \quad \textbf{(2)}$$

Where:

- ρ is the pheromone evaporation rate.
- $\Delta\tau_{ij}^{k}$ does the k-th and deposits the pheromone on the path (i, j).

Ant Colony Optimization (ACO) for Crop Planning:

1. Initialization: Start with an initial configuration, representing a potential crop plan.
2. Ant Movement: Deploy virtual ants to explore different planting strategies.
3. Pheromone Update: Adjust pheromone levels on paths based on the quality of solutions.
4. Solution Evaluation: Assess the fitness of each crop plan based on factors like soil quality and climate conditions.
5. Pheromone Evaporation: Gradually reduce pheromone levels on all paths to simulate natural decay.
6. Path Selection: Ants choose paths with higher pheromone concentrations, favoring better solutions.
7. Iteration: Repeat steps 2-6 for multiple cycles.
8. Convergence: As iterations progress, the algorithm converges towards an optimal crop plan.
9. Result: The obtained crop plan enhances yield and resource efficiency in agriculture
10. Solution Retrieval: Extract the best crop plan with the highest pheromone concentration.

Particle Swarm Optimization for Resource Allocation

Particle Swarm Optimization (PSO) is a nature-inspired algorithm that mimics the:

Collective behavior of birds or insects to solve optimization problems. In the context of resource allocation in horticulture, PSO can be employed to determine the optimal allocation of resources such as water, fertilizers, labor, and land to maximize crop yields while adhering to various constraints. This swarm intelligence approach aids in AI-enabled green and sustainable resource management in horticulture, helping optimize resource usage, minimize waste, and contribute to environmentally friendly and efficient agricultural practices, as shown in Fig. (**3**).

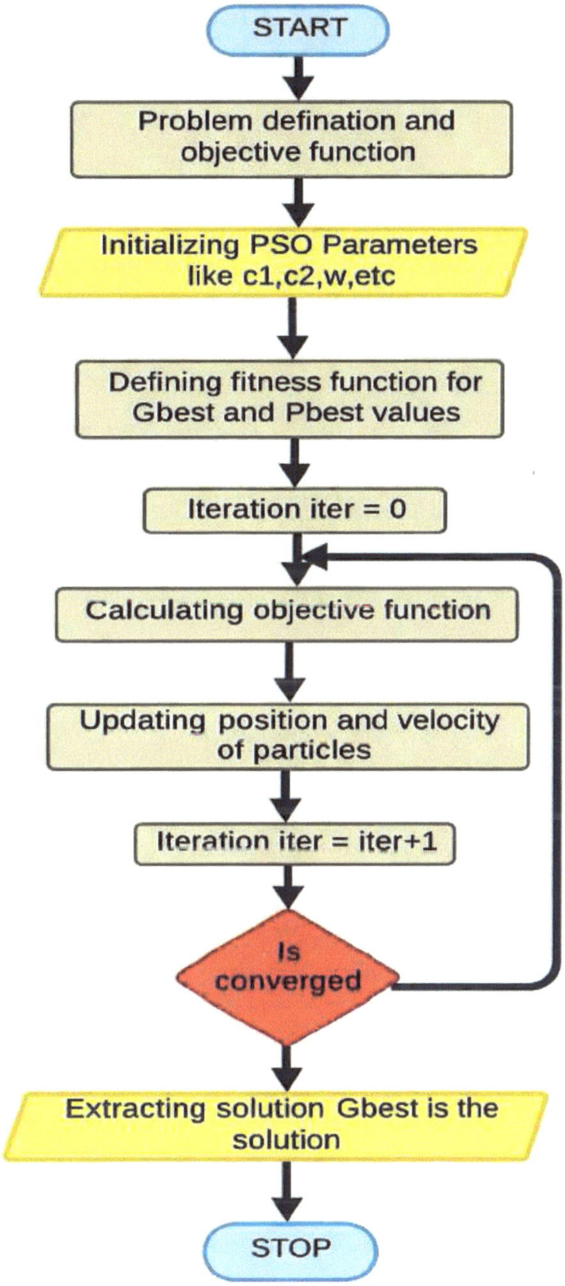

Fig. (3). Flow of particle optimization for resource allocation.

Mathematical Model

- *Objective Function:*

Define the objective function, denoted as f(x), where x represents the allocation of resources to different crops. The objective function quantifies the goals of resource allocation, such as maximizing crop yield while minimizing resource consumption. The function may include terms for crop-specific yields, resource costs, and penalties for exceeding constraints.

$$f(x)=\text{Maximize } (\textstyle\sum_{i=1}^{N} \; y_i(x) - \sum_{j=1}^{M} \; C_i(x) \tag{3}$$

N is the number of crops.

M is the number of resource types.

Y_i (x) represents the yield of crop i based on resource allocation x.

C_j (x) represents the cost of resource j based on allocation x.

Decision Variables:

Define the decision variables, X_ij, representing the allocation of resource i to crop j. These variables determine the resource allocation plan.

$$X_{ij} \geq 0, \forall_{i,j}$$

- Constraints: Specify constraints that must be satisfied, such as water availability, labor availability, budget constraints, and land size limitations. These constraints can be represented as equations or inequalities.
- Water Constraint stated in formula 4:

$$\textstyle\sum_{j=1}^{N} \; A_{ij}X_{ij} \; \leq \; W_i\forall_i \tag{4}$$

where A_{ij} is the water requirement for crop j and W_i Is the available water for crops?

- Labor Constraint:

$$\textstyle\sum_{j=1}^{N} \; L_{ij}X_{ij} \; \leq \; W_i\forall_i \tag{5}$$

Where L_ijis the labor requirement for crop j and L_i is the available labor for crop I in formula 5.

Particle Swarm Optimization (PSO): Implement the PSO algorithm to optimize the resource allocation plan. The PSO algorithm consists of the following components:

- Initialization: Initialize a swarm of particles, where each particle represents a resource allocation plan. Initialize the particle positions and velocities within the defined constraints.
- Fitness Function: Define the fitness function f(x) as described earlier, which evaluates the quality of each resource allocation plan based on the defined objectives and constraints.
- Particle Movement: Update particle positions and velocities according to the PSO equations stated in 6,7 formulas:

Several Benefits and Limitations

Ant Colony Optimization (ACO) and Particle Swarm Optimization (PSO) offer distinct advantages for horticultural crop planning. ACO is adept at global exploration in complex and dynamic contexts, inspired by ant foraging behavior. It systematically explores various crop designs, accommodating diverse constraints and objectives. However, ACO demands significant computational resources and careful parameter tuning, potentially impacting scalability and convergence speed. On the other hand, PSO excels in resource allocation, such as water, labor, and land, among crops. It adapts well to changing conditions, is user-friendly, and handles complex allocation problems with fewer parameters. Nevertheless, PSO may converge to local optima in intricate scenarios, require sensitive parameter choices, and struggle with nonlinear or discontinuous search spaces, sometimes leading to less interpretable plans. Ultimately, the choice between ACO and PSO should consider the specific horticultural problem, available computing resources, and the need for solution robustness and interpretability.

Neural Network in Horticulture

Artificial neural networks, or neural nets, are foundational in machine learning and AI. Inspired by the human brain, they consist of interconnected neurons organized into layers: input, hidden, and output. Neurons perform calculations and pass information to the next layer, enabling tasks like classification and decision-making. Neural networks have transformed industries, from audio and image recognition to natural language processing and autonomous vehicles, by iteratively learning and improving their efficiency [10]. Neural networks have proven to be incredibly successful across various domains. Convolutional Neural Networks (CNNs) excel in image recognition tasks, playing a pivotal role in computer vision for tasks like object detection, facial recognition, and image categorization. They have revolutionized the field, driving many cutting-edge AI applications. Recurrent Neural Networks (RNNs) are designed for processing sequential data by maintaining context through looping connections [11]. This makes them ideal for tasks like time series analysis, speech recognition, and natural language processing, leveraging features extracted by convolutional layers to enhance their performance. Overall, neural networks, including CNNs and RNNs, have transformed the landscape of computer vision and text analysis [12] [13].

Convolutional Neural Network for Disease Detection

A Deep Learning technique called a convolutional neural network employs a convolution operation rather than straightforward matrix multiplication. When compared to other Deep Learning methods, CNN is most effective at handling images. From the input Heatedos, it extracts various spatial and temporal properties that are crucial for image classification and other computer vision applications. One Input layer, one Output layer, a collection of Convolutional layers (each with an activation function), pooling layers, and Fully Connected layers (each with an activation function) make up the architecture of a standard.

CNN. In the CNN, the convolution operation is carried out by the convolutional layer. Simple lower-level features of an image are extracted by the beginning convolutional layers of a CNN, while the subsequent layers extract sophisticated higher-level features.

Proposed System Architecture

The proposed system architecture, shown in Fig. (**4**), is used for the detection of various diseases, such as Black rot, Leaf spot, Black measles, and numerous others, over the leaves of horticulture plants like Grapevine, orange, pomegranate, papaya, *etc*. It can also be used over the leaves of some vegetable plants, such as tomatoes. The system module functions by acquiring pHeatedos, capturing them with a mobile camera, pre-processing them, and then segmenting the pre-processed images. The segmented images would then be max-pooled for precise feature extraction and classification of the numerous images in defined categories. The system is given a dataset that is divided into two parts: one set is denoted as a training dataset, and the other is named a testing dataset. The feature extraction and other various steps of the algorithm will take place for both sets of images.

The features from the testing set that were retrieved are compared to the features from the training set, which are regarded as permanent features [14].

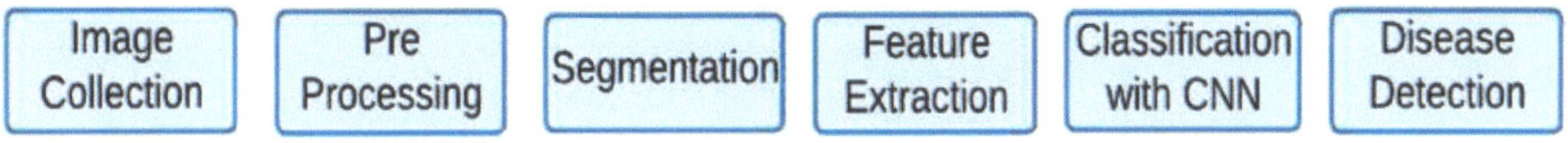

Fig. (4). Design of the CNN module for disease detection.

Image Pre-processing: The information image will be resized during image pre-processing to increase the precision of disease detection. Noise, shadow, and brightness effects are eliminated during this step.

Image Segmentation: By dividing the input image into numerous segments that show similarities between the pixels, an image can be segmented. The goal of segmentation is to simplify the representation of an image while also making it more pertinent and intelligible.

Feature Extraction: Feature extraction is a process that converts raw data into manageable numerical features while preserving the original data set's information. CNN removes features from the heatmaps it receives. The input image serves as the starting point for the feature extraction network. The neural network classifies using the retrieved feature signals [15].

Classification: CNN applies a filter to each area of the image, picking out the most important details (such as edge information, color, texture, *etc.*), and using those details to categorize the image. Each image in the labeled dataset used to train the model is associated with a certain disease class. Classification enables the automatic and effective identification of diseases in patients, aiding in decision-making for diagnosis and therapy [16].

Precision: The ratio of True Positives (TP, correct predictions), which is the sum of True Positives (TP) and False Positives (FP), to the total number of relevant outcomes given in formula 8. P is the average of the classes for situations involving multi-class categorization. The formula for precision is as follows:

$$P = \frac{TP}{TP+FP} \tag{6}$$

Recall: The percentage of false negatives (FN) and total positives (TP) that are TP is the Recall value, computed using formula 9. R is averaged across all classes in issues involving multi-class categorization. The recall formula is as follows:

$$R = \ TP/(TP + FN) \tag{7}$$

F1 Score: The harmonic mean of precision and recall. For multi-class classification problems, F1 gets averaged among all the classes. The 10 formula for the F1 score is given below:

$$F1 = 2 * \frac{TP*FP}{TP+FP} \tag{8}$$

ReLU Layer: It keeps the "active neuron feature" and maps out these features *via* nonlinear functions, which is crucial for the neural network to handle the challenging nonlinear problem. The activation function adds nonlinear elements to eliminate redundant data while maintaining features. ReLU layers give the CNN model nonlinearity by substituting zeros for negative input values while leaving positive values alone by trimming non-essential details and enhancing essential ones.

$$f(x) = \begin{cases} x & x \geq 0 \\ a\left(\frac{x}{|x|+1}\right) & x < 0 \end{cases} \tag{9}$$

In equation 12, the function represents a nonlinear activation function, where x is the input, and a represents the variable hyperparameters. When a=0, the function is the ReLU function [17].

Max Pooling: Max pooling maintains the strongest activation in each pooling zone by choosing the highest value there, which helps to capture important patterns associated with the black rot sickness. Max pooling facilitates the extraction of higher-level characteristics by reducing the spatial dimensions of some spatial data and discarding it. As a result, the model can more easily generalize and spot patterns associated with disease in pictures of grape leaves that have the condition black rot. Additionally, max pooling strengthens the model's resistance to modifications in the disease's outward appearance, such as size, rotation, or translation alterations.

Recurrent Neural Network for Yield Prediction

Accurate crop yield prediction is essential for global food preservation and generation. It plays a pivotal role in agricultural planning, aiding farmers, decision-makers, and stakeholders in making informed choices regarding planting schedules and resource allocation. This forecasting is vital for efficient resource utilization, reducing waste, and enhancing resilience to climate change. Precise predictions empower farmers to implement strategies like crop rotation and improved irrigation, ultimately boosting yields. Monitoring crop growth and forecasts is also critical for national economies, directly impacting local, national, and international economic stability. Nevertheless, estimating agricultural productivity remains challenging due to the myriad of factors influencing it, including soil quality, weather conditions, farming techniques, and crop genetics [18].

System Architecture

The system module designed is used to predict the yield of the crop well before using various parameters, which include Maximum temperature, Minimum temperature, Humidity, Pressure, and Wind Speed. The module is designed by incorporating different layers of recurrent neural networks, which include the Input layer, recurrent layer, and Output layer. The input layer Receives Sequential data, such as time series, word sequences, or any other kind of sequential data. A feature vector or embedding is often used to represent each element of the sequence and is used as the RNN's input. Depending on the particular issue, these vectors can come in a variety of sizes. The core of an RNN is the recurrent layer. It analyzes the sequential input while keeping track of information from earlier time steps in a hidden state, also known as the memory state. Depending on the goal, the output layer may use the hidden state from the recurrent layer to generate a different type of output. *Image Pre-processing and Data Segmentation:* The module pre-processes the input images by scaling them down to extract information and then resizing them accordingly. The given image dataset would be divided into two datasets, *i.e.*, the training dataset and the testing dataset [19]. The network consists of an output layer that predicts a single value, a hidden layer with four LSTM blocks, and a visible layer with one input. The recurrent neural network called the Long Short-Term Memory network, or LSTM network, is trained using backpropagation. Memory blocks in LSTM networks are connected by layers in place of neurons. A block has features that enable it to be more intelligent than a traditional neuron and has a memory for recent sequences. The conditionality of the change of state and addition of information flowing through the block is achieved by using the sigmoid activation units to control whether each gate within a block is triggered or not. Gates that control a block's state, output, and reaction to an input sequence are found within a block. We can predict how well the model will perform on the train and test datasets after it has been trained. This will enable us to use new models as a point of reference. A batch size of 1 is utilized while the network is trained across 50 epochs, to guarantee that performance is given in the same units as the original data, the predictions must be made before calculating error scores. For a complete fit module, the epoch iteration and batch size are also taken into account, along with the model input data class that is employed, which is X-train, and the labels are Y-train. It provides the model training history, which includes losses and is visualized after each epoch. Since the dataset in this case is very large, a batch size must be assigned. It separates the data into batches of equal size, uploads a sample of each batch into memory, and processes them. The neural network will be trained after 100 epochs, which will take about a minute. The loss function has been trained up to an RMSE of about 0.010 [20].

Fundamentals of Fuzzy Logic

This study examines the use of fuzzy logic in horticulture, a subject essential for sustaining agriculture in the face of mounting global difficulties. Horticulture's traditional decision-making processes sometimes oversimplify complicated and ambiguous elements, which reduces their usefulness. By accounting for imprecise and uncertain data, fuzzy logic offers a nuanced approach that enables horticulturists to make more informed and adaptive judgments. This paper emphasizes fuzzy logic's potential to improve precision, yield, and sustainability in crop production by examining its theoretical underpinnings and practical applications. This makes fuzzy logic an invaluable tool for the contemporary horticulturist looking to address the complex and dynamic issues of agricultural management. Fuzzy logic provides a fundamental paradigm shift in horticultural practices. It offers a more accurate comprehension of elements, including soil quality, climate variability, and plant health, improving resource allocation, managing pests and diseases, irrigation, and crop performance as a whole. Horticulturists can create robust and adaptive farming systems that can react quickly to shifting environmental conditions by embracing fuzzy logic. This study highlights the revolutionary potential of fuzzy logic in horticulture by pointing the way to improved crop production techniques that are necessary to meet the world's expanding food demand and environmental concerns.

System Design

The primary objective of the fuzzy logic-based methodology, which utilizes degrees of truth to handle incomplete data, is to facilitate decision-making. This method, as shown in Fig. (**5**), enables the management of incomplete and uncertain information. Membership functions increase the flexibility of elements with experience rather than factual correctness, thus fuzzy sets encompass classical sets. The fuzzy inference system uses the weighted average method. A fuzzy logic control system makes use of four key blocks. Based on membership levels, fuzzy inputs are created from crisp inputs. The inference engine uses if-then rules to infer fuzzy outcomes from these inputs. These guidelines specify how inputs and outputs relate to one another. Membership functions are used to categorize fuzzified inputs and outputs. The inference engine's fuzzy output is subsequently converted into a precise output by the controller.

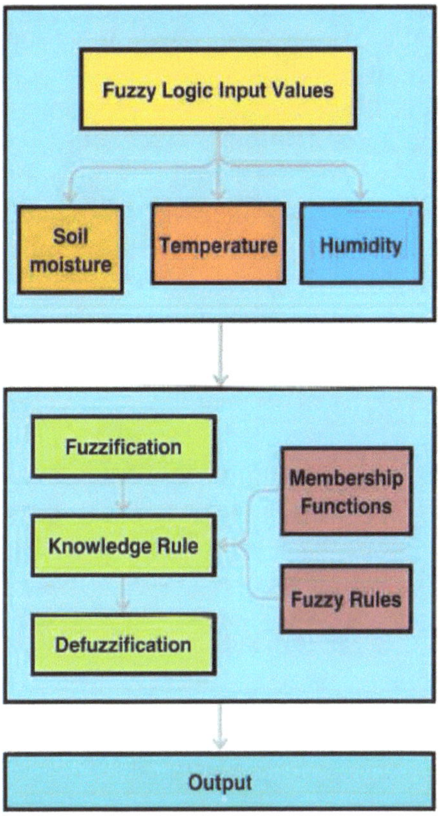

Fig. (5). Fuzzy logic system.

Membership Functions

i. *Temperature:* The definition of membership functions for temperature is the initial stage. The language typically employs phrases such as "Frosty," "Moderate," and "Heated," each corresponding to its own fuzzy set. For instance, the terms "Frosty" and "Heated" might each have a triangle membership function that is centered on a particular temperature, and "Frosty" might also have a triangular function that is centered on a higher temperature.

ii. *Soil Moisture:* For levels of soil moisture, you would define membership functions that may include words like "Dry," "Moist," and "Wet." The forms of these membership functions would vary depending on the requirements of your particular soil and plants.

iii. *Humidity:* Membership categories like "Low," "Medium," and "High" could be developed for humidity. Once more, the features of the local climate would dictate the forms of these functions.

- Fuzzy Rules: The irrigation system's response will then be determined by a series of fuzzy rules that are developed based on the input values (temperature, soil moisture, and humidity) and their respective membership functions."IF-THEN" statements are commonly used to represent these principles. As an illustration, "IF Temperature is Frosty AND Soil Moisture is Dry THEN Increase Irrigation."To cover the different conceivable combinations of input conditions, you would develop a collection of such rules.3. Fuzzy Inference System (FIS): The real temperature, soil moisture, and humidity readings are used as inputs by the fuzzy inference system, which then evaluates them following the established membership functions and rules. It determines the "firing strength," or the extent to which each rule is met. It then aggregates these firing intensities to determine the fuzzy system's overall output.

- Defuzzification: The aggregated output of the fuzzy inference system must be defuzzified to provide a crisp value that represents the quantity of irrigation to be used. One of the many defuzzification techniques available is centroid defuzzification, which determines the center of mass of the combined fuzzy output.

Mathematical Model

The decision-making objective is the main emphasis of the fuzzy logic-based methodology. It is primarily used to gather partial information, enabling decisions to be made based on the concepts of degrees of truth and true or false. The membership function is shown in Figs. (**6a**, **b**, and **c**). Attribute is used for implementing the fuzziness of set elements whose solution depends more on experience than on knowledge. The weighted average approach is used to implement the membership function in the fuzzy inference system. The outputs are produced using the fuzzy rule base system by the supplied input to the system. Three input parameters are considered in this study, each of which is composed of three membership functions, as shown by the equations. The number of rules is decided based on the membership function of each input parameter. Each parameter, therefore, has three membership functions. There are now a total of 27 regulations (Table **1**).

Table 1. Fuzzy rule table with various categories of input and output parameters.

Rule	Soil Moisture	Temperature	Humidity Level	Motor pump
1	Clay	Frosty	Low	On
2	Clay	warm	Low	On
3	Clay	Heated	Low	On

(Table 1) cont.....

Rule	Soil Moisture	Temperature	Humidity Level	Motor pump
4	Clay	Frosty	Moderate	On
5	Clay	warm	Moderate	On
6	Clay	Heated	Moderate	On
7	Clay	Frosty	High	On
8	Clay	warm	High	On
9	Clay	Heated	High	On
10	Moderate	Frosty	Low	Off
11	Moderate	warm	Low	Off
12	Moderate	Heated	Low	On
13	Moderate	Frosty	Moderate	Off
14	Moderate	warm	Moderate	Off
15	Moderate	Heated	Moderate	Off
16	Moderate	Frosty	High	Off
17	Moderate	warm	High	Off
18	Moderate	Heated	High	Off
19	Moist	Frosty	Low	Off
20	Moist	warm	Low	Off
21	Moist	Heated	Low	Off
22	Moist	Frosty	Moderate	Off
23	Moist	warm	Moderate	Off
24	Moist	Heated	Moderate	Off
25	Moist	Frosty	High	Off
26	Moist	warm	High	Off
27	Moist	Heated	High	Off

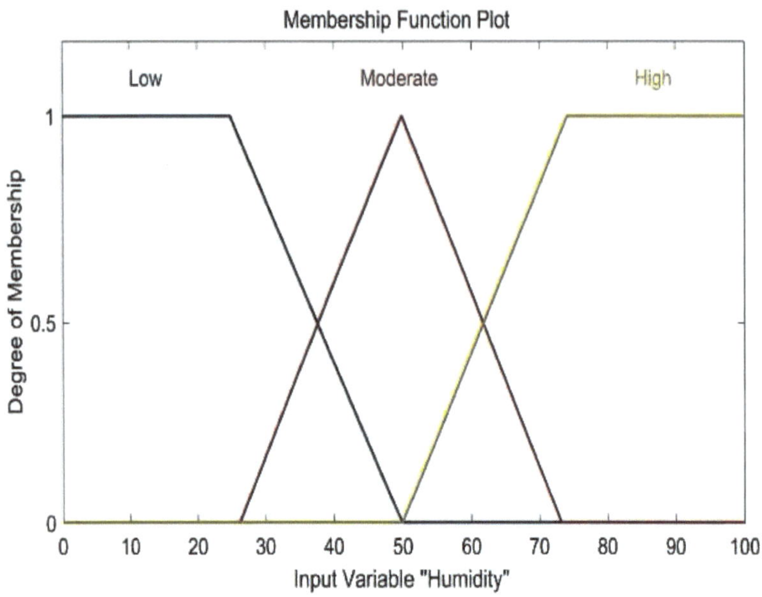

Fig. (6a). Membership function of humidity.

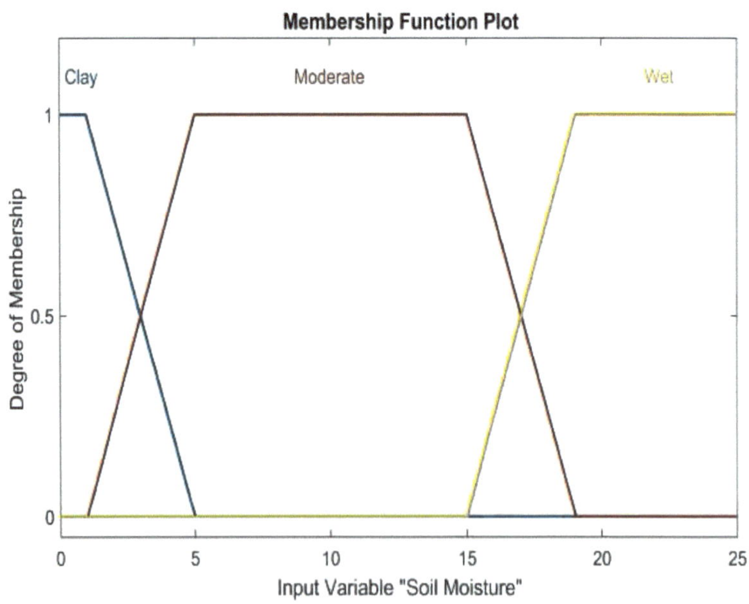

Fig. (6b). Soil moisture membership function.

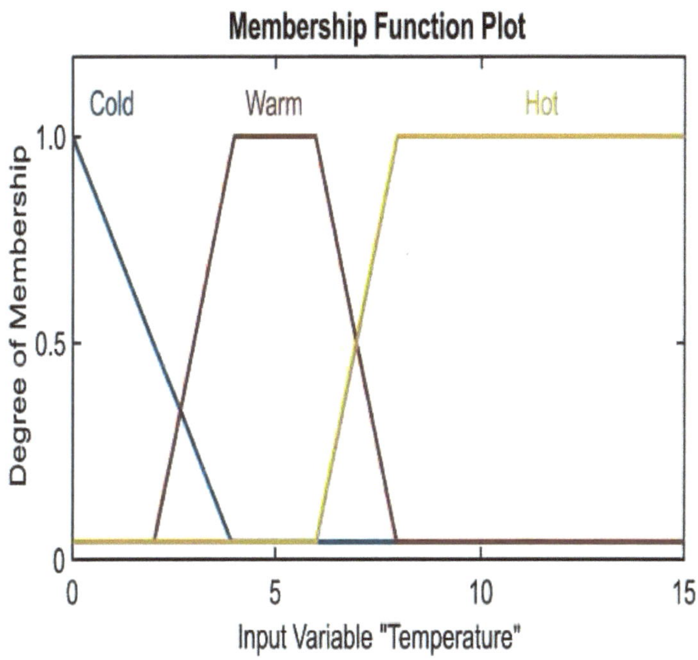

Fig. (6c). Temperature membership function.

Real-Time Usage of AI-Enabled Green and Sustainable Resources In Horticulture

The four basic parts of the smart agriculture irrigation control and plant disease monitoring system are the end device node, coordinator node, web server node, and mobile (controlling unit), as shown in Figs. (**7** and **8**). The end device node is composed of the plant leaf picture, soil moisture sensor, motor, temperature sensor, humidity sensor, and Arduino controller. The microcontroller device functions as both the coordinator and end devices in the wireless sensor network. It is used for data communication in the network. Data is continuously gathered from sensors and transferred to the web server system through the RS232 serial data bus. For real-time monitoring of farming parameters, data collection is carried out on the web server. Data can be retrieved from the server and seen on the Android phone. After that, the Android app automatically sends the control signal to the coordinator node. The coordinator node sends a signal to the endpoint device, which then replies by controlling the motor's status, either turning it on or off. A fuzzy logic framework is used to control the motor's activation and deactivation procedure for irrigation purposes. This device enables farmers to control water and motor usage according to their unique agricultural needs, and also allows for remote monitoring of their agricultural areas. Both the

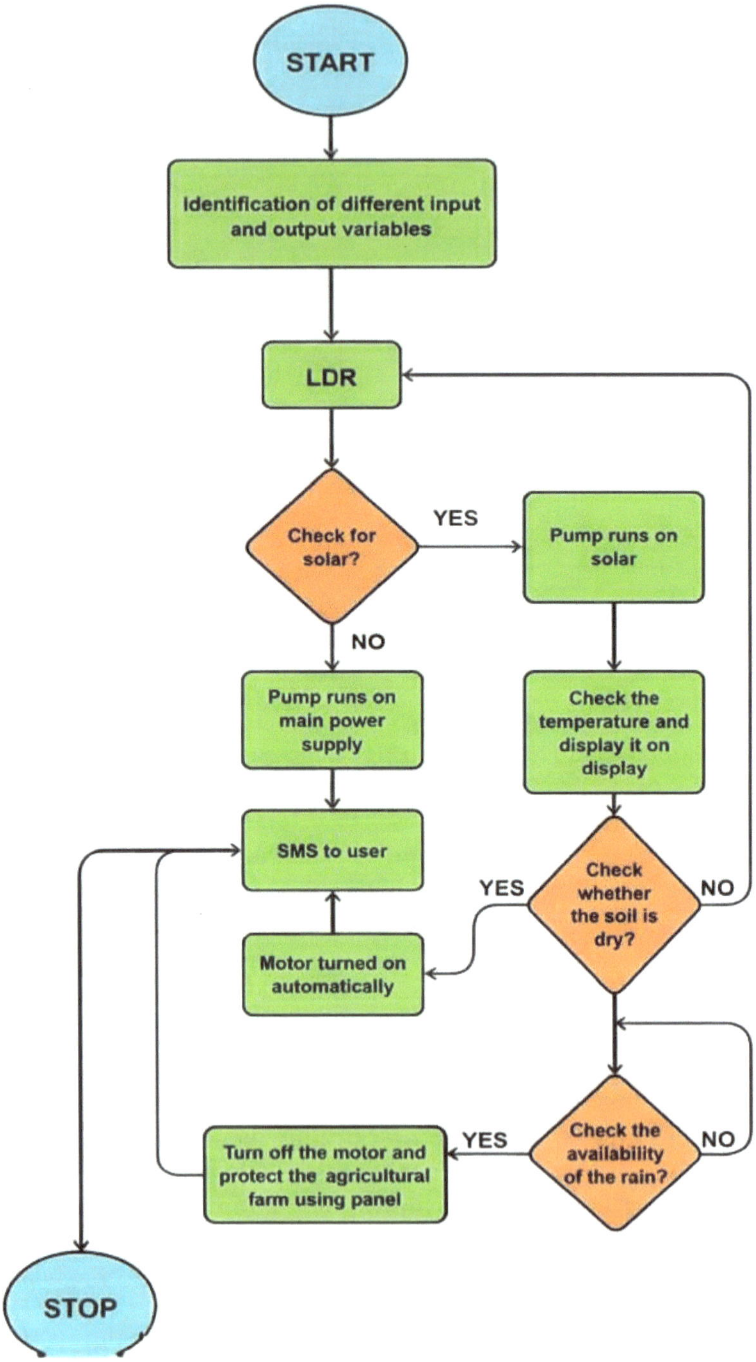

Fig. (7). Workflow diagram of the proposed system.

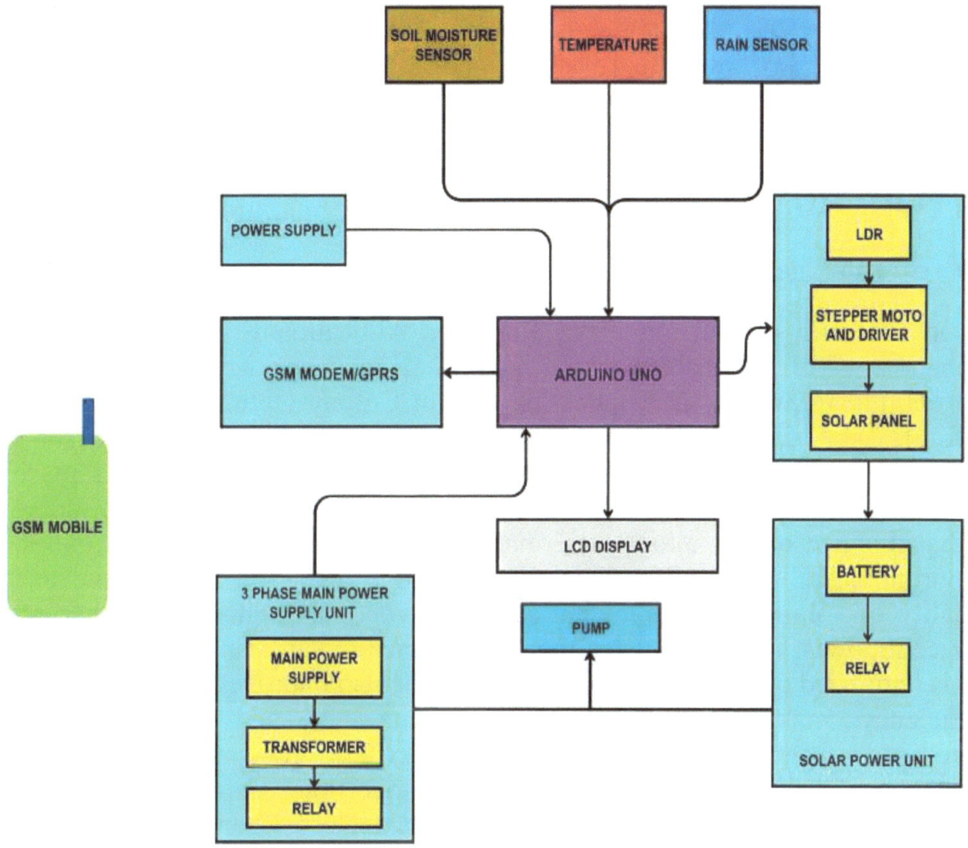

Fig. (8). Working strategy.

Arduino and the GSM modem/GPRS are initialized when the power supply is turned on. Users are given the option to select either manual or automatic operation modes after this initialization process. A Light Dependent Resistor (LDR), which recognizes sunshine, is used by the Arduino to assess the availability of solar energy while it is operating in automated mode. The solar panel is mounted atop a stepper motor to track the sun's movement and maximize sunlight exposure. In the absence of solar energy, the system automatically switches to battery operation. The system is equipped with a water level sensor that is connected to the tank in the agricultural field. A relay is linked to the pump, which activates the water pumping process when the moisture sensor detects dry conditions in the land where crops are grown. The moisture sensor is responsible for gauging the soil moisture content in the cropland, while a temperature sensor monitors the ambient temperature of the agricultural field. In the event of rainfall, an automated mechanism is in place to halt the water pumping process, thereby conserving electricity. Simultaneously, the system notifies the user of this status change *via* GSM/GPRS communication. Additionally, protective panels are automatically closed to shield the crops from the rain. In manual mode, updates regarding the agricultural field are provided to the user only upon calling a pre-authorized number.

APPLICATIONS AND DISCUSSION

Swarm Intelligence

Crop Planning Optimization and Resource Allocation Efficiency are critical components of AI-enabled green and sustainable resource management in horticulture. Through the application of Ant Colony Optimization (ACO), the optimization of crop planning involves a dynamic process where virtual ants explore different planting strategies, guided by pheromone levels and heuristic information. The results of this approach have shown significant promise in enhancing resource allocation, maximizing crop yield, and minimizing environmental impact. By adjusting pheromone levels on paths based on the quality of solutions and allowing ants to favor paths with higher pheromone concentrations, ACO facilitates the convergence towards an optimal crop plan. This optimized plan not only enhances yield but also improves resource utilization efficiency, making better use of water, nutrients, and pesticides. Swarm intelligence, a concept inspired by social insects like ants, further aids in sustainable horticulture by decentralizing decision-making and promoting collaboration among individual components of the ecosystem. The principles of swarm intelligence align with the collective behavior of insects like ants, bees, and termites, where positive and negative feedback mechanisms, amplification of fluctuations, and multiple interactions ensure efficient resource utilization and ecosystem stability. This natural inspiration results in more eco-friendly and efficient horticultural practices, contributing to sustainable growth and reduced environmental impact.

Neural Network

Potential Check of AI for Disease Detection

Our module had a test loss of 0.10484 and an accuracy of 96.57% when used to detect diseases on a grapevine plant leaf. Below, we also covered how to visualize training and validation accuracy using graphs. In Fig. (**9**), we displayed the many illnesses that our module has recognized and classified.

Fig. (9). Disease identified by the module.

In terms of revolutionizing disease detection in horticulture, Convolutional Neural Networks (CNNs) hold enormous promise. These cutting-edge deep-learning models can greatly improve the speed and precision of disease identification in plants and crops. One important use of CNNs is in the detection of leaf diseases. CNNs can examine leaf photos and find minute visual clues that indicate illnesses like powdery mildew, rust, or blight [21]. To examine the quality of fruit, CNNs can also be used to look for blemishes, rot, or other anomalies that could indicate disease. By examining pictures of the entire plant and looking for any unusual growth patterns or discolorations, they can track the health of specific trees or vines in orchards and vineyards. In addition, CNNs can assist farmers in conducting targeted pest control techniques by identifying prevalent pests on leaves or fruits.

AI Enabled Crop Yield Prediction Performance

Accurate crop yield prediction is instrumental in driving sustainable growth in horticulture. It empowers farmers and stakeholders with the information needed to optimize resource allocation efficiently, reduce waste, and adapt to changing climates. Precise predictions enable farmers to adjust planting schedules, diversify crops, and make data-driven decisions. They also facilitate market planning, reducing post-harvest losses and promoting environmental sustainability. Furthermore, these predictions contribute to economic stability at various levels, from individual farms to national economies. In essence, yield predictions are a cornerstone of sustainable horticultural practices, supporting informed, efficient, and environmentally conscious decision-making for a prosperous and resilient industry.

Fuzzy Logic

In the proposed work, we looked at how fuzzy logic might be used in sustainable horticulture. We were able to simulate and optimize several horticulture practices, including irrigation, insect control, and crop yield prediction, through the creation and application of fuzzy logic systems as stated in the outcomes have shown in Fig. (**10**) that fuzzy logic is useful in providing decision support and control strategies that improve resource efficiency, lessen environmental impacts, and increase overall sustainability in horticulture operations. In summary, the application of fuzzy logic to sustainable horticulture has enormous potential for the development of agriculture. The results of this study highlight fuzzy logic systems' potential for dealing with the complex and dynamic character of horticulture systems. Fuzzy logic can help horticulturists and other professionals make more educated and flexible decisions, which will ultimately lead to greater resource efficiency and smaller environmental footprints. Fuzzy logic models must be further investigated and improved as we move forward, keeping in mind the changing nature of technology and the difficulties posed by the environment. We can prepare horticulture and agriculture in general for a future that is more robust and sustainable through ongoing research and useful applications.

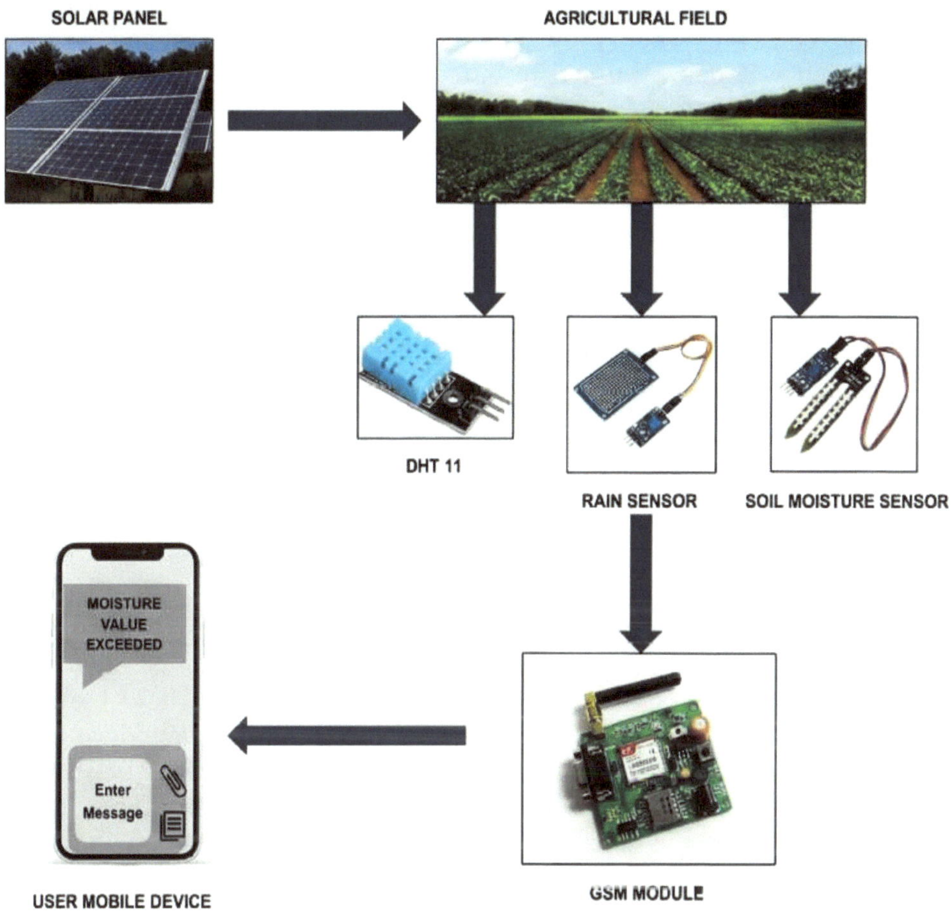

Fig. (10). proposed model.

Precision Farming

For instance, John Deere's See and Spray technology employs artificial intelligence-driven cameras to identify weeds and administer targeted herbicides, achieving a 90% reduction in chemical usage. The process involves AI evaluating images captured by cameras installed on tractors, recognizing weeds, and determining the most effective herbicide application.

In order to ascertain the precise water requirements, AI-powered irrigation systems, such as those found in vineyards and orchards, evaluate real-time data from sensors in the soil and plants. These systems forecast water needs using AI algorithms that take into account plant health, soil moisture content, and weather patterns.

Benefits: AI-based precision irrigation reduces water waste, boosts agricultural output, and conserves energy by delivering water only when and where it's needed. When water is a limited resource in dry or drought-prone areas, this strategy is beneficial.

Monitoring the Environment to Conserve Biodiversity

AI-based sensors in farming ecosystems track how agricultural practices affect regional wildlife and plants. This may involve monitoring soil microbiomes, insect diversity, and bird populations. To make sure sustainable practices are followed, sensors in coffee plantations, for example, monitor biodiversity data.

Benefits: By warning farmers about possible disturbances and enabling them to modify their methods to prevent damage to biodiversity, AI insights support the maintenance of balanced ecosystems. This supports the objectives of environmental sustainability by promoting harmony between agriculture and the natural world.

Greenhouse Climate Management

Example: GreenSense utilizes artificial intelligence to enhance the regulation of temperature, humidity, and carbon dioxide concentrations. The AI evaluates sensor information and modifies climate settings to maximize plant development. By optimising environmental conditions and reducing dependency on artificial heating or cooling, AI-managed greenhouses lower energy usage. This results in lower greenhouse gas emissions and energy savings.

Exact Fertilizer Application

AI is able to evaluate soil and generate detailed plans for applying the appropriate quantity of fertilizer. This allows a farmer who grows flowers or vegetables to focus on areas with low nutrition levels. Benefits include preventing soil damage, saving money, and lowering chemical runoff into neighboring rivers and lakes when the proper amount of fertilizer is applied. Cleaner ecosystems and sustainable farming are supported by healthier soil.

CONCLUSION

Ant Colony Optimization (ACO) and Particle Swarm Optimization (PSO) have emerged as powerful tools in the realm of sustainable horticulture. ACO's prowess lies in its ability to optimize crop planning by selecting the most suitable crop types and planting schedules, factoring in variables such as soil conditions and market demand. This approach ensures efficient land use and resource allocation, fostering increased crop diversity and bolstering market competitiveness within the sustainable horticulture sector. On the other hand, PSO excels in resource allocation within horticultural operations. It efficiently distributes vital resources such as labor, fertilizers, and water, leading to improved crop yields while minimizing waste. PSO significantly contributes to resource efficiency and sustainability by optimizing the allocation of critical inputs. In the domain of disease management, Convolutional Neural Networks (CNNs) have brought about a revolutionary shift. By analyzing images with remarkable accuracy, CNNs have become indispensable in the early detection of diseases in horticultural crops. This early detection allows for timely intervention, reducing crop losses and minimizing the need for chemical treatments. Additionally, Recurrent Neural Networks (RNNs) play a pivotal role in predicting crop yields. Leveraging historical data, RNNs provide more precise and dynamic forecasts, facilitating better planning and resource management. This heightened predictability supports sustainable practices by reducing uncertainty in crop yield outcomes. In the context of resource conservation, Fuzzy Logic Control has made significant strides in irrigation systems. Fuzzy logic-based irrigation systems enable precise water allocation, ensuring that plants receive the optimal amount of water required for healthy growth. This approach not only minimizes water wastage but also reduces energy consumption, promoting sustainable water management practices in horticulture. Furthermore, fuzzy inference systems have ushered in a new era in pest management. By adapting pest control strategies to changing conditions, these systems enhance the efficiency of pest control efforts, reduce reliance on chemical pesticides, and minimize environmental impact while safeguarding crop health. These developments collectively underscore the transformative role of advanced technologies in promoting sustainability and efficiency in horticulture. Further research can be conducted to develop an efficient system using a different algorithm to detect the disease over a crop with more efficiency and accuracy than the one proposed in the following chapter. The chapter also opens a wide scope of research in the field of AI to increase horticulture growth with the help of creating different AI-embedded modules. A chapter can also be created to develop a module for predicting the most suitable soil type for a given crop.

REFERENCES

[1] FAO, "UN Report: Global hunger numbers rose to as many as 828 million in 2021," Newsroom, Jul. 06, 2022. https://www.fao.org/newsroom/detail/un-report-global-hunger-SOFI-2022-FAO/enSingh

[2] R. Singh, R. Singh, A. Gehlot, S.V. Akram, N. Priyadarshi, and B. Twala, "Horticulture 4.0: adoption of industry 4.0 technologies in horticulture for meeting sustainable farming", *Appl. Sci. (Basel),* vol. 12, no. 24, p. 12557, 2022. [http://dx.doi.org/10.3390/app122412557]

[3] Mamta Saxena, Advisor(Horticulture), "Horticultural Statistics at a Glance 2018 ", Department of Agriculture, "Ministry of Agriculture and Farmers Welfare", Government of India.

[4] D.M. Sharath, S.A. Kumar, M.G. Rohan, and K.V. Akhilesh, Suresh and C. Prathap, "Disease detection in plants using convolutional neural network", *2020 Third International Conference on Smart Systems and Inventive Technology (ICCSIT),* pp. 389-394, 2020.Tirunelveli, India [http://dx.doi.org/10.1109/ICSSIT48917.2020.9214159]

[5] K. Lamm, A. Powell, and L. Lombardini, "Identifying Critical Issues in the Horticulture Industry: A Delphi Analysis during the COVID-19 Pandemic", *Horticulturae,* vol. 7, no. 11, p. 416, 2021. [http://dx.doi.org/10.3390/horticulturae7110416]

[6] H. Bhavana, and A. Bhagwan, "Review on Role of robotics in horticulture", *J. Pharmacogn. Phytochem.,* vol. 10, no. 1S, pp. 306-309, 2021.

[7] S. Chetty, and A.O. Adewumi, "Comparison study of swarm intelligence techniques for the annual crop planning problem", *IEEE Trans. Evol. Comput.,* vol. 18, no. 2, pp. 258-268, 2014. [http://dx.doi.org/10.1109/TEVC.2013.2256427]

[8] Z. Doshi, S. Nadkarni, R. Agrawal, and N. Shah, "Agro consultant: intelligent crop recommendation system using machine learning algorithms", *2018 Fourth International Conference on Computing Communication Control and Automation (ICCUBEA),* pp. 1-6, 2019.

[9] Z. E. Ahmed, R. A. Saeed, A. Mukherjee, and S. N. Ghorpade, *Energy optimization in low-power wide area networks by using heuristic techniques.,* 2020. [http://dx.doi.org/10.1016/B978-0-12-818880-4.00011-9]

[10] Oludare Isaac Abiodun, *State-of-The-Art in Artificial Neural Network Applications: A survey.,* 2018. [http://dx.doi.org/10.1016/j.heliyon.2018.e00938]

[11] S. Albawi, T.A. Mohammed, and S. Al-Zawi, "Understanding of a convolutional neural network", *2017 International Conference on Engineering and Technology (ICET),* pp. 1-6, 2017.Antalya, Turkey [http://dx.doi.org/10.1109/ICEngTechnol.2017.8308186]

[12] A. Santoro, R. Faulkner, D. Raposo, J. Rae, M. Chrzanowski, T. Weber, D. Wierstra, O. Vinyals, R. Pascanu, and T. Lillicrap, *Relational recurrent neural networks.* Curran Associates, Inc, 2018.

[13] P. Bedi, and P. Gole, "Plant disease detection using hybrid model based on convolutional autoencoder and convolutional neural network", *Artificial Intelligence in Agriculture,* vol. 5, pp. 90-101, 2021. [http://dx.doi.org/10.1016/j.aiia.2021.05.002]

[14] P. Mehta, S. Sapkal, T. Lichade, C. Kulkarni, and Y. Patil, *Recognition of Diseases on Horticultural Leaves Using Machine Learning Approach.,* vol. 25, pp. 1-5, 2023. [http://dx.doi.org/10.1109/ASIANCON58793.2023.10270074]

[15] M. Jogin, and M.S. Mohana, Madhulika, G. D. Divya, R. K. Meghana and S. Apoorva, "Feature extraction using convolution neural networks (CNN) and deep learning," 2018 3rd IEEE International Conference on Recent Trends in Electronics, Information & Communication Technology (RTEICT), Bangalore, India, 2018, pp. 2319-2323. [http://dx.doi.org/10.1109/RTEICT42901.2018.9012507]

[16] A.M. Reshmi, Prameeja Prasidhha, "Leaf disease detection using CNN", International Journal of Creative Research Thoughts (IJCRT), ISSN: 2320-2882, Volume.10, Issue 3, pp. f235-f241, March 2022.

[17] G. Lin, and W. Shen, "Research on convolutional neural network based on improved Relu piecewise activation function", *Procedia Comput. Sci.,* vol. 131, pp. 977-984, 2018. [http://dx.doi.org/10.1016/j.procs.2018.04.239]

[18] S. Khaki, and L. Wang, "Crop yield prediction using deep neural networks", *Front. Plant Sci.,* vol. 10, p. 621, 2019. [http://dx.doi.org/10.3389/fpls.2019.00621] [PMID: 31191564]

[19] S Chaithanya, A Punith Raj, and N Rajesh Rahul, Mrs. Sujatha Hiremath and Dr. Veena Devi, "Rice crop yield prediction using recurrent neural networks", International Research Journal of Engineering

and Technology (IRJET), Volume: 07, July 2020.

[20] P. Sivanandhini, and J. Prakash, "Crop yield prediction analysis using feed-forward and recurrent neural network", *International Journal of Innovative Science and Research Technology,* vol. 5, no. 5, pp. 1092-1096, 2020.

[21] S.D. Sapkal, P.S. Mehta, and G. Chillarge, "Smart cultivation and prediction system for agriculture", *Int. J. Grid Distrib. Comput.,* vol. 13, no. 02, pp. 2380-2388, 2021.

CHAPTER 13

Artificial Intelligence: Utilizing a Cost-Safety Matrix to Assess Risk in Material Handling Systems

Randhir Singh Baghel[1,*], **Govind Shay Sharma**[2] and **Harkaran Singh**[3]

[1] *Department of Mathematics, Poornima University, Jaipur-303905, Rajasthan, India*

[2] *Department of Mathematics, Vivekananda Global University, Jaipur-303012, Rajasthan, India*

[3] *Foundation Education Centre, Kangan Institute, Broadmeadows VIC 3047, Australia*

Abstract: This chapter focuses on route selection by simultaneously evaluating the safety performance and transportation cost associated with each alternative path. It introduces the concept of a Cost–Safety Matrix as a tool for risk analysis of transportation routes. In this framework, the cost matrix quantifies the transportation expenditure for each route, whereas the safety matrix characterizes the safety-related attributes of those routes. The combined cost–safety matrix incorporates both the economic considerations and the inherent risk present on each individual path. The corresponding risk matrix is developed using a defined numerical scale derived from historical (past) data. The cost of transportation and risk level combine to make a matrix that can be divided into three parts. The categories used to describe the danger level are low, moderate, and high. This matrix may be used to pick a route before commencing the transport. Integrating Artificial Intelligence (AI) into material handling procedures is critical for increasing productivity and maintaining worker safety. The primary purpose of this study is to identify and reduce potential dangers associated with lifting, transporting, and handling products. The primary focus is on using AI to estimate the danger of material handling jobs. The study uses machine learning techniques, data analytics, and sensor technologies to examine large datasets relevant to material handling processes. By harnessing the power of AI, the research aims to develop a robust risk assessment framework that can automatically detect, predict, and mitigate potential risks associated with falling materials, collapsing loads, improper lifting techniques, and struck-by hazards.

Keywords: Artificial intelligence, Cost-safety matrix, Material handling, Risk analysis, Transportation.

[*] **Corresponding author Randhir Singh Baghel:** Department of Mathematics, Poornima University, Jaipur-303905, Rajasthan, India; E-mail: randhirsng@gmail.com

Subir Gupta, Indrajit Ghosal, Keshav Kaushik & Monika Dandotiya (Eds.)

INTRODUCTION

Risk assessment principles have been established to provide a systematic basis for conceptualizing and managing risk, with a focus on refining core concepts, analytical methods, and the role of "risk thinking" in decision-making. In modern business practice, risk assessment and management are treated as science-based processes aimed at identifying, evaluating, and controlling factors that could distort managerial judgment, thereby safeguarding organizational performance and long-term viability [1].

In the context of materials management, structured risk management programmes provide an overarching strategy and framework for controlling uncertainties in material handling and associated operations [1]. Material management itself spans procurement, supply, and the movement of materials from warehouses to points of distribution, where delays in dispatch are recognized as a critical challenge for project time performance [2]. In industrial practice, risk management extends across procurement, storage, processing, internal logistics, supply chains, and outbound transportation of finished products. Construction-sector studies highlight that inadequate handling practices at the site level can compromise worker safety and productivity, and therefore emphasize systematic analysis of material-handling safety and corresponding countermeasures. Inventory-related risks have been modelled using multi-criteria tools such as the Analytic Hierarchy Process (AHP), providing a structured basis for prioritizing hazards and selecting appropriate control actions in inventory management. From an ergonomic standpoint, manual material handling is identified as a high-risk activity, and sensor-based, machine-learning approaches have been proposed for automated assessment of workers' postures and movements. Risk matrix methods have also been applied to material distribution processes to evaluate handling performance and to highlight critical stages in the internal flow of materials. Effective safety management in these contexts depends on competent professionals and appropriate mechanical handling equipment, particularly at construction and industrial sites where accident potential is high. Beyond physical operations, risk management in material handling increasingly intersects with information and communication technologies, with research on IT-system risk analysis proposing qualitative and quantitative frameworks for evaluating vulnerabilities in information systems that support logistics and inventory control. In parallel, industrial studies stress that the design and selection of material-handling systems, including material-flow configurations and technology choices, strongly influence profitability and operational efficiency. Automation through Programmable Logic Controller (PLC)-based systems is promoted as a means to reduce or completely replace manual handling in tasks such as filling, sorting, packaging, and loading. The development of integrated material-handling systems in manufacturing has been shown to enhance organizational productivity while reducing overall manufacturing cost. Methodologically, several decision-support techniques have been integrated into material-handling planning; for example, artificial neural networks have been explored for forecasting and decision-making in engineering and logistics applications, offering predictive capability for material demand and system performance. Equipment selection has been optimized using multi-criteria decision models for choosing among alternatives such as conveyors, trolleys, and automated guided vehicles, particularly in sectors like pharmaceuticals, where reliability and throughput are critical. Complementary work on the classification and attributes of material-handling equipment provides structured guidelines for matching equipment types to operational requirements, cost constraints, and safety objectives [3]. Within this broader literature, material handling is consistently defined as the coordinated movement, protection, storage, and control of materials and products across manufacturing, warehousing, distribution, consumption, and disposal, supported by technologies such as forklifts, conveyors, cranes, pallet racking, automated storage and retrieval systems, inventory management systems, warehouse management systems, barcoding, and RFID to ensure safe, efficient, and cost-effective flow of goods.

Transport Equipment

Automated devices that transport goods along a preset route are called conveyors.

Pallets and big items can be lifted and moved by forklifts.

Pallet Jacks: Equipment, either electric or manual, used to move palletized items.

Storage Equipment

Pallet Racks: Systems with many levels for storing palletized items.

Shelving Units: Used to store boxes and smaller objects.

AS/RS: Automated systems with low human interaction that store and retrieve objects.

Unit Load Formation Equipment

Pallets: Platforms for stacking and transporting products. Containers are used for bulk storage and transportation.

Positioning Equipment

Robotic Arms: Used for precise handling in production.

Turntables: Used to rotate components during assembly or inspection.

Identification and Control Equipment

Barcode scanners: Used to track and manage inventories.

RFID systems are used to track the position of items in real-time.

Principles of Material Handling

The planning principle guarantees that all elements of material management are considered, from design to implementation. The standardization principle states that standardized equipment and procedures can increase efficiency and compatibility.

Work Principle: Minimizing needless motions and handling.

Ergonomic Principle: Designing material handling systems to decrease physical strain and promote worker safety. The unit load principle states that commodities should be handled in standardized units to facilitate transit and storage.

The Space Utilization Principle states that storage space should be used efficiently to enhance capacity and accessibility. The system principle is to integrate material handling with other activities to increase overall efficiency.

Automation Principle: Utilizing automation to reduce labor costs and enhance precision.

Environmental Principle: Use eco-friendly material handling procedures such as recycling and energy-efficient equipment.

Benefits of Effective Material Handling

Increased efficiency: Processes were streamlined, and handling time was lowered.

Cost savings: Automation and enhanced systems save labor and operating expenses.

Safety: Proper equipment and procedures reduce the risk of injury and accident.

Improved Inventory Management: Enhanced material tracking and management lead to fewer shortages and overages.

Increased Customer Satisfaction: Orders are fulfilled faster and more accurately.

During the construction phase, delays in the delivery of materials decreased overall worker efficiency. The study identified the material management aspects that most strongly influenced the time performance of the Banda Aceh flyover project and concluded that effective control of both work outputs and processes has a direct impact on construction schedule performance [3]. This is the effect of material management risk on control and control variables. They used multiple linear regressions to study risk variables and timing performance in flyover projects. Ten risk variables have a favourable impact on material management, according to their linear regression analysis. According to the positive consequences, the project's transition schedule has been improved, and one of the risk factors in material management is well controlled. Material handling systems, in particular, are recognized as a major source of serious and fatal accidents during construction activities. To evaluate the significance of safety-related factors in material handling, one investigation conducted a structured survey of site practices and applied t-test analysis to determine the statistical importance of different safety variables [4].

Within the metal production chain, the principal safety issues and corresponding control measures were systematically mapped and analyzed [5]. To identify and prioritize optimal risk-control strategies for these hazards, the Analytic Hierarchy Process (AHP) was employed. The results indicated that risk is embedded in every stage of management, ranging from inventory and storage of materials to processing operations and other production-related activities.

Material handling refers to the activities involved in the movement, protection, storage, and control of materials within a facility or a short distance. It focuses on optimizing the movement of materials within manufacturing plants, warehouses, and distribution centers.

Key Aspects of Material Handling

Movement: The short-distance movement of items within a facility, utilizing equipment such as conveyors, forklifts, and pallet lifts. Storage is the process of organizing goods by employing racks, shelves, or automated systems. Protection refers to ensuring that items are neither damaged nor lost during handling and storage.

Control involves managing inventories and tracking commodities inside a facility, utilizing technologies such as Warehouse Management Systems (WMS) and inventory management systems.

Transportation, on the other hand, refers to the movement of goods over long distances, typically between different geographic locations. This involves the logistics of shipping products from suppliers to manufacturers, between manufacturing plants, and from manufacturers to distributors and retailers.

Key Aspects of Transportation

Movement: Long-distance movement of goods using various modes of transportation such as trucks, trains, ships, and airplanes.

Logistics: Planning and managing the routes, schedules, and methods of transporting goods to ensure timely delivery.

Cost Management: Managing transportation costs by optimizing routes, consolidating shipments, and negotiating with carriers.

Regulatory Compliance: Ensuring that transportation complies with regulations and standards, such as those related to safety, hazardous materials, and international trade. Each company should have a risk plan for every step and section, including processes and operations, that are cost-effective. The analysis revealed that excessive consumption relative to demand poses the greatest risk. Information obtained from brainstorming sessions and questionnaire surveys was used to formulate a comprehensive risk management plan for employees. At every organizational level, a structured risk plan should be established to address key dimensions such as cost overrun, material control, excess inventory, and other relevant operational parameters. Accordingly, risks are typically classified into demand risk, supply risk, and material-handling risk at each management tier. From an ergonomic perspective, Mudiyanselage *et al.* [6] demonstrate that manual material handling is highly unsafe and employ machine-learning techniques on surface electromyogram (sEMG) signals to detect harmful body movements. Sugito *et al.* [7] highlight that material-handling activities constitute a critical component of production performance, using root-cause analysis and a risk matrix—supported by adequate manpower to identify and evaluate major risk factors.

Pethaperumal and Sivakumar [8] emphasize that effective safety management requires highly qualified managers and professionals capable of understanding and implementing appropriate safety requirements. Their work shows that industrial accidents frequently result from inadequate safety measures and poorly controlled operations, with construction sites identified as among the most hazardous workplaces. In this context, they assessed safety-measurement systems at construction sites, proposed multi-level safety norms, collected survey data on material-handling practices, and statistically validated their recommendations using t-test analysis. Sulaman *et al.* [9] provide a comprehensive mapping of risk-information systems and review IT-system risk analysis methods based on both qualitative and quantitative approaches. Dongre and Mohite [10] examine material-flow design and the evolution of material-handling technologies in industry, concluding that material handling is a core activity in manufacturing that directly influences a company's profit margin.

They concluded that MH systems play a major role in productivity, Distribution, and manufacturing, providing optimization to increase productivity and reduce costs [11]. Presented a PLC-based system to replace the manual material handling system. In this model, they studied the filing, sorting, packaging, and loading of material. They concluded that manual material handling can be replaced by automation with minimal or no human effort [12]. Analyze the ginning machine to identify and locate wasteful activities in material handling. This paper concluded that materials handling systems are important for manufacturing industries. An organization's productivity may increase, and manufacturing costs may be decreased with the use of material handling systems [13]. The Analytical Hierarchy Process (AHP) is focused on material handling equipment selection to optimize the material handling system. They found that automated guided vehicles are more suitable for material handling in the pharmaceutical industry than trolleys and conveyor belts [14, 15]. The goal of a material handling system is to deliver the right amount of material at the right time to the desired destination at the lowest possible cost. Material handling equipment is continuously automated with new inventions in technology. The MHS selection depends on the cost of handling and adoption of the system.

Artificial Intelligence (AI) has significant potential to enhance safety in the transportation sector through various applications and technologies. Here are some ways AI can be effectively utilized for safety measures in transportation:

Autonomous Vehicles

Self-driving cars: One main contributor to auto accidents is human mistakes, which Artificial Intelligence (AI) may remove. They can safely traverse roadways, avoid obstructions, and make judgments in real time thanks to sensors, cameras, and machine learning algorithms. Artificial Intelligence (AI) is used by Advanced Driver Assistance Systems (ADAS) to deliver functions including adaptive cruise control, lane-keeping assistance, and automated emergency braking. AI can improve traffic signal timing to reduce gridlock and accidents at intersections.

Traffic pattern monitoring by Artificial Intelligence (AI) can detect potential risks or traffic jams, allowing for proactive traffic control and safe route rerouting.

Predictive Maintenance

Tracking the health of a vehicle: By monitoring various components and identifying issues early on, intelligent systems can prevent accidents and expedite repairs in the event of mechanical failures. Tracking the state of roads, bridges, and other infrastructure may be done with Artificial Intelligence (AI) to identify issues before they become serious or result in accidents. Enhanced detection and identification of accidents: Real-time monitoring: Artificial Intelligence (AI)-based surveillance systems can see and notify authorities of potentially harmful events or scenarios while simultaneously monitoring highways and intersections. Artificial intelligence is capable of detecting anomalies, such as erratic driving or road debris, by recognizing odd patterns or behaviours.

Public Transportation Safety

Passenger monitoring: AI programs can analyze public transit usage patterns to identify potential security threats, such as misplaced bags or hostile behavior. This makes safer and more proactive interventions possible.

Automated Control Systems: AI provides improved safety measures to buses and railroads. Artificial Intelligence reduces the possibility of mishaps and ensures efficient functioning by monitoring and adjusting operational factors.

Unmanned Helicopters: Drones equipped with Artificial Intelligence (AI) provide a flexible means of keeping an eye on large regions through aerial surveillance. They may control traffic flow, conduct accident investigations, and examine infrastructure, all of which can yield insightful information and increase overall productivity.

Emergency Reaction

Accident Operations: AI may assist in times of need by evaluating accident data to identify the best course of action and resource allocation. Catastrophe management: AI can assist in the management of evacuation routes and guarantee the security and smooth functioning of transportation networks in the event of a natural catastrophe. Planning policies with data analysis: Risk assessment: Artificial Intelligence (AI) can analyze big data sets to pinpoint the locations and timing of high-risk incidents, which improves infrastructure and policy planning. Safety Patterns: Regular examination of transportation data reveals trends and insights that help improve safety rules and guidelines.

Preliminary: The material handling system is a special case of transportation problems. The material transport from one manufacturing unit to consumers depends on the cost. Many routes connect the manufacturing unit to the supplier. The route selection of transportation depends on customer demand, which is influenced by distance or cost. To increase productivity and boost the production factor, certain sectors did, nonetheless, implement the Material Handling technique. To begin with, create a mathematical model and network representation for transportation problems. The network is typically used to illustrate the transportation paradigm. Every source and destination, represented by a node, has m and n, respectively. The arcs show routes connecting the origins and destinations. Two pieces of information are carried *via* the arc (i,j) from source i to destination j: the amount sent, x_{ij}, and the transportation cost per unit, C_{ij}.

Table **1** shows that there are n choices to S_1 source for delivery of the material at (D_1, D_2 … ….. D_n) destination. Similarly, D_1 the destination hasm choices (S_1, S_2 … … ... S_m) to take the material. However, management has a task to choose the most suitable path for transportation. There are many hazards between the path of the source and the destination. They required risk calculation in each path of transportation and the process of handling the material. We will use the concept of the Transportation model for cost optimization.

Table 1. Path of transportation process.

Source(S_1)	Demand (d_1)
S_1	D_1
S_2	D_2
....	....
S_{m-1}	D_{n-1}
S_m	D_n

Minimize the total cost:

$$\text{Minz} = \sum_{i}^{m} \sum_{j}^{n} C_{ij} X_{ij}$$

$$\text{S.t} \quad \sum_{\substack{i=0 \\ i \neq j}}^{n} x_{ij} = 1$$

Now, the path selection can be done according to the risk in the path. Risk is a collective hazard and the probability of occurrence of the incident. Risk can be assessed by evaluating the potential risk in the process (Path). A quantitative analysis of risk in the material handling system will be necessary. We can determine the optimum cost of transportation using the Vogel method or the North Corner method, and then prepare the safety matrix. We provide a novel approach to transportation path selection: the cost-safety matrix.

Methodology: The cost risk matrix is a novel notion that we provide. The safer and more economical method of material conveyance should always be taken into consideration when shipping any kind of material. Road conditions and modes of transportation influence the process of creating a matrix that displays safety ratings first. The path with the lowest safety aspect score in the matrix is the one we favor. Transport paths with less manual involvement are assigned a lower mark. In material handling, we aim to eliminate physical labor wherever possible, as we believe it may lead to accidents. A risk-cost-safety matrix with AI involves assessing the impact of various risks, along with their associated costs and potential safety implications. An AI-driven risk analysis model that scores, categorizes, and visualizes risks based on probability, cost impact, and safety consequences.

Cost Impact: This refers to the potential financial impact of each risk. Financial records, past cost analysis, and previous incidents can be considered to frame this cost estimation.

Safety Impact: This can include historical incident data, regulatory compliance records, and expert input on potential safety hazards.

In the safety matrix, we assign values from 1 to 5. Grade 1 means a very safe procedure with a very low probability of dangerous situations. The method has low risk if we issue a 2 mark, and medium risk if we provide a 3 mark. Four and five indicate the high and very high processes in this matrix. The allocation of marks can be based on experience or on accidental data. The main matrix is a complete package for safe and economical material transportation.

Incidents are very rare ------ S_a

Incidents are rare and unlikely ------ S_b

Incidents are moderately likely ------- S_c

Incidents are moderately likely -------- S_d

Chances of any incident are very high -------- S_e

If a procedure identifies a mark of 5, we should seek an alternative route of transportation instead of taking it. The safety analysis of the way should be prepared in the event of four marks, and the standard method should be adhered to precisely. The safer method, denoted by a safety mark of less than three, is always preferred by the management.

We create the cost matrix and assign a score between 1 and 5 in the same manner. A score of 1 indicates how inexpensive and low-cost the method is. Marks 2 and 3 demonstrate how inexpensive the method is. Every time, the management strives to implement the procedure that locates markings 2 and 3. The expensive procedures with a cost of 4 and 5 are indicated in this matrix. Accepting these kinds of material handling and transportation methods is not advantageous for industries. The management finds it difficult to decide on a material handling system and a transportation route.

The cost of handling and transportation is very low ------ C_a

Minimal Transportation Costs ------ C_b

The middle price for any kind of transportation -------- C_c

The high expense of any kind of transportation -------- C_d

We now calculate the range of the product of the Cost factor rank and the safety factor rank. If the product of both rankings falls within the desired range, the path is suitable for material transportation. The product of ranking is higher than it should be, which is why we should avoid this path. The rage of the product can be present as P_a, P_b, P_c, For the modeling, we take the common safety index S_u and C_v.

$$S_u * C_v = P_a where u = a, b, c, d, e and v = a, b, c, d, e$$
$$P_a \leq S_u * C_v \leq P_b$$
$$P_b \leq S_u * C_v \leq P_c$$
$$S_u * S_v \geq P_c$$

Now we create a matrix that takes into account both cost and safety.

To obtain the grade of Table **2**, multiply the cost factor and the safety factor in the given matrix. Although more efficient and productive, the strategy produces low scores.

This matrix shows three zones.

1. Red Zone
2. Yellow Zone
3. Green Zone

Table 2. Cost – Safety matrix-I.

		Safety				
		S_a	S_b	S_c	S_d	S_e
Cost	C_a	$S_a * C_a$	$S_b * C_a$	$S_c * C_a$	$S_d * C_a$	$S_e * C_a$
	C_b	$S_a * C_b$	$S_b * C_b$	$S_c * C_b$	$S_d * C_b$	$S_e * C_b$
	C_c	$S_a * C_c$	$S_b * C_c$	$S_c * C_c$	$S_d * C_c$	$S_e * C_c$
	C_d	$S_a * C_d$	$S_b * C_d$	$S_c * C_d$	$S_d * C_d$	$S_e * C_d$
	C_e	$S_a * C_e$	$S_b * C_e$	$S_c * C_e$	$S_d * C_e$	$S_e * C_e$

The area where the marks are obtained above the range is shown by the red zone in the matrix. This sign denotes that there are financial and safety hazards involved with the delivery of materials. This illustrates how expensive and lengthy the material transportation route may be. The yellow zone encircles Mark's modest position. This might be categorized as a medium-level danger. Transportation costs are not extremely high, and the procedure is not very dangerous in this zone. However, the method is medium because, while the cost of the procedure is inexpensive, it is not substantially safer for transportation. Similarly, while the method is safe, the expense of the transportation system is on the higher side. In this matrix, any sector can benefit from the green zone. This zone shows a mark of less than eight. This location has reasonably priced transportation. A safer approach is that which is superior.

Now the Safety ratio with cost can be calculated for $S_a = \frac{S_a}{(S_a+S_b+S_c+S_b+S_e)}$

The safety ratio with cost can be calculated for $S_b = \frac{S_b}{(S_a+S_b+S_c+S_b+S_e)}$

The safety ratio with cost can be calculated for $S_c = \frac{S_c}{(S_a+S_b+S_c+S_b+S_e)}$

We provide a score of 1 to 5 to the safety matrix, where 1 indicates an extremely safe procedure with a very low chance of an event. When we give a procedure a 2 mark, it indicates minimal danger, while a 3 mark indicates medium risk. The high and very high processes in this matrix are indicated by the numbers 4 and 5.

Extremely little likelihood of any occurrence ------ 1

Minimal and insignificant likelihood of an incidence ------ 2

Moderate likelihood of any event ------- 3

A high likelihood of any occurrence -------- 4

Extremely high likelihood of any event -------- 5

If a procedure encounters mark 5, we should avoid that route and seek an alternative. When there are four marks, the safety analysis of the way should be prepared, and the standard method should be adhered to properly. The safer procedure has a safety mark below 3, which is what management always prefers. We also create a cost matrix and assign a score from 1 to 5. A score of 1 indicates that the procedure is cheap and very affordable. The minimal cost of the technique is demonstrated by markings 2 and 3. The management consistently attempts to implement the procedure that identifies marks 2 and 3. The payback period is short for this kind of technique. The expensive procedures with a cost of 4 and 5 are indicated in this matrix. Accepting this kind of material handling and transportation method is not advantageous for the industry. The management finds it difficult to decide on a material handling system and a transportation route.

Extremely minimal handling and shipping costs ------ 1

Minimal Transportation Costs ------ 2

The middle price for any kind of transportation ------- 3

The high expense of any kind of transportation ------- 4

Extremely expensive for any kind of transportation -------- 5

We are now developing a matrix that considers both cost and safety:

Table 3. Cost – Safety matrix-II.

	Safety					
		1	2	3	4	5
Cost	1	1	2	3	4	5
	2	2	4	6	8	10
	3	3	6	9	12	15
	4	4	8	12	16	20
	5	5	10	15	20	25

In Table **3**, the area of the matrix with the red zone is where the part receives scores higher than 15. This sign denotes the possibility of financial and safety concerns in the delivery of materials. This demonstrates that both the cost and the route of material transportation are quite high. Between markings 8 and 15, there is a yellow zone. This might be categorized as a medium-level danger. Transportation costs are not extremely high, and the procedure is not very dangerous in this zone. Nonetheless, the technique is deemed medium since, while it may be inexpensive, it is not particularly safe for transportation. In a similar vein, the procedure could be secure, but the transportation system is more expensive. The green zone in this matrix is ideal for all industries. The marks in this zone are fewer than eight. Transportation costs are on the lower side in this area. Similar to how handling or shipping procedures are safer than others.

We create the cost matrix and assign a score between 1 and 5 that represents:

1. This cost-safety matrix can be used to evaluate job site risks, balancing cost impact and safety outcomes. Safety risks with high financial impact, like falls or equipment malfunctions, receive high priority and trigger preventive measures. This matrix enhances worker safety on-site by directing resources toward the most hazardous activities while keeping project costs manageable.
2. In the oil and gas sector, companies apply a cost-safety matrix to manage the integrity of assets like pipelines, platforms, and refineries. Risks with lower costs and significant safety measures may be prioritized using a cost-safety matrix.
3. The cost-safety matrix is used to assess risks in aircraft maintenance, operations, and passenger safety. An AI model predicts maintenance needs based on component wear data and assesses the probability of failures. Critical parts with both high repair costs and significant safety impact, like engine components, are prioritized.
4. The cost-safety matrix is used to balance the risk of supply chain disruptions with the safety implications of equipment, processes, or materials handling in Logistics and Supply chain.
5. Insurance companies use a cost-safety matrix to evaluate risks associated with various claims, weighing the cost of claims against potential safety impacts.

Artificial Intelligence in Risk Management: The National Institute of Standards and Technology (NIST) has been actively involved in developing standards and frameworks to support the trustworthy use of emerging technologies, including artificial intelligence. Its work on AI risk management aims to provide structured guidance for identifying, assessing, and mitigating risks associated with AI systems across their lifecycle. A NIST AI risk management framework typically emphasizes key principles such as reliability, robustness, security, transparency, and accountability. It encourages organizations to consider not only technical performance, but also ethical, legal, and societal implications when deploying AI.

By following such guidance, stakeholders can better align AI applications with organizational objectives, regulatory expectations, and public trust. For detailed and up-to-date information on NIST's AI risk management activities, practitioners should refer to the official NIST publications and related resources, which describe specific concepts, functions, and recommended practices for managing AI-related risks.

Integrating Artificial Intelligence (AI) and Machine Learning (ML) into risk management is a popular trend in many industries, including banking. Here are some key ways in which AI/ML is making an impact in the field of risk management:

Efficiency and Productivity: AI and ML technologies can easily handle large volumes of data, especially unstructured data, which traditional systems often struggle with. Because these technologies can quickly uncover patterns and trends that may be difficult for humans to detect, they can automate data analysis operations, increasing productivity and efficiency.

Production costs can be significantly reduced by leveraging labor-intensive, creative processes that incorporate AI and ML. Organizations may write risk assessments and procedures to cut expenses and increase accuracy. Decision-making and data analysis: AI and ML algorithms excel at analyzing data, enabling businesses to make quick, well-informed judgments. These tools have the ability to assess previous performance, pinpoint issue origins, and impart problem-solving skills. Lending choices: Banks and other financial organizations' lending decisions will be greatly impacted by artificial intelligence and machine learning. AI algorithms can make more accurate and quicker decisions about the truth than human reviewers by examining a borrower's credit history, transactions, and other pertinent data.

Fraud detection: AI-based systems can be invaluable in fraud detection because they are very smart at detecting anomalies. These systems continuously monitor user activity and events, allowing for quick identification of suspicious activity and referral for further investigation.

AI/ML: An AI/ML application of predictive analytics that predicts risks and trends based on historical data. Organizations can identify risks before they occur and mitigate their impact.

Portfolio Management: Artificial intelligence is used in portfolio analysis and asset management to estimate the return profile. This helps portfolio managers select investments based on risk tolerance and investment objectives.

Companies continue to use artificial intelligence and machine learning to manage risk, while increasingly realizing the potential benefits in terms of cost savings, efficiency, and accuracy. However, concerns about data security, ethical dilemmas, and the need for AI decision-making systems must be taken into account. If you want to build a performance-critical model, it is best to choose multiple variables, especially when working with a large data set. For a better selection process, consider design and materials.

DISCUSSION AND CONCLUSION

This document helps you identify threats to your device management system. The risk matrix takes into account the transport costs and safety aspects of each route. Based on the cost security matrix, managers must choose a path to the green zone. Implementing an inventory management solution can improve productivity, cost-effectiveness, and decision-making.

AI offers several potential advantages. Optimizing inventory may be achieved by applying AI systems to analyze past data, present consumption trends, and other factors. By doing this, you can make sure that your organization has adequate cash on hand to pay obligations, avoid overspending, and maintain adequate reserves.

Accurate forecasts are produced by artificial intelligence using a range of data sources, such as past sales information, market patterns, and outside factors like the state of the economy or the climate. As a result, choices on production scheduling and replenishment have a better knowledge base.

Out of Stock and Over Stock: Having precise inventory projections reduces the likelihood of stockpiling or running out of stock.

Enhance Order Fulfillment: Products are kept in stock for the appropriate length of time when needed, and order fulfillment procedures can be sped up. Order processing and delivery times are accelerated for customers.

AI systems can modify order points and quantities in response to shifts in market circumstances and demand patterns by using real-time data. This process is known as dynamic reordering.

Supply chain optimization: AI technology can be applied to optimize not only within a company but also throughout the supply chain. Preparing for potential disruptions, maintaining relationships with suppliers, and streamlining the supply chain are all part of this, which accelerates the evaluation of large amounts of data, which improves decision-making. This helps those responsible for production planning, inventory management, and resource allocation make better decisions.

Tailored inventory techniques: Because different products have different demand patterns, AI can tailor inventory techniques to specific product categories or customer segments. Real-time Monitoring: AI systems can continuously track inventory levels and provide up-to-date stock status information. This facilitates anticipatory decision-making and prompt responses to shifts in demand or disruptions in the supply chain.

It should be emphasized that good implementation requires a strategic approach in addition to current technologies. This requires ensuring data integrity, incorporating artificial intelligence into current methods, and promoting data-driven decision-making.

REFERENCES

[1] T. Aven, "Risk assessment and risk management: Review of recent advances on their foundation", *Eur. J. Oper. Res.,* vol. 253, no. 1, pp. 1-13, 2016. [http://dx.doi.org/10.1016/j.ejor.2015.12.023]

[2] M.V. Krishna, "Satyanarayana, D.: Rao, K. S. Risk management is the key enabler in materials management (A study on the significance of risk management in materials management)", *Int. J. Appl. Res.,* pp. 392-394, 2017.

[3] A.H. Rani, "Syammaun, T. The identification of material management risk factors affecting the time performance in fly over project construction", *International Conference on Industrial Engineering and Operations Management,* 2019.

[4] C.N. Kumar, M. Sakthivel, R.K. Elangovan, and M. Arularasu, "Analysis of material handling safety in construction sites and countermeasures for effective enhancement", *The Scientific World Journal,* 2015.

[5] A.C. Monteiro Sales, "Gondim, L.: Guimarães, A.: Veiga Neto, A. R. Risk assessment model in inventory management using the AHP method", *Gest. Prod.,* vol. 27, p. 3, 2020.

[6] E.S. Mudiyanselage, Dat Nguyen, P. H.: Sadra Rajabi, M. "Automated workers' ergonomic risk assessment in manual material handling using sEMGWearable sensors and machine learning", *Electronics (Basel),* 2021. [http://dx.doi.org/10.3390/electronics10202558]

[7] E. Sugito, Ampuh Hadiguna, R.: Hasibuan, R. P. *Identification of Material Distribution Process to Improve Material Handling Performance Using Risk Matrix Analysis (Case Study at Paper Manufacturing).* International Information and Engineering Technology Association, 2021, pp. 369-378.

[8] H. Pethaperumal, and N. Sivakumar, "Effectiveness of mechanical material handling equipment safety in construction sites for operation safety and environment health", *International Journal of Applied Environmental Sciences,* 2017.

[9] S.M. Sulaman, Weyns, K.: Höst, M. A. "Review of Research on Risk Analysis Methods for IT Systems", *International Conference on Evaluation and Assessment in Software Engineering,* Association for Computing Machinery: Porto de Galinhas Brazil, pp. 86-96, 2015.

[10] A. Dongre, and N. Mohite, "Significance of selection of material handling system design in industry – a review", *International Journal of Engineering Research and General Science,* 2015.

[11] H. Kumar, and S. Kamboj, "Modelling of automatic material handling system using PLC", *International Journal of Advanced Trends in Computer Science and Engineering,* 2019.

[12] P. Sundaram, and E. Viswanathan, "Development of material handling system in a manufacturing company", *Int. J. Innov. Res. Sci. Eng. Technol.,* 2014.

[13] G.S. Sharma, R.S. Baghel, and H. Singh, *A study of artificial neural networks using MATLAB and its future application in forecasting.,* 2024.

[14] M. Zubair, S. Maqsood, M. Omair, and I. Noor, "Optimization of material handling system through material handling equipment selection", *International Journal of Progressive Sciences and Technologies,* pp. 235-243, 2019.

[15] A. Kamble, and P. Patil, "Selection of material handling equipment: classifications & attributes", *International Journal for Innovative Research in Science & Technology,* 2019.

SUBJECT INDEX

T

U

V

W

X

www.ingramcontent.com/pod-product-compliance
Lightning Source LLC
LaVergne TN
LVHW070948210926
848482LV00002B/132

9789815324051